Tarot of the Future

Raising Spiritual Consciousness

May your travels be
clear and satisfying !

Art Rosengarten

TAROT OF THE FUTURE

Raising Spiritual Consciousness

Arthur Rosengarten

Paragon House

First Edition 2018

Published in the United States by
Paragon House
www.paragonhouse.com

Copyright © 2018 by Paragon House

Library of Congress Cataloging-in-Publication Data

Names: Rosengarten, Arthur, 1950- author.
Title: Tarot of the future : raising spiritual consciousness / by Arthur
  Rosengarten.
Description: First [edition]. | St. Paul, MN : Paragon House, 2018. |
  Includes index.
Identifiers: LCCN 2017043120 | ISBN 9781557789334 (pbk. : alk. paper)
Subjects: LCSH: Tarot. | Spiritual life. | Spirituality. | Consciousness.
Classification: LCC BF1879.T2 R675 2018 | DDC 133.3/2424--dc23 LC record
available at https://lccn.loc.gov/2017043120

The paper used in this publication meets the minimum requirements of American National Standard for Information Sciences—Permanence of Paper for Printed Library Materials, ANSI standard Z39.48-1992.
Manufactured in the United States of America
10 9 8 7 6 5 4 3 2 1

For current information about all releases from Paragon House, visit the website at http://www.paragonhouse.com

To all Travelers—may your journey be clear and satisfying.

Contents

Introduction

Like most of us, I think about the passage of Time periodically. Time has a way of making us ponder late into the night, for instance, the fact that Change is constant, but rarely do we see its operation in action, only its effect. Past, present, future—are they facts, or ideas? Do they exist outside of the mind? Am I really different than who I was before, or just grayer and less thin?

Our minds can grow restive and questions abound, especially in the late hours of the night when the buffering sensations of daylight are deprived. In what increments do we define the present? Minutes, seconds, or moments? Do I exist in time, or space, both, or neither? And who (or *what*) exactly am I referring to when I say "I" or "me?" Can it be pointed to or found in the body? Can this be verified? And so, for me, periodically, if only as an effect of too much caffeine, are the riddles of Time sustainable in thought, or else I fall increasingly less sane.

Eventually, things do seem to run out. We don't know this for a fact, we take it on faith from our beliefs and perceptions, and also our imagination, born from a mental apparatus that itself is still running. Is it qualified to judge? What happens to Time when we expire? Is it absolute as Newton believed, independent of an observer, and therefore goes on ticking, or a relative phenomenon intimately tied to subjective experience? "Death is certain," the Buddhists are kind to remind us, "but the time of death unknown." "Tomorrow or the next life? Which comes first we never know" go their thoughtful slogans. And so periodically we must ponder. It's part of being human. Then, gladly, we roll back over and get some sleep.

Whether or not Time really exists, it cannot be denied, we feel its ghostly presence. It begs us to consider the future, where it's all going, and where we are going with it? What will happen when we get there? What role do I have in Time's making? So many things to consider, but we must do this only periodically, otherwise we start to bang our faces into the unyielding walls of the present. Turn right here, stop there, take a step to the left, and keep walking.

Time speculation does not serve in navigation through our moment-to-moment reality when, say, going downstairs to the kitchen to make a sandwich. "Always in motion is the future," we are told by Yoda, while the Nobel laureate Bob Dylan bemoans, "The future for me is already a thing of the past." It's the periodic enigma and riddle of all riddles. Certainly the past and future provide background music to the present. We hear tinges of it when doing things, if audible only at a whisper. But what we call the "present"—is it the same experience as what we mean by "now?" Is there a difference? Alan Watts tells us in *The Way of Zen:*

> All time is in this body, which is the body of Buddha. The past exists in its memory and the future in its anticipation, and both of these are now, for when the world is inspected directly, and clearly, past and future times are nowhere to be found.[1]

You, my alert reader, for instance... are you speculating about Time now? Can you hear its whispers in the background of your mind as you read this text? "Where is this book going...um?" Or maybe, "Just time for a few more pages, then I'll..." If you confess as much, you are forgiven. It's hard to be completely free of the indignities of Time even when you are engaged in activities. The thought "What comes next?" is omnipresent, even when providing the smallest dint of anticipatory sensation, technically it qualifies, nonetheless, as Time speculation, does it not? If you are unsure, I suspect it is because the passage of Time can only be thought about periodically, that is, from time to time and then you will cease if only from the boredom.

Otherwise, as noted, the nose gets bruised and misshapen by the hard plaster of physical reality that surrounds us, we start to lose blood, and it's simply not worth it. Fortune-telling is like this. So, too, is politics. Too much of it and we lose sight of the real work in front of us. But periodically, when the moment feels right, it is a well-spent, even necessary part of the task of living. Indirectly, that's what this book is about. Is it clear now?

---

1. Alan Watts, *The Way of Zen*, 1959.

FUTURE SPECULATIONS

Many will remember a time not so long ago when "future speculation" was in, and actually quite a pleasant and exciting indulgence. Think back to circa 2000 CE, only sixteen years prior to the writing of this book. A wild culture craze (and small cottage industry) of future speculation was sweeping planet Earth then, you may recall; it was to be an epic moment, slated to become a universal milestone in human civilization—Y2K— and the coming of the new millennium! Remember that? It was not so long ago.

Everyone was thinking quite a lot about the future then, some anxiously, some brimming with hope, some sitting on the sidelines with cynical indifference, mildly amused by all the hoopla. A collective "Spring" was upon many of us, and it was palpably felt in the collective consciousness of the planet. Change of veritable millennial proportions was in the air, and few out of hand could deny it, even if they tried. And as always before momentous, immanent change is expected to occur, questions abounded. Would the technological wheels and springs upon which the modern world was wound continue to function, or come to a resounding halt? Would the angels of Aquarius descend upon our small planet bringing good tidings for the new age, some mused in earnest, if only to themselves... Would time-honored prophecies of "a coming" of religious proportions be actualized, or forever dismantled by their failure to appear? Rich forebodings, at long last, for the tired blue planet we call home!

And then, not a hop, skip, and a jump down the royal Y2K highway, only months after its largely uneventful, anticlimactic no show had fizzled, the date 9/11 (2001) happened, blowing up the Spring illusion into a million fragments of shard and glass, bodies jumping off towers, the horror... and the dream of radical transformation suddenly morphed into its opposite, radical destruction, a wicked storm of dread, death, vengeance, rampant paranoia, and all in an instance, it seemed, the magical promise of the new millennium vanished in the night. Darkness had fallen.

For me, three personal events occurred during the liminal 21 month span—from late December, 1999 and September 11, 2001—between, that is, the inception of a burgeoning, glorious "new age" and the inferno of a smoldering terror of an annihilating "old age," which still linger in my thoughts, even today while writing this book. Each of the three events carried seeds of possibility for the coming future. Each, in turn, had chilled my spine with hope and purpose, as well as some dread and terror, and each, sadly, might have died tragically on the vine from the unforeseen bitter frost on that September day in America, which dramatically and irreversibly traumatized much of the world as well.

But the initial hopes and purposes did not die, they simply went into an extended, patient dormancy, that is, underground. And only now, some sixteen years later, with a little push from recent political developments in the year 2016, they are ready to sprout. As we will learn, 2016 in Tarot parlance, is a "9 year."

THE THREE EVENTS

Every adult living today surely has a "story about time" hinged squarely around Y2K, but it is likely a more vivid and enduring memory that remains around the terrorist attacks of 9/11/2001. Time suffered a severe head trauma that day, even if remembered only periodically, no different than did humanity as a whole. Overnight it seemed that the beginning was at the end, you might say. The day-to-day news cycle superseded everything else; the past lost its relevancy, and the future felt ominous and highly uncertain. In some respects, it is not very different now on the political front. As for 9/11, the act of forgetting, of course, helps to free up bandwidth, and much has been forgotten of that surreal period accordingly. But retrieval of the forgotten can sometimes be trigger-fast, owing to the marvels of the human mind and the sheer magnitude and emotional force of what was displaced. You might try to recall some of your own memories of that period.

For our purposes, it will be well worth remembering the words of George Orwell: "Who controls the past controls the future. Who controls the present controls the past." It should not be difficult to ascertain who and what controls the present, certainly in this country, and I would suggest we underscore the word "control" as it will become germane to the groundwork we are setting for the Tarot of the Future. There is no need in this work to revisit the trauma at length but, rather, to pick up some of the pieces, as I have done, that were lost in the fire, see what if anything can be salvaged, and move forward.

In my case, the embers lost in the fire, remarkably, were each concerned with, of all things, tarot cards. You know, those magical little creatures of the imagination used in so-called fortunetelling? And here comes my first disclaimer. It may seem an odd and curious fact that as a clinical psychologist and philosopher for over four decades now, nearly all of my writing and research has been about tarot cards. I often shake my head at this myself, but have otherwise learned to accept this fate and make the best of it.

For me, the study of psychology, philosophy, language, spirituality, and Tarot come together as a synergy, the creative blending of a diverse set of contributors. Synergy, in the biological sciences, is the causal agency that accounts for the progressive evolution of complexity in living systems over the course of Time. The Tarot itself can be thought of as a living system. The accepted thesis, in a nutshell, is that synergistic effects from a diverse set of contributors provide functional advantages in relation to survival and reproduction of the living system and have been favored by natural selection. The cooperating parts, in effect, become functional "units" of selection in evolutionary change.

I mention synergy because all three of my aforementioned events spanning the "millennial bubble" greatly impacted the making of the present work. The *final act,* or third of the trio, began on the auspicious day of September 10, 2001, that is, the day before September 11th, though chronologically, I will begin earlier with the second of the three events in my re-telling.

It was mid-April, 2000, and marked the release of my first published book on this topic, *Tarot and Psychology: Spectrums of Possibility.* The book arrived, that is, in the bubbly, numinous days four months into the New Millennium. How perfect! I had just turned 50, and the timing felt so right. The book was an accessible synthesis of the dissertation I had written in the mid-eighties, the first doctoral study of Tarot readings, comparing their reliability and validity to those of dream analysis and projective story-telling (TAT). In my just-released book, however, I made a kind of prognostication of sorts: "Tarot," I declared, "is a potential high-powered psychospiritual instrument for the 21st century." Though I was quick to add:

> It is not the author's contention, however, that the deck of possibility is some perfectly formulated, all-inclusive, well-oiled, and complete dream machine of psychospiritual omniscience. It too has evolved and will need to evolve further. Rather, I believe Tarot is indeed one finely-tuned, intricately engineered, new class of psychological vehicle with a surplus of horsepower and great versatility for traveling far and wide through the cosmos of the human psyche. For those not yet initiated, I would simply ask them in for a test drive.[2]

That was one of the big events for me, the arrival of *Tarot and Psychology*, a product of decades of work, onto the printed page. We'll leave this for the time being, and move onto the third event, which occurred the very week of 9/11. On September 10, I had flown into Chicago for a major conference and went a few days early to visit with an old friend. I was slated to be a featured presenter at the Second World Tarot Congress, sponsored by the International Tarot Society, and was planning to use this platform before many of the world's leading Tarot experts and authors, to present my long-held theory regarding the urgent need to update the Tarot map for our coming age.

The Major Arcana, the most sacred and important cards of Tarot's 600 year history, I believed, was unfinished and incomplete, and I was prepared to prove this somewhat audacious claim, and reveal my "correction-expansion thesis" developed over many years of research and experimentation. While most people might think such puttering with an old map not that big a deal, I suspected it would be a veritable bombshell to those who made their careers with it; I was fully prepared to stake my

---

2. Arthur Rosengarten, PhD, *Tarot and Psychology: Spectrums of Possibility,* 2000.

claim, however, though a tad nervous as many highly-respected European and American scholars I admired would be in attendance. I expected to be either widely lauded for the originality of my thesis, or handed my head in a basket of hanged men for this provocative, fanciful, even heretical hypothesis.

In retrospect, as we now know, I had locked onto the wrong bombshell! The conference was, of course, canceled, given what had shockingly transpired, and the world, it now seemed, was at war. What difference would my little theory of a hidden number code laying dormant in a 600 year canon make at this historic moment, when all the major airports in America had been put on high emergency alert, and airport security at O'Hare Airport, I soon discovered while desperately trying to fly home to California to be with my wife and kids, had taken the morbid safety precaution of substituting plastic forks and spoons for their silverware (no plastic knives were allowed even in the Concourse).

Never had I seen anything like this. The airport glaringly seemed like the first and last line of defense. The skies were now eerily empty over Chicago. Among other things, modern travel was now under assault. All flights in the US were summarily canceled, and one did not know when or even *if* they would be able to return home. In retrospect now, things soon began to coalesce around our new normal; the conference was rescheduled for the next year, my presentation was delivered, though to a much smaller and far less enthusiastic audience, and, I too, under the circumstances of the Bush Administration, had lost the wind at my sails. So went event two, though I might add, the theme of "travel," as we shall see, was duly noted.

The last of the three (though first chronologically, in linear time), was not directly tarot-related, though to me, it spelled-out in neon letters the future of Tarot immediately. Instead, it concerned the future of American Psychology. It occurred four months before my book was released, in late December, 1999, about the time the Great Transfer to the new future was to begin. An article published in a special "Millennial Edition" of the *APA Monitor,* the main journal of the American Psychological Association, said it all loud and clear. The journal had asked several of the country's leading field researchers—with expertise specifically with regard to future trends within the field of Psychology—to make their best predictions for the next hundred years about likely changes they foresaw for the field of Psychology through the 21st century.

Specifically, the experts were asked to speculate about how clinical practices, and the discipline as a whole, would be affected. One essay in particular, written by University of Texas professor, author/researcher, Rand B. Evans, PhD completely lit me up for its implications, prophecies (many of which have already proved false), and long view of the field in which I make my career. In my eyes, the article predicts both some good news and bad news for the profession, and I will mention here the parts I found particularly striking.

In his long essay, Dr. Evans first addresses the triumphs and impact of science over the next hundred years, and predicts that clinical psychology would be altered fundamentally by the conclusion of the human genome project (though shortly later, I must note, the project was declared completed in 2003). The result? Too early to say, but nothing especially ground-breaking of this nature has come across my dealings as a therapist since that time that I know of... No fundamental alteration post-Genome Project yet, but I know there is more to go on this front.

Evans also predicted that much of mental illness will be prevented through biomedical discoveries, and more profound ailments (schizophrenia, bipolar etc.) will be dealt with using gene therapy. This remains on the cutting board also today, and it is still early to judge. It is an attractive hope for many that one day may be realized, but Evans neglects to mention the thorny reality that today, more than ever, pits pure science with its less pure ramifications, namely, the competing market-driven realities that often over-ride not only biomedical research, but the power politics and controversy behind defining, naming, and treating mental illness itself. As such, what we call "mental illness" carries a political dimension not often understood by the public. Writes Dr. Ofer Zur, Director of the Zur Institute in Northern California:

Over the years, as psychology, psychotherapy, psychopharmacology, the DSM [Diagnostic Statistical Manual], and the culture at large have co-evolved, and varying diagnoses have taken center stage... The question then becomes, to what degree do these historical shifts in diagnostic focus reflect deep evolutionary structural changes in the nature of the psyche, and to what degree do these shifts reflect the ways in which diagnosis in general, and how the changes in the DSM, are determined by cultural and professional fads, driven by professional self-interest and the business economics of the psycho-therapeutic and psychiatric treatment market, rather than by scientific process?[3]

"Prediction," cautioned Noble Laureate, and founding contributor of quantum theory, Neils Bohr, ironically, "is very difficult, especially if it's about the future." We must appreciate, however, that pure scientific research, for all its genius, when taken from the psychological perspective, remains but a powerful myth. Many myths come true, of course, when they are believed, yet at base, they are mythic constructions like everything else. The sacred stamp of approval given today to so-called "evidence-based" outcomes, must still be inspected for their construct validity, as well as their hidden biases of professional self-interest and business economics, no different than the softer disciplines of Psychotherapy and Tarot. Interestingly, contrary to popular misconceptions, the art of prediction actually falls more squarely within the province of science, than fortunetelling. As a card reader, I am loathe to offer hard predictions about the future, unless the cards come right out and bite me if I do not! But partially, this is because I question what the future really means, and this philosophical concern very much continues in the present study.

Evans also predicts that advances in *brain research* will lead to precise biochemical and noninvasive techniques to correct chemical imbalances and neural ailments, and this knowledge will lead to *designer drugs* which will reshape personality patterns. Certainly, efforts in this direction are hotly pursued currently, and new generational medications can be a

---

3. Zur, O. and Nordmarken, N. (2015). *DSM: Diagnosing for Status and Money Summary Critique of the DSM-5.*

godsend to many suffering mental disorders with a biological component.

But so-called "designer drugs," unfortunately, have taken a different turn today than Professor Evans envisioned. They are known more for increasing calls to US poison control centers, and the incidence of drug problems in emergency departments (EDs), hospitals, and other medical settings. Only a small percentage of those using designer drugs will come into contact with the health-care system, but their consequences of use can be severe. The *Journal of Addiction Science and Clinical Practice* reports: "Familiarity with designer drugs can help clinicians recognize common adverse reactions and life-threatening consequences that can arise in their abuse."[4]

The attraction and virulence that mood-altering drugs have played in social, cultural, political, and psychological directions has long been underestimated, or wrongly predicted by the experts, and this is not a new story. Evans is more prescient, however, regarding the tail winds of addiction and withdrawal, that is, psycho-socially speaking, prevalent today, even at this still early test phase of his century-long vision; he quite accurately predicts an uptick in addictions of a social nature, including *information addiction*, which will continue to escalate.

People will increasingly withdraw from direct social interaction, says Evans, due to escalating dispersion of the workplace. The need for human interaction will be satisfied through *virtual interactive liaisons* mediated by the Internet or its replacement. This, says Evans correctly, will produce addictive and psychologically-based obsessive behaviors brought about by poor development of interpersonal skills in a society of increasingly isolated (and, I might add, mean-spirited) individuals as witnessed today in the underbelly of the internet and social media, reeking havoc with cyber-bullying, fake news, global hacking, propaganda, cyber warfare, and the whole lot of it. But even these important issues around cyber addiction outlined by Evans, were not what I personally found most compelling about the article.

---

4. *Journal of Addiction Science & Clinical Practice* (2015) [Volume 10 (1):8].

The Good News About the Future

It was "the good news" about the future that Professor Evans envisioned that I still find inspiring and relevant to the book in your hands. It speaks of a future I too foresee, when something quite different and positive will come into focus, albeit, probably not on a mass level at first. Evans predicts a future in which a small segment of the population will be motivated to seek out more soulful and essential forms of psychological treatments. He writes:

1. As mental illness/emotional problems are dealt with through biochemistry, a strong *spiritual and mental counter-movement* will arise, dedicated to coping in a world without chemical or mechanical aids.

2. These movements will develop *radical therapies* and group cultures, rejecting all but the most primary and personally human relationships.

3. They will deal with *hope, self-actualization, self-worth, and spirituality.*

4. Such movements will be looked on with disdain by the biomedical Establishment but *will gain strength* as the 21st century ends.

This good news vision, I believe, is a clarion call to transformational practices of all kinds, including the Tarot of the future. But one final point should be made clear from the outset: no one is suggesting that tarot cards alone can heal the world, make the critical changes that are needed, or transform the complex and difficult global landscape of the 21st century. It is people—individuals who take actions and do important things—that will make the difference in how things transpire, and this point should be obvious and understood throughout this book. But individuals are far more than what they think and do in the outside world, far more than what conventional wisdom says about them, and they assume themselves to be. More consequentially, they are also the keepers of their interior worlds, individually and collectively, those immensely private inner spaces within the self wherein lies the human heart, soul, and Man's innate wisdom to become whole and complete.

Tarot cards, uniquely, provide special access to this sacred universal reservoir of mind, and can lend guidance in shaping and reflecting a deeper understanding of who (or *what*) we really are, and where, in fact, we are really going. It is in this spirit and with this intention that the present book is written.

AR

SECTION 1

DEPARTURE (X)

CHAPTER 1

The Scientific Attitude

Strange Bedfellows Once More

It was another year to remember—2016—though many would soon prefer to forget. The morning air of early March in Clackamas, Oregon was clear as the glisten of dew on the brier. Inside the hotel conference room, I was about to begin preaching to a Tarot Symposium near Portland, and the packed and lively throng of intuitive healers, aging New Agers, gentle meditative artists, nose-ringed occultists, metaphysical curiosity-seekers, and alternative thinkers of many stripes and persuasions, was my choir. Thankfully the majority were lovely women! Though perhaps 30 percent of the attendees were male and equally lovely, it was not an uncommon mix for a Tarot conference.

My topic was blandly titled: "Psychological Tarot-Empirical Studies"for a very specific purpose. A carefully chosen emphasis placed on the words "Psychological" and "Empirical" would surely conjure up shades of the dreaded lab-rat psychologist, especially for those unfamiliar with my work, and hardly the sexy enticement for this "sublime magical art" that several hundred enthusiasts had come to honor and to praise, grow their beloved craft in arcane knowledge, commune spiritually with fellow diviners, and hone their cartomantic skills with the 600-year-old "deck of possibility" as I call the Tarot. If I was up to something, well, it was for "heuristic" reasons.

I quite expected, and did not mind, the usual skeptical projections planted onto my clinical profession as was bound to occur, and actually, my lecture topic handily invited them. The lone psychologist at a festive party of pre-Freudian pagans—the guy with the "scientific attitude"—I knew my audience well, and I relished the opportunity to disabuse them. I have shamelessly courted these very strange bedfellows, Tarot and Psychology, since well before my book bearing that title was released in 2000, and though I may be a little paranoid, I can usually sense the apprehension in the room (in the mildly fearful sense) when a psychologist takes the lectern in a Tarot auditorium. After all, he sits on the other side of the aisle, does he not?

Apprehension is a curious word, with two rather disparate meanings. As it has evolved in common modern usage, it suggests a vague fear or anxiousness about possible future occurrences. Etymologically, however, the word derives from *prehension,* the act of seizing or grasping, without mention of fearfulness. Hence by extension, apprehension is the mental, conscious, grasping of the nature of a stimulus or event. Psychologically, apprehension is treated as a rather primitive, immediate act, and distinguished from comprehension, which involves more in the way of reflection and interpretation.[1] A crucial feature in this book, however, will be to speak quite forcefully in favor of this kind of apprehension regarding the proper initial approach to a tarot card.

In either respect, I now imagined my audience would first perceive me in the guise of the lowly mental healthcare worker, perhaps like the one at their niece's recovery center. It would not offend me in the least. Or perhaps, as the witless pawn of the anxiety and depression industry there to hawk their latest wares? Well, there were many of them, I conceded. I continued down the list. Might Dr. Empirical be one of those eager brain studies geeks raving about neuroplasticity in all its manifestations, and somehow try to saddle their sacred tarot cards onto the hemispheres of the brain? It happens, you just don't know. Maybe even, the snarky academic scholar of mentality he was, here to lecture at us on "William James, the American Mystic" or worse still (and I smiled at my own warped reverie momentarily)—the polished clinical shaman! Groovy with the cards, but that scientific attitude of his... No thanks! So

---

1. Arthur S. Reber, *Dictionary of Psychology.*

many transferences the poor psychologist endures, I thought with some amusement, to say nothing of his unavoidable counter-transferences!

None of it mattered. The attendees of the tarot conference would be in for a surprise. "Let the projections begin," I declared to my inner audience, "I'm ready to roll." Truth be told, it was precisely my intention to get all this out on the table quickly. After all, I am both a psychologist and a Tarot reader, and make no bones about either one. Projection, I believe, is the first and last bastion of the ignorant, and much like skepticism, it runs both ways, as my esteemed colleagues in the helping professions would be quick to comment; but here at the lovely Monarch Hotel Conference Center, a transformation of stereotypes was the order of the day.

Experience had shown the inadvisability of stretching standard-fare psychology topics into the misty land of Tarot, that is, without the proper alternative papers in hand. "Politics," of course, are as alive and well in business and professional circles as they are in government, they just manifest a bit more subtly. It's human nature, after all. There would no doubt be some spoken and hidden boundary issues that must first be addressed as this smaller circle of often isolated, ridiculed, and unappreciated Tarot professionals were greatly vulnerable before the established Goliaths of mental health and sickness, as well as consciousness research, the social and cognitive scientists.

In the more conservative backwaters of mainstream American psychology, the opposite sort of invasion and redress would be met by even fiercer resistance as I have witnessed up close; something so scurrilous as tarot cards brought into the august, hermetically-sealed, chambers of the clinical consulting room would likely signal a fat flashing red light to the imperious Ethics Committees of the APA (Principle D-Justice came to mind: "Psychologists exercise reasonable judgment and take precautions to ensure that their potential biases, the boundaries of their competence and the limitations of their expertise do not lead to or condone unjust practices."); even though thirty years prior, I had completed the first accredited experimental doctoral dissertation on this same controversial admixture of mainstream and alternative healing disciplines.[2] What was learned then, beyond the encouraging results of my study, was that most naysayers and scientific skeptics had never actually experienced a tarot reading themselves. Was that in keeping with the scientific attitude? I thought this was weak and uninformed, though not surprising at all.

But here at the Northwest Tarot Symposium on a clear late morning in March, Tarot most certainly was on center stage. If there would be edgy subliminal rumblings of turf war to the tune of "Whose cards are these anyway, Doctor?" I welcomed them. I feel it is essential that these misguided internecine battles do not persist any longer, as the world should be adult enough today to examine anything and everything fairly presented that might bring some light to our muddled and polarized societal and mental condition. While conventional psychology is generally loathe to consider the merits of the metaphysical level, it's fair to say that the clinical community—psychologists, social workers, family therapists, mental health workers, academics, researchers, and especially psychiatrists (the evil pimps of psychopharmacology)—remain outright suspect in Tarot quarters, as well.

The psychologist may wax poetic on multi-generational family dynamics of morbid obesity, or the atypical character disorders, *ad nauseam*. He may exude over the marvels of cognitive reframing until he's blue-in-the-face, or trumpet with modest pride his beloved "evidence-based" treatments which now corner the market on legitimacy. Or, extol the down-right cleverness and future horizons of cutting-edge depression-elimination pills, and laud the stunning breakthroughs of their rising young mental science. Simply put, however, deep spirituality, mysticism, magic, oracular divination, occult correspondences, ancient wisdom teachings, and the so-called "perennial philosophy" as posed by Aldous Huxley in 1945, were simply *not* his thing.

It was clear as the twitter of birds, as my lecture was now about to begin. Yet given the opportunity presented to me here, I sought to show

---

2. *Accessing the Unconscious: An Experimental Study of Dreams, TAT, and Tarot*; Arthur E. Rosengarten, doctoral dissertation, 1985.

these kind tarot folk that there was no inherent reason to worry over the dangers of psychologism in my topic for the day. In fact, as a shrink myself, I was more in their camp than they realized.

Tarot in the Modern Age

And so I began my brief sketch of the decidedly psychological turn that modern Tarot has taken over the past hundred years, due in large part to the work of Carl Jung and the Post-Jungians, Abraham Maslow and the Human Potentials Movement, and incrementally, furthered along by a refreshing blend of exotic Eastern and shamanic psychological flavors that had sifted into the edges of the profession, and been quietly incorporated in a net of humanistic, transpersonal, nondual, and integral theorists of progressive psychology practices today. After all, they too were psychologists to be reckoned with, and they too acknowledged the transformative power of archetypal symbols, meditation, ancient wisdom teachings, and (non-religious) spirituality. Many of these more progressive types, in fact, freely encouraged their followers to engage in scientific experimentation and empirical research to further its development, lend greater reach, and legitimacy to these "new" therapeutic methods. To date, however, in the slow evolution of so-called "Tarot science," regrettably, I have been something of a lone sailor in this sea of prescient waters.

The discussion now veered into Empirical Studies proper, the meat of my morning potatoes. I explained that primarily I earned my living as a psychotherapist in private practice, not a researcher at all, and that I too was over-wired on the right side of my brain much like them. I too was constitutionally more the intuitive philosopher-artist type, by disposition and ability, and not given easily to statistical analysis, design protocols, or the administering and scoring of tests—the sorts of things conventional psychology lauded as evidence of their validity and reliability in matters of the elusive mind. Of course, the irony was not lost on me that, for any seriously science-minded reader of this book (and I know you are out there), it may already be obvious that putting me in the role of "science advocate" is not dissimilar to inviting Boy George to host a retrospective of British Rock Star Titans of the late 1960s. Hardly the right man for the job, but someone has to do it!

I felt called upon like some dutiful "citizen-scientist" to pick up that dreaded lab coat, and raise the bar for Tarot Studies such that it was, unless the sea of prescient waters rise irreversibly over our beloved, though fragile, disappearing arcanum. I then quoted some inspiring words of the "Father of Humanistic Psychology" himself—Abraham Maslow, writing in the Preface of his legendary 1964 book *Religion, Values, and Peak Experiences* who said the following:

> I speak about astrology, the I Ching, numerology, Tarot cards, and fortune telling, which—so far as I know—have no empirical support at all...What I say to my friends and readers...is not that these things are necessarily wrong or false, but that I just don't know about them because there is no evidence. I also ask them, if they have a hunch that there is something to numerology, or Tarot cards etc., why don't they put it to the test? Why don't you do some research on it?

Some may have been surprised to hear such reasonable support coming fifty years prior from a giant of 20th century psychology. Yet there was a second point that I wished to convey regarding the merits of the true so-called *scientific attitude,* a point far more important than the first. It was this. Beyond simply lending greater reach and legitimacy to our methods, it is through the liberating principles of "experimentation," (competently undertaken in the freest and most creative sense of the word), applied to Tarot readings, that one soon discovers other special benefits and rewards are served both the experimenter and subject (querent) alike. What benefits and rewards?

The short answer is this: the unseen and invisible worlds that operate beneath the Tarot process will thereby be brought into clearer focus, awareness, understanding, and vision. Their applicability and relevance, therefore, will surely increase. This would include both the unseen and mysterious *mechanism* of Tarot's operation, which we shall call "synchronicity" in this work, and of equal value, the unseen and mysterious *template* of Tarot's profound wisdom, which here shall be called The Matrix or the map, that is, the Major Arcana.

Without The Labcoat

With this long aside, I was beginning to freelance a bit, my time was not long, and though pleasant enough in the great Northwest, I knew the Pacific Ballroom of the Monarch Hotel in Clackamas was hardly the place to say anything further regarding the deepest mysteries and secrets of this monumental deck of cards. Better saved for an expansive grassy pasture rich in green acreage that friendly cows may graze upon blithely on a long and sunny afternoon. This book is such a pasture, I believe, and in time, the cows will be coming home.

Instead, I rattled on about my general empirical interest in *patterns,* that is, those things that occur with discernible regularity and precision. How previously in the handful of Tarot studies I have undertaken to date, my main research approach has primarily been about close observation of card patterns and frequencies, administered in a variety of different contexts and populations, and later speculated upon as for their meanings.

And particularly to the majority of women in the audience, I was happy to assure them that contrary to expectations (even if this sounds a tad sexist, forgive me), no antiseptic lab coat was really necessary for this sort of research actually, to the contrary, *in vivo,* natural Tarot settings (and apparel) were the laboratory of Tarot research—your kitchen table, the office desk, a living room floor, or coffee table if you have one, and one may wear anything one likes.

For the more adventurous researchers like myself who like to travel, certain extraordinary physical and historical settings can powerfully add fascinating and sobering context to a study. I described, for example, "experiments" I had recently undertaken at Stonehenge, and inside newly formed crop circles in Wiltshire, England, as well as various sacred sites I had visited with deck in hand over the years doing Tarot "field work," including ancient Egyptian temples like Denderah and Karnak in 1981, Hindu and Buddhist sacred sites in the north Indian Himalayas in 1989, as well as other interesting places of spiritual context closer to home—a Tibetan Buddhist retreat center in Northern California throughout the 1990s, and, of course, the mystical red rocks of Sedona, Arizona over the wildly electric Harmonic Convergence in August of 1987.

But equally rewarding was my study of male perpetrators of domestic violence who volunteered to receive Tarot readings from me at their court-mandated facility in Southern California with the understanding that readings must address their abuse. That study called The Tarot Research Project, presented in *Tarot and Psychology*, also included my visitation of female victims of domestic violence living in shelters, and similarly sought from them volunteers who would receive readings that dealt with their experiences as victims.

All were fascinating and fruitful settings to quietly launch experiments, and as Maslow said, "put it to the test," but here I am thinking about the wider meaning of experimentation, not necessarily the narrow application of strict scientific procedures, but more generally "taking a course of action tentatively adopted without being sure of the eventual outcome" as the word "experiment" is defined in the Oxford English Dictionary. "To try out new concepts or ways of doing things," from the Latin *experiri* or "try." "Try it!" was the message. In a sense, all Tarot readings are nothing more than experiments, as indeed, much of everything we do in life as a whole is experimental—we try it and see what happens, and what can be learned from it. This is the epitome of the true scientific attitude.

Studying card patterns that appear "randomly" (i.e. synchronistically) via divination, and doing so in a slightly more scientific manner does require a little more structure and procedure. My own way has first been to contemplate the manifest structure, and possible meanings, of a given pattern (or spread) in a reading, and then take the additional steps of methodically quantifying, comparing, contrasting, wondering about, analyzing, and eventually, assembling and organizing this data into a formal study of sorts, one that could be coherently presented to others (though not likely replicated, a cornerstone of hard science, which cannot easily be done here, as we shall see, due to the very nature of nature); this essentially is what empirical investigation of Tarot has meant to me.

The essence of my scientific attitude is, in effect, "try it," and then ask the question, "What can be learned from this?"

Study subjects (querents, or questioners in Tarot) are abundant and can be found literally anywhere—ordinary life, friends, family, complete strangers, or else from special populations, from presidential candidates to truck drivers at truck stops, fleeing Syrians, you name it, can be studied through the synchronistic (and richly insightful) lens of readings, as could college students, people named Wendel, spiritual gurus, or even other tarot readers. Why not? In my doctoral research (1985), my first study used eight members of an experimental dream group I was conducting in San Francisco.

Subjects should not to be limited by time or space either. They could be your friends and neighbors today or, just as easily, public and historical figures of the past, fictional characters, even larger entities, such as nation-states, ethnicities, gender studies, planets in the solar system, or rats in the castle. A little creativity, and it can be done. Not only people or things, but events and phenomena themselves can by studied through Tarot readings as well, like the American Revolution, the break-up of the Beatles, cancer research, the Quarterly Board Meeting of Apple, football games, animal companions in the afterlife, crazy ideas, nocturnal dreams, lurid fantasies, the jokes of George Carlin, and even particular trees in a forest. One only needs to try it, and see what can be learned. Some readings I've tried have been addressed to the dead. Some might be addressed to the "yet-to-be born." Some to the "undead," or the "seeming dead" like your Aunt Agnes or Uncle Joe. There really is no limit as to whom or what an experiment might be directed towards, or invited in for questioning.

As with all good science, the experimenter must come to the investigation with an unbiased and open mind. This is no different that the proper attitude of a Tarot reader coming to a reading, a psychotherapist coming to a therapy session, or a nuclear scientist coming to an electron. In fact, it may be a general rule of life. Rule number one—Leave your "ego" behind, it's contaminated. This includes your personal beliefs, theories, preferences, credentials, accomplishments, and opinions, even your knowledge itself, leave them at the door. Later we will learn why this is actually regarded as baggage in the divinatory process.

Observe the patterns that arise freshly, and try to understand them. This is truly a most welcomed invitation for the Tarot experimenter in particular, as it frees her up tremendously to do what she does best: read the cards. There is no need to be particularly informed or opinionated about the question at hand, nor must one have advanced learning or initiation into cartomancy (card reading). Often in fact, and happily, the less one knows, the better. Your own personal reactions (should they arise) may be included in the data, but are of secondary importance.

Case in point: over the years I have been a frequent guest on a popular late night radio show *Coast to Coast AM* with host George Noory. The show invites authors and researchers on cutting-edge, though often very controversial topics, including a potpourri of conspiracy theories, UFOs, extreme weather, lost civilizations, miracles, impending disasters, alternative health, backdoor politics, and the like. My topic on the show, naturally, has been Tarot.

On occasion, the host would ask me to give live demonstrations on various hot topics that had come into focus, involving many things that I frankly, and openly, had little or no special knowledge about at all, (and frequently had conflicting personal opinions about to be quite honest), but none of this is ever a problem for a tarot experimenter, that is, with the correct scientific attitude. His or her job is simply to interpret the cards in the moment as skillfully as possible, and leave the conclusions for "accuracy" to the audience. Invariably, what will be revealed is not so much accuracy as relevancy, and it will be reported as such by the readee. In general, we leave it to the Tarot gods to do the heavy lifting. And the more we empower the process and place our supreme trust in its working, the more power and wisdom issues forth from the experiment.

Sometimes people say they don't have a question. I tell them "questionless" questions are always welcome, just as those that have form. The rub here is that simply by engaging in a reading, you essentially are entering into a question. The same basic procedure and analysis applies. Some researchers use "intuitive inquiry" as their method of analysis, a formal procedure which can be brought to both quantitative and qualitative studies, but in terms of questions and questioners for the Tarot experiment, the sky's the limit. Obviously, the grand field of experimental possibility outlined here greatly exceeds the far narrower accepted bounds of ordinary applied science, which awkwardly is limited to the gathering of physical evidence alone, in most cases. But then one may wonder, "By what special allowance is the Tarot researcher granted freedoms that the conventional researcher is not?" The answer is stated quite plainly in the introduction of author Cynthia Giles' excellent book, *Tarot: History, Mystery, and Lore:*

> Tarot begins in the realm of the imagination. Imagination is the faculty that allows us to experience the immaterial. Ordinary perception operates through the senses, and so is confined entirely to experience of the material world, but imagination is not bound by the rules of space and time which govern materiality. Through the mode of imagination, it is possible to travel instantaneously into the past or future, to other lands, beyond the earth, and even to realms that don't exist in the material dimension.[3]

What Oracles Do Psychologically

The general reader of this book, *Tarot of the Future,* perhaps not well-acquainted with tarot cards yet, or for that matter, divination, the occult, Depth Psychology, fortunetelling, or any kind of oracle work, may not quite grasp the driving force behind so much excitement around these wily little illustrated cards? What's all the fuss? Here, however, to my Clackamas audience, I was literally preaching to the choir, but this book is not exclusively written for the tarot-initiated.

Quite correctly, for all those who have not experienced first hand the power and the magic of Tarot, the question arising must be, "So what's the big deal?" So what if Tarot speaks in discernable patterns worthy of interest? So what if it's mysterious manner of operation may even have descended from ancient metaphysical teachings? Doesn't astrology do the same thing? What about the Hebrew Kabbala? Hypnosis, by no means metaphysical, is known to operate invisibly, it's been around for hundreds

---

3. Cynthia Giles, *Tarot: History, Mystery, and Lore,* p. ix.

of years, and produces so-called "evidence-based" results; guided imagery techniques too have shown promising results in treating various psychological maladies, including trauma. Why, therefore, tarot cards? Especially with so much conventional disdain and the "smirk factor" they engender, skepticism by the rationalist intellectuals, or at least "noise" associated with them in the public trust? Most people when hearing of tarot cards think of gypsy fortune-telling hucksters, raffish occult wizards, or New Age rainbow lollipops? Tarot card reading is a parlor trick on the order of Ouija boards, table-tipping, or something their deceased grandmother practiced when they were little. Do I really need to study another metaphysical system, another technique or practice that promises one more *whatever?* In so many words, "What makes Tarot different?"

The answer is quite simple: Tarot is an oracle. An oracle comes from its own side, and speaks through its medium, in this case, the cards and reader. This is something different, and the more one sees it in operation, something beyond interesting. Sadly, however, as a consequence of modernism, scientism, and the ubiquitous technological turn of this century, the world today has largely forgotten how to revere the extraordinary subjective workings of oracular phenomena.

An analogy of the miner may illustrate this point. Oracle tools and techniques differ from those of "the miner," which are meant to extract known objects buried in the mine—say gold, diamonds, or coal (and their mental equivalents)—things known or suspected to exist down there, and whose task it is to bring them home, to be utilized. In effect, the miner is an extractor of the known. An oracle, on the other hand, is a kind of alien intelligence of unknown origin or appearance. It is not guided by human knowledge or ego-based perceptions. One never knows what we will be found down there in the oracle's cavern, but learns to trust its import and relevance. An oracle, therefore, is an extractor of the unknown.

It is not dissimilar to the disagreement between Freud and Jung on the nature of a true symbol. Freud, in this sense, was more a miner of the known—things like castration anxiety, the elektra complex, and penis envy. They were the stuff Freud believed lay hidden down in the mine.

Jung decried this as mistaking the baby for the bathwater, that is, mistaking a true symbol for a sign. A true symbol, according to the Swiss psychoanalyst Jung, was always something mysterious and unknown until explored openly in the light of day. In effect, we don't really know what is down there, but will explore it respectfully when we find it. Coming from its own side means exactly this, surprising us with what it brings. The uncanny fact that it seems always to bring precisely what is needed or most relevant, subjectively-speaking, makes the surprise well worth waiting for. Honoring such a practice, even in this electric age of lost mystery, is part of my intention in writing this book.

Of course, when preaching to my choir of tarotists, I hardly needed to spend time on this point. For the initiated, it is abundantly obvious and re-experienced every time the deck is shuffled, every time a new pattern is laid out, every time a card is turned. Scholars of Tarot's ancient Chinese divinatory cousin, the classical *I Ching* or *Book of Changes,* Carl Ritsema and Stephen Karchar, in a ten-year study sponsored by the Jung Institute in Switzerland, translated into modern, easily understandable terms the three things that oracles do psychologically: namely, they translate, mirror, and reveal. More precisely, an oracle:

Translates a problem or question into an image language like that of dreams.

Mirrors the unconscious forces shaping any given moment or situation.

Reveals that in every symptom, conflict, or problem, an inner spirit is trying to communicate to us.

Such Things That Occur With Discernable Regularity

As I spoke on this summarily, I showed a slide of a blank Tarot spread configuration used in many of my experiments, both for clinical and personal use, commonly known as the Celtic Cross Spread. The format may vary slightly from reader to reader, but it is a basic ten-card configuration (see Figure 1) that I fondly refer to as "the bread and butter" of serious Tarot readers. I have outlined the spread positions in some detail in *Tarot and Psychology* (pp. 53-58) including my original "cluster" descriptions which provide readers a more sophisticated way to approach the complexity of this ten card pattern.

FIGURE 1. CELTIC CROSS SPREAD

A general reflection of your present state of mind or consciousness; an indicator of emotional, physical, and spiritual considerations. This layout is designed to access from the unconscious unusual creative opportunities and talents, as well as possible tests for lesson-learning.

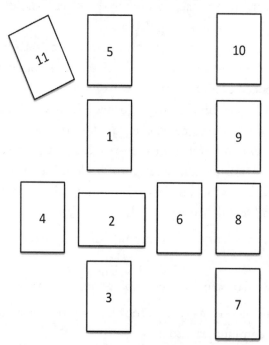

PRESENT STATE OF CONSCIOUSNESS

1. Present situation: how you come to the reading or focus now.

2. The obstacle or issue you need to work through or properly align with that now blocks your your energy.

3. The foundation or root of the situation. The ground of your being here.

4. Past karma: the previous patterns and influences operating behind the situation. S. Perfect pictures: your conscious ideals for the situation; includes goals, visions, ideations.

6. Coming soon: what is immediately beyond your obstacle or issue depending on how you deal with it.

7. How you see yourself: your ego identity in the matter at hand; who you think you are.

8. How others see you: how others perceive you; concerns over what other people think.

9. Hopes and Fears: a two-bladed sword: what you both wish for but may also fear.

10. Outcome: long range resolution of the situation. Something you may work towards or try to resist, but will be in your destiny and will need to be reckoned with.

11. Gift & Guide: A hidden factor outside your situation which will serve you as a gift and for guidance. (Blindly selected by the reader).

Excerpted from Rosengarten, *Tarot and Psychology: Spectrums of Possibility,* 2000.

Typically, after a full reading is completed in about 25-40 minutes, including card preparation and selection, a "cluster analysis," is a rational way of breaking a spread down into its psychodynamics or clusters, always with an eye to the uniqueness of the pattern in question. This refines our perception of the complexity of each individual reading, and better translates the reading into an image language like that found in a dream. One then may ask: "What unconscious forces are shaping this moment or situation? What is the 'inner spirit' here trying to tell us?"

Over the thousands of readings I've given in my career, I daresay no two patterns have ever been exactly alike. This I find quite interesting and intriguing, though not at all surprising, given the obvious fact that no two people are exactly alike, no two stories or life contexts are exactly alike, and no two moments in time and space are exactly the same. It is the nature of reality, and in this experiment we find replication only to be a particularly thorny issue for statistical analysis.

I've come to regard each divined spread to be a kind of snowflake of psychical proportions. Certainly there are similarities, and obvious differences from one reading to the next; a distinctive *flavor* each reading carries, varying first impressions generated, and one soon learns to recognize if a noticeable prevalence or omission has occurred in the pattern, of color perhaps, figure, number, element, or gender, as well as other striking interior trends and themes within specialty groupings.

When a series of readings are given and studied over time (for example, every month for three months), one often observes remarkable carryovers, repeats, reversals, and continuations from previous experiments that begin to flesh out an evolving, full-bodied, narrative. The oracle is speaking to us. Actual snowflakes are the best comparison, in that they display a wide variety of intricate shapes, often of great beauty and fascination in their uniqueness, leading to the popular expression "no two snowflakes are alike." Although theoretically it is possible for two snowflakes (like two readings), to be identical, it is highly unlikely, and in practice rarely seen.

Russian photographer Alexey Kljatov has devised a clever way to bring the wonder of macrophotography to the minuscule world of snowflakes which I find analogous with Tarot readings. Using a homemade rig comprised of a working camera lens, a wooden board, some screws and old camera parts, Kljatov captures the breathtaking intricacies of snow, with its six-sided symmetry, in the following examples:

Figure 2. Snowflakes photographed by Alexey Kijatov, 2014

A second example, a shade more controversial, is with crop circles. In Wiltshire, England last year, the epicenter of this mysterious global phenomenon, I had the pleasure of meeting with Michael Glickman, a former architect, inventor, and professor, who brings a wealth of practical experience to the crop circle subject from the world of designing, making, and manipulating solid matter in the material world. With more than twenty years of involvement with the crop circles, Glickman has made a veritable art form of the deconstruction of crop circle designs to better understand their symbolism and, most importantly, their geometric properties. As a result, his work on the geometry of the circles is respected throughout the crop circle research community worldwide.

Glickman writes:

> Looking back, I realise [sic] it is not simply the geometry that intrigues me. I constantly sense an order behind the geometry and an intent behind that order. The pursuit of the source and origin of that intent, its programme, its goal and ultimately its identity must surely be the obligation of everyone interested in crop circles.[4]

Figure 3. Crop Circle Patterns

---

4. *Crop Circles: The Bones of God,* Michael Glickman (2009).

Example of a Tarot Pattern

To illustrate a similar sort of "pattern uniqueness" in Tarot, I presented a reading given several months earlier for a person named DJ, and then briefly offered my initial impressions. In Figure 4, using a standard Waite deck, DJs "snowflake" or "crop circle" appeared thusly:

Figure 4. DJ's Snowflake

With the little remaining time I had for my lecture, I summarized the distinctive *flavor* I felt regarding the spread. There had been no particular question in this case, and I shared my first impressions, things that struck me, or seemed obvious (even by their omission), and invited the audience to add their own observations. For instance, I was quickly troubled by Position 2: The Obstacle—held by the Knight of Cups (a questor of Love) stuck in the center of the reading. It was surrounded, and seemed adversely "hemmed-in" by four powerful major Keys: The Moon, Death, The Hierophant Reversed, and The Wheel of Fortune. This suggested to me a psychological context of great emotional pressure and turbulence, and lack of conscious control. Because the Major Keys (e.g. Moon, Death, Hierophant, and Fortune) always bear far stronger, more impersonal, archetypal weight in Tarot, I sensed tremendous inside pressure bearing down on all sides, quite a large challenge to get right for a purported Knight who was now constrained (or out of alignment) as he was in Position 2 (The Obstacle).

I was also struck by a preponderance of reversed cards, usually signaling blockage or the shadow side of said card. Most concerning for me was the very confused self-image observed in the Ego Position (7) "How I see myself" holding the 7 of Cups Reversed ("Hamlet in Purgatory" I think of it); followed by The Hermit Reversed in Position 8 "How Others see us," suggesting aloofness, being walled off, insular, and isolated. Simultaneously, however, from the next card up the ladder in Position 9, a person possessing a great desire for stardom or celebrity in— Hopes and Fears ("A two-sided sword")—where sat still another major Key—(17) The Star itself, "illumination," perhaps egging poor DJ into battle, I wondered, despite so much weight and confusion surrounding him. The "Fear side" of Position 9, I imagined, failed Star power, would be one of unbearable humiliation and deflation, should the mission be unscuccessful.

Many additional comments came from the audience of considerable insight and ingenuity. What I neglected to tell the audience until the end, however, in adherence to the principle of non-bias as a hallmark of the proper scientific attitude, was that this reading was originally done two months earlier on January 7, 2016, discussed in an interview on *Coast to Coast* AM that night, was of D. J. Trump! At the time, DJ was generally perceived publically as a smug, button-pushing, political long shot, who flamed populist frustrations on the right with some success, and was an enormously controversial presidential candidate to say the least; it was a month before primary season, and I thought he would make an interesting subject for a reading experiment. I ended my talk there, simply as another unique Tarot flake to behold, and took questions from the audience.

CHAPTER 2

Traveling

Figure 1. All But the Brain Dead and Fully Enlightened

Many years ago a graduate professor of mine with expertise in social psychology and Buddhist mind theory remarked during class, *"For Westerners, there is one question, above all others, that most quickly triggers instant anxiety, no matter who is being asked, or what their age. What is it?"*

One student blurted out the obvious "fire!" No, that was not a question, nor was it the correct answer, the professor curtly said. Another tried, "Did you notice a strange rash on your genitals when you woke up the next morning?" Funny, but still not correct. A few more stabs yielded predictable concerns with respect to tax audits, root canal, penis size, wet dreams, embarrassing moments, etc., "the full catastrophe," as you'd expect of graduate students in the mid-1970s, for such purposes. All wrong. The Professor grew tired of our weak attempts and came right out with it. The question is: *"So what do you want to be when you grow up?"* It came like a thud. I thought it was a pretty lame answer, frankly, for such an inviting build-up, but upon closer examination, I supposed it did show some merit for the stated intent. But at any age? It eclipsed around the meaning of "being" I figured. Interesting... But after some decades to reflect upon this curiosity, I now think the better questions are *"Who are you really,* and *where are you really going?"*

At first glance, it seems innocent enough. "So, Mary, who are you really and where are you really going?" The identity part might be the easier of the two, at least in the beginning (to which we will come back later), but where one is going is a perhaps little more thought-provoking. Not in the obvious, immediate, or concrete sense of going places, rather in terms of direction, purpose, and destination in the grander scheme. Where, in fact, are *you* going? Try asking yourself this right now: "Where am *I* going?" Surely you must be going somewhere? Whether or not it is precisely known, muddled, or unknown (at the present moment), it hardly needs to be said that human beings are wired to go places all the time and on many levels. Its complete absence, on another level, calls to mind the Zen slogan "Nowhere to go, nothing to do."

Most places we are consciously going to, it turns out, fall into the category of physical destinations in outer space, or "PDs" in shorthand. PDs are three dimensional places like the office, home, the park, the restaurant, the moon, etc., and this movement typically occurs volitionally around daily routines of ordinary life, and in present time. For instance, you might say: I am going to "the job I dislike," "run some errands," "pay the electric bill," "visit a friend (or lover)," "shopping for shoes," "to brush my teeth," "take a run," "walk the dog," "play my guitar," "make dinner for my family," "play mindlessly on the computer," "the doctor for my bladder infection," "drink a cold beer," "meditate on kindness," "the bathroom at the end of the hall," "my daughter's basketball practice," "catch a movie I really want to see," or "get some much needed sleep," etc. So many places go I! Remove the "coloring," however, the specific qualifiers, descriptors, and particulars—and examine structurally just the rudimentary things that remain, we find our collective goings to be rather finite and predictable: we go to work, maintenance and upkeep, socializing, sex, consumption, hygiene, exercise, care-taking, creativity, eating, playing, health care, mood alteration, bodily functions, parenting, entertainment, and sleep. By no means a complete list, but these are among the common destinations today that most people in modern culture will identify as the objects of their goings.

But is this not obvious, and do mundane destinations such as these really strike terror just at their mention? No, they categorically do not! About what, then, is all the fuss? Weren't we talking about the Tarot of the future? We will get to that, but there is more here to ponder...for we are ultimately talking about our life purpose: "Where are we really going?" also includes what is the true direction and purpose of our movements in view of a future destination.

Physical destinations, as such, are not typically the category of goings by which instant existential anxiety is generated as posed by the cardinal questions. To the contrary, PDs are generally familiar places, unremarkable, and often satisfying. If anything, they provide comfort and pleasure, not distress. Whatever anxiety PDs may provoke, they will more likely fall into second order effects such as one's attitude, preference, memory, and interpretation about them. "Did I do it well enough?" "Was it appreciated sufficiently?" "I wasn't happy the last time I tried it," "Will it come back to haunt me later?" etc.

But the places we reflexively associate as our "going objects," i.e. physical destinations in outer space, actually comprise only a fraction of the content that we have come to know as "our lives," and occupy perhaps no more than 50 percent of our goings, (unscientifically, I would wager), and here I'm being over-generous. If someone asked you simply "Where are you going?" on the PD level you might simply answer "I'm going to the store," add some explanatory note, and think nothing more of it.

As I wrote this chapter, a meaningful synchronicity occurred with what we are discussing. Namely, sad news of the passing of the legendary heavyweight boxer, Mohammed Ali, on May 3, 2016, in my opinion, among the great ones of our time, and for so many, a favorite hero for me throughout my life. I find such striking parallels to what I am engaged in writing often to be fertile ground for momentary reflection. Scanning through major media coverage of Ali's passing, I found an old interview with Ali back at age 35, given before a live audience in England. A kid asks The Champ what he will do when he retires? Ali's answer speaks directly to our point here:

> When I retire from boxing I really don't know, but I want to say something here...Life is real short. So if you add up all your traveling, all your sleeping, your school, your entertainment, you probably been half your life doing nothing. So now I'm 35 years old. 30 more years I'll be 65. We don't have any more influence, we can't do nothing much at 65—your wife will tell you that...when you're 65, ain't too much more to do. So, did you know in 30 years I'll be 65? In those thirty years I have to sleep 9 years, I don't have 30 years of daylight. I have to travel back to America, takes 6/7 hours. All my travelling, probably 4 years of traveling in the next 30 years, about 9 years of sleeping. Television, movies, and entertainment, probably about 3 years of entertainment. I might have 16 years to be productive. So this is how we can all break our individual lives down. What am I going to do in the next 16 years? What's the best thing I can do? Get ready to meet God.

Especially when we consider what changes when the sexy modifier "*really*" is added to our formulation, "So where are you *really* going?" a light punch in the gut may now be discernible. Take a look. If the answer is that you are frankly uncertain, you haven't given it much thought, or instead you default to another PD in outer space, then it is likely that a second gnawing question will soon loom in the outer hallways of your mind: *"Is this all there is? Is this where my life is really heading?"* To a retirement community in Scottsdale, Arizona or its equivalent. To visit all the PDs in North America you can with your husband in your recreation vehicle (providing he's still around)? To your last confused breath on Earth, and then, hopefully, to cash in on the free rent and good food in heaven? Is *that* really where you are going?

Travel

In this book's terminology, I substitute for the phrase: *the act of going places,* a better, technically more accurate, single word, namely, "travel" or "traveling" as in "Where am I traveling to?" The most basic definition of travel, is simply *"moving from one place to another."* It applies both to outer space and inner space. We are traveling constantly, and on many levels of travel remaining perfectly still seems nearly impossible (assuming you are alive) for all but the brain dead or the fully enlightened, the alpha and omegas of complete stillness.

We are travelers by nature, instinct, functionality, tradition, desire, enjoyment, habit, wisdom, both involuntarily, and by choice. We are always going somewhere, it seems, and this is as clear as the cloudless hour. Even without a physical destination, we are moving from one place to another. Travel, of course, by no means is limited to its ordinary modern connotation—the thing we do on business trips or vacations to Europe, or to our sister's house in Des Moines. The depressed person who spends hours of her days ruminating over a recent break-up travels in anguish looking for relief. The college student may travel late into the night in his books (and simultaneously, as well, an inner space of myriad fantasies which shall remain nameless), looking for knowledge, ideas, stimulation, and understanding. The profoundly spiritual or mystical among us may even be traveling in awareness to find enlightenment, or so they believe.

The computer age has certainly played a dominant role in not only *where* but *how* we travel today; it crosses the borders of inner and outer space, and within its portals has rendered travel times and distances virtually instantaneous and theoretically unlimited in reach. Software today is rapidly transforming the outer world that once was. Vast possibilities for new applications continue to be imagined and created with no end in sight, fed and nourished by the massive amount of human index data now available. Driven by rapidly expanding access to ever-strengthening software and hardware capabilities, the information superhighway discovered at its inception, however, a critical and essential necessity and reliance that all travel requires to function: navigation tools. As computer software today is rapidly transforming the world that once was, Reid Hoffman, co-founder of Linkedin and called "the most connected man in Silicon Valley," recently observed in an interview on CNN:

> All of human life can be thought of as navigation—you are navigating your career, you are navigating your education, you are navigating your personal life, you are navigating your entertainment, and you are navigating your health. And all of that navigation can now be used as "human index data to build entirely new kinds of navigation" (CNN, GPS with Fareed Zacharia, May 29, 2016).

Thus it is that we are all traveling in the purest sense, moving from one place (physical, virtual, or mental) to another, constantly, and with little guidance beyond our navigation tools. This intrinsic condition of being human is what psychologists call the "process" of how we find ourselves to exist: moving through impermanence, and the constant flux of "traveling." In the Buddha's formulation 2500 years ago, it is the very source of the first of The Four Noble Truths, Suffering (dukkha):

> Life in this mundane world, with its impermanent states and things, is dukkha, suffering, and unsatisfactory.

The fact that all the constituents of our being, bodily and mental, are in constant travel (motion or movement), arising and passing away in rapid succession from moment to moment, without any persistent underlying substance, further begs the questions: *"To where?"* and also, *"Who is it that's going?*" (or perhaps, *"what"* is it that is going?). The Buddha's fundamental insight suggests that the very things we identify with, and hold to, as the basis for happiness, rightly seen, are also the very basis for the suffering we dread.

> All beings in whom ignorance and craving remain present wander on in the cycle of repeated existence, samsara, in which each turn brings them the suffering of new birth, ageing, illness, and death. All states of existence within samsara, being necessarily transitory and subject to change, are incapable of providing lasting security. Life in any world is unstable, it is swept away, it has no shelter and protector, nothing of its own. (Trans. By Ven. Bhikkhu Bodhi)[1]

Mind Travel

Sometimes we human beings are conscious of our ceaseless wandering, other times less so, particularly when it eclipses with inner space. We tend to go on "automatic" like driving in our cars, for instance, when we may forget *why*, or even *where*, we are going, until, of course, we actually arrive there. This is the interior dimension of travel, which operates, as we shall discuss, on many levels.

Interior travel characteristically carries the subjective perception of either "entering or exiting" some thing (a physical or virtual place, a thought, or experience of any kind), of comings and goings, departures and arrivals. And as the saying goes, we often don't know "if we're coming or going?" Like walking, chewing gum, and texting at the same time, the untrained mind has difficulty perceiving doing each, simultaneously. Though equally true, we can shift our frame of reference on a dime owing to the nimbleness of the human mind. "Now I am exiting the elevator. Now I am entering the office, etc.," but regardless, perceptions of this kind occur in single linear units, even under rapid fire.

To extend the metaphor, new drivers often find it hard to experience exiting the off-ramp and entering onto the freeway in one unified motion,

---

1. Bhikkhu Bodhi, "What are the Four Noble Truths?" *Tricycle,* https://tricycle. org/magazine/impermanence-and-four-noble-truths/.

a juggling of sorts is required, even though both are always dynamically occuring simltaneously during travel. Werner Erhard, the controversial American consciousness guru of the 1970s and founder of est, has more recently observed: "the future that one lives into shapes one's present."[2] Much indeed, depends upon one's frame of reference and skills of observation. By the same token, entering/exiting is never really occurring (as single linear units) in reality, only the mind makes it so.

Air travel, working rather nicely for our discussion, extends the time ratio between departures and arrivals because greater distances are accorded, thereby slowing the process down perceptually, such that experientially we can visualize the dynamic process in our minds of departing Los Angeles say, transferring in Kuala Lampur, and then arriving in New Delhi, simultaneously. We have time to visualize the whole pathway, and hold it easily in our imagination. A significant gap of time between start and finish, with a middle phase of transfer (or transition), gives our minds the needed time span necessary to "feel into" the psychological experience of traveling in its full context.

Figure 2. Commonly Viewed in Airports:

(c) brankica www.fotosearch.com Stock Photography

---

2.   Erhard, Werner, *A Breakthrough in Individual and Social Transformation,* The Eranos Conference, Ascona, Switzerland (2006).

As we routinely observe now with air travel, both international and domestic, a "gap" phase between departures and arrivals is clearly indicated in the itinerary: the sometimes dreaded "stop-over," change of planes, commonly called "transfer" in the language of travel, provides a travel gap. Whether it's Oakland-transfer in Dallas-to JFK (New York), or San Diego-transfer in Amsterdam-to Kiev, the gap occurs "in transit," and as we shall soon discover, in the *Tarot of the Nine Paths* (TNP), this too is an integral aspect of passage, and herein will be referred to simply as "Transfer."

On the everyday level, the transfer gap is akin to what happens on your way to getting where you are going. If it is not navigated properly, you could get stranded. Like John Lennon's famous snipe: "Life is what happens while you are busy making other plans." The three-fold process: departure-transfer-arrival can be noted more sparingly in practical functioning as simply: home-car-work, letter-stamp-mailbox, or perhaps, planning-life-outcome. So-called "transfer gaps" are crucial to outcomes and arrivals, they can be long or short, rich in texture like all that may occur between the first kiss and the point of orgasm, or hardly noticed like the click of a mouse ("sending") between the points of composition and reception (write-send-receive) in an email. But you may astutely ask "What about the baggage?" Uniquely, in the way of *The Nine Paths,* the baggage stays home, or at least, if it is brought it will weigh heavily upon your freedom to travel lightly and openly.

Conscious Mind Travel

Mindfulness meditation and other awareness practices teach us not only to be present in the here-and-now with all manner of mental contents, but also to observe the gaps between thoughts, and at much shorter distances, namely, the spaces between "arisings" and their fallings away. Soon we will see a parallel in the Tarot to this "transfer phase" which corresponds on the "map" with the middle row (Y) of the TNP Matrix, sandwiched, that is, between Departures (X) and Arrivals (Z). If the reader has not the foggiest idea of what I am referring to here, he or she may be commended for paying attention. The so-called TNP Matrix has not been mentioned to this point, and quite rightly, you must therefore wait in joyful "not knowing" until the following chapter. In any event, for now it is enough to understand that we experience our world in single linear units of comings and goings, that a gap exists between identified or designated points, whether registered in awareness mindfully, or occurring automatically or unconsciously.

The second level of travel that we have already begun discussing occurs simultaneously to physical destination travel (PDs), but is untied to it. It is mental by nature, and we may think of it as mental travel, or "mind travel." I'm not speaking here of the more exotic astral travel or thought projection done by yogis, seers, and such. Everyone but the brain dead and the fully enlightened mind travels. Mind travel may (or may not) be relevant or in sync with parallel outer realities, physical, or even virtual destinations. Often it is entirely independent and unrelated to where we are going on a physical level (PDs). It may be derided as mere "day dreaming," "being in your head," "spacing out," "mind-tripping," "not knowing where you are going," or God forbid, "thinking." In contemplation, we reside fully in mind travel.

We are mind traveling, as well, in the constant subtext and self-talk of day-to day thinking, a kind of primary process, with silent murmurings of our tallying inner voices running commentary it seems on every stimulus that has broken into our field of attention. Momentarily, we deem each thing with a "like" or "dislike" just as on Facebook. And not only do our minds travel through space, but through time as well; mind travel may (or may not) be tied to present time or circumstance also, unlike physical travel. Little, it seems, escapes our nimble perceiving centers. It (our mind) often moves incredibly swiftly, capable of traveling faster than the speed of light, in principle, should one choose to travel mentally to Saturn or Mars, or even beyond the far reaches of the Milky Way. It can be achieved in an instant, that is, at the soaring speed of imagination (not light), and rather efficiently without the clunky need for expensive space ships, alien propulsion, or cantankerous crew. Yes, imaginary meanderings are not the same thing of course, but as you can see, the laws of classical physics do not necessarily apply in this realm. Time-wise, of course, mind travels can be entirely occupied in the "past," "present," or "future," and even "the timeless Now." They tend to alternate between these in any combination, in fact, and at any moment. Generally, however, Newtonian linear time is not much of a factor here at all.

Also to be considered, mind travel is generally only vaguely experienced, or even completely unconscious for many engaged in it, no matter that everyone but the brain dead and the fully enlightened do it, ceaselessly. With practice and development, it can be directed with conscious intention and awareness. This is where the power of symbols may lend a critical hand. In waking hours, while playing tennis, rolling a joint, or delivering the State of The Union Address before Congress and the world it is happening, and it is still happening even when we are dreaming. With mind travel, however, our hackneyed question, "So where are you really going?" stimulates a new and quite different set of possibilities and potentialities, as well as uncertainties and unknowns. Especially as time and space no longer carry the same limiting factors, you might now also wonder, *"Are there places I would really like to go in my imagination?"*

Cognitive Science

In the Western world, the area of mind travel given greatest consideration today is cognition. Cognition refers to the mental processes involved in gaining knowledge and comprehension. These processes include thinking, knowing, remembering, judging and problem-solving. The aforementioned are considered the higher-level functions of the brain and encompass language, imagination, perception and planning. This is a very large topic in the brain science of today, so without going too far afield from the subjects discussed in this book, a few key points are worth mentioning here.

What cognition fully entails and how it comes about is a subject open to debate. Cognition research places great stock in the scientific method: first a type of work, problem-solving skill, or deficit is theorized, and then a study is designed to test and validate said theory. A scientist does not so much *find* a type of cognition, as he constructs it, and then places his construction into the laboratory to determine whether it has merit. The point to remember is "that one type of thinking being different from another" is firstly a human construction. There are differences in kind of cognition, but smart people called scientists ultimately decide which kinds are the differences that matter, depending on their beliefs and purposes, training in the sciences, those of the culture at large, as well as those of the research-funding entity that subsidizes their efforts. Differences, as such, are not inherently true, but more in keeping with the way researchers have decided to divide and categorize them.

It can be, and is often, split differently by different researchers. A slice out of the pie is thus validated if it meets certain statistical criteria, but the slices do not already exist as such. A new form of cognition can be "discovered," therefore, if a case for why or how it is different from other forms of cognition is well crafted. In that sense a new kind of cognition is part discovery and part invention. It is thus "disco-invented" (discovery/invention) on the spot. A hobbit brain researcher, one imagines, might choose to study the cognitive differences in daily meal consumption, finding varying brain receptors activated for Breakfast at 7am, Second Breakfast at 9, Elevenses at 11 am, Lunch at 1 pm, Afternoon tea at 3pm, Dinner at 6 pm, and of course, Supper at 9 pm. (They are hungry little fellows!)

Brain imaging techniques do not provide the answer here either. Cognitive functions such as problem-solving, decision making, abstract thinking, or logical reasoning, it turns out, are not categories that neatly fit within each other and do not, therefore, correlate to single areas of the brain perfectly. In research studies, cognitive scientists start with a skill or type of activity, and then look at what brain areas are associated with it; they do not start with the brain areas, and then look at what kind of activities it produces. The problem, they have found, is that every area of the brain is related to multiple things, so correlation does not mean that much without a theory to support it. The brain, in fact, is a Great Web, and largely still a mystery.

The current Western infatuation with cognitive science and the mysteries of the brain (often to the bane of cognitive scientists them-selves), is driven home in a *New Yorker* review by Louis Menard, on of all things, the business of sports:

> For people who think that if, instead of saying that people are happy when their team wins, you say, "Activity increased in a region called the ventral striatum," or, instead of talking about stress, you talk about " a surge of cortisol," then you are on to something.
>
> What you're on to is physicalism, which (leaving the metaphysics aside) is simply a method of *redescription* [italics mine]. We're con-scious of our thoughts and feelings; what we're not conscious of is their physical correlates, the chemical states in our bodies that con-stitute them and without which nothing could be felt or thought. "The experience of rooting for your favorite team can actually be captured at a neural level"... This is true, because so can the experi-ence of everything. ("Show Them The Money," *New Yorker,* May 16, 2016, pg. 90).

But as transpersonal psychologist Stanley Krippner, author of *Varieties of Anomalous Experience,* writes:

> There are other epistemologies, "ways of knowing" relying on the body, on feelings, on intuition, and on transpersonal and anomalous experiences, that are capable of taking us to realms that mainstream science has yet to acknowledge, much less to appreciate.[3]

Let's turn now to the East, where another dimension of mental travel has long been developed, well before the precursors of modern-day Western science first took to examining the nature of their minds. And also to a parallel stream found in Western wisdom teachings, with its own long tradition of metaphysical thought, often overshadowed or debunked by the dominant purveyors of modern Science and Religion. It is in these traditions that the taproots of Tarot first took shape, and retain their timeless wisdom.

---

3. "Quotes by Stanley Krippner," awaken.com, http://www.awaken.com/2013/01/quotes-by-stanley-krippner/.

CHAPTER 3

Traveling East and West

If one wants to form a picture of the symbolic process, the series of pictures found in alchemy are good examples, though the symbols they contain are for the most part traditional despite their obscure origin and significance. An excellent Eastern example is the Tantric chakra system, or the mystical nerve system of Chinese yoga. It also seems as if the set of pictures in the Tarot cards were distantly descended from the archetypes of transformation, a view that has been confirmed for me in a very enlightening lecture by professor Bernoulli. The symbolic process is an experience in images and of images. Its development usually shows an enantiodromian structure like the text of the I Ching, and so presents a rhythm of negative and positive, loss and gain, dark and light.

—Jung, in *The Archetypes of the Collective Unconscious*

RESONANCE

Joseph Needham writes about the Chinese worldview in his major work *Science and Civilization in China:*

The key-word in Chinese thought is Order and above all Pattern... The symbolic correlations or correspondences all formed part of one colossal pattern. Things behaved in particular ways not necessarily because of prior actions or impulses of other things, but because their position in the ever-moving cyclical universe was such that they were endowed with intrinsic natures which made that behaviour inevitable for them.[1]

---

1. As quoted by Robert Aziz in *C.G. Jung's Psychology of Religion and Synchronicity,* p. 136.

In every pattern, every journey, a discernible story with a beginning, middle, and ending is unfolding. In a tarot reading, the Tarot oracle itself is co-author, storyteller, and guide. You are the questioner, the "querent," and comprise the other half. It is a dance between two very strange bedfellows: ourselves and the alien intelligence; together we co-create an original, shared pattern, and authentic work of art, called a "reading." It can never be perfectly replicated because we ourselves, and each passing moment, are never the same. *"You cannot step into the same river twice,"* the ancient Greek philosopher-mystic Heraclitus observed, adding *"for fresh waters are ever flowing in upon you."* From the Western psychological view, we attribute the source to the deep unconscious from which all symbols spring, in keeping with Carl Jung's view that the unconscious is "the matrix of the human mind and its inventions."

In tarot readings, narratives based entirely on the random selection and distribution of symbols regularly display meaningful correlations between one card-symbol and another, often uncanny in their impact. As well, meaningful correlations (or "coincidences") will regularly be found between card(s) and outer events (or circumstances) within the event horizon in question. It was this same curious fact using a related and far more ancient oracle-tool—the *I Ching,* or the Chinese *Book of Changes*—that led Jung to formulate his momentous theory of "synchronicity" or "meaningful coincidence," which Jung defined "acasual connection through meaning."

When connections are *acausal,* it implies that no exchange of energy or cause-and-effect relation passed between them, yet still, to our amazement, they are clearly interconnected. This would include, of course, psychological influence as well, such as fear causing my hand to tremble, or love my heart to flutter, which do meet the criterion of causal energy exchange, and therefore, strictly speaking, are not synchronistic. The idea flatly challenges the Western mechanistic paradigm of causality, which Jung did not deny, but suggested, under certain conditions (e.g. *abaissement du niveau mental,* or lowering of thresholds), causality was not the exclusive operating factor.

When things are called "meaningful" in this respect, it is important to understand that we are not merely suggesting they are logically, analytically, or intellectually meaningful only. *Meaning* here has a palpable feeling quality. One can feel it in their bones. For lack of a better term, Jungian analyst Robert Johnson points to this quality as "clicking."[2] We can sense its resonance with our natural being and imagine it to harmonize with some larger pattern. It clicks in our gut, and feels intuitively certain and whole, and delivers a "felt sense" of correctness deep within our interior centers. We can say, it "resonates," or "clicks" in our sacred interior.

On the tragic night of 9/11, for instance, a tarot reader would surely feel the click if a preponderance of Tower and Death cards were inordinately turned during an evening of readings. But what significance would this have if true? Beyond the obvious synchronicity shown most tellingly between these card illustrations and the chaos and mayhem of the outer event itself, far more provocative would be the underlying implications with regard to linkages in general, between outer and inner worlds. Something important and uncanny is seemingly occurring here, but only from our modern vantage point that sees outer space and inner space as separate and unrelated.

In the Western metaphysical tradition of symbolism, stemming largely from alchemy and Hermeticism, this linkage is called *correspondence*. The approach recognizes that all natural and cultural objects may be invested with a symbolic layer and function, which in turn, emphasizes their essential qualities and linkages, and therefore, lends them to spiritual or metaphysical interpretation. A car, for example, is a vehicle for transport. Symbolically, it corresponds with a chariot, a rocket ship, an ocean liner, a Boeing 747, a bicycle, a mule, a crane, a map, a tray, an algorithm, a referendum, an education etc. All things, in effect, may also find deep structural sympathy in a corresponding tarot card, or similar symbol system. "The reality of the symbol," notes Spanish symbolist J.E. Cirlot, "is founded upon the idea that the ultimate reality of an object

2. Robert Johnson, *Inner Work: Using Dreams and Active Imagination for Personal Growth* (1986).

lies in its spiritual rhythm—which it incarnates."[3] It is through these rhythms, we may say, that all things are interlinked.

The distinguished English author and Christian Qabalist of the early 20th century, Dion Fortune, brings it a step further:

> It is said that thought grew out of language, not language out of thought. What words are to thought, symbols are to intuition. Curious as it may seem, the symbol precedes the elucidation; that is why we declare that the Qabalah is a growing system, not a historic monument. There is more to be got out of the Qabalistic symbols today than there was in the time of the old dispensation because our mental content is richer in ideas.[4]

In addition to interlinking objects and patterns of correspondence, of equal import in cartomancy are meaningful *cause-and-effect* patterns arising. These connections often appear unavoidably obvious to reader and querent alike, and likewise, they can manifest between card-to-card, and/or card-to-event, occurring either simultaneously or within the scope of the event horizon. In Eastern philosophy, this causal dimension is more properly understood as *karma* that includes psychological and moral causation, and can extend over previous lifetimes. As we delve a little further into these two seminal principles for their relevance to the Tarot of the future, we do so lightly, in keeping with our initial phase of departure, and the reader is advised to simply follow "the clicks" in their experience for verification.

UNDERPINNINGS

For the Tarot practitioner and researcher, the doctrines of karma and correspondence, East and West, fall roundly within the underpinnings and presuppositions of his philosophical base, and it is well to define these important terms at this early stage. Of correspondence, the distinguished University of Chicago philosopher and professor of religion, Mircea Eliade, observed:

---

3. J. E. Cirlot, *A Dictionary of Symbols,* 1962.
4. Dion Fortune, *The Mystical Qabalah,* 1935, p. 16.

Nothing is isolated inside its own existence: everything is linked by a system of correspondences and assimilations.

A central understanding found in Hermeticism, which greatly influenced Western esoteric tradition during the Renaissance, is the doctrine of correspondence. Rather than reducing "Happiness," to "a warm gun," as the beloved Beatles did most playfully, hermetically-speaking, we would prefer, "Happiness corresponds to a warm gun" (even though the song's meter suffers atrociously). Correspondence, however, is but an aspect of a still deeper linchpin of metaphysical thought, namely, "the method of analogy." The traditional formula setting forth the method of analogy is well known. It is the second verse of the storied Emerald Tablet *(Tabula Smaragdina)* of Hermes Trismegistus, a mysterious text first appearing in Arabic between the sixth and eighth centuries, highly regarded by European alchemists as the foundation of their art and its Hermetic tradition. The classic verse in the text we will return to later in view of The Nine Paths, is the honored passage:

> That which is above is like to that which is below and that which is below is like to that which is above, to accomplish the miracles of (the) one thing.

In addition to the classic "as above/so below" axiom of the Emerald Tablet, tarot scholar Robert M. Place notes there are six cornerstones that define the esoteric or occult view subscribed by modern Western Hermeticists: 1) the world is a living being held together by a World Soul or Anima Mundi (found similarly in recent years in the Gaia Hypothesis proposed by James Lovelock); 2) the value of imagination, understood as the door for entering the reality of the soul or the unconscious mind; 3) the idea of correspondence as mentioned above, which recognizes no separation between internal and external reality, in keeping with "synchronicity" which points to a connection between psyche and matter, and we believe accounts for the operating mechanism behind Tarot divination; 4) the belief in a transmutation of the self, such that the goal of life is gnosis, or a mystical union with spiritual oneness; 5) the perennial philosophy which upholds the belief that all cultures and religions share the same yearning for this mystical union; 6) and the necessity for a spiritual journey, where truth and realization can be gained through transmission or initiation, by a reenactment of the hero's journey, which in Tarot is commonly termed as The Fool's Journey.

Place, and other historians, have shown that all of the images and symbols in the early Tarot can be found in other works of popular art from the Italian Renaissance, generally accepted by historians as Tarot's birthplace in the early 15th century. The Tarot is mystical, says Place, because the secular arts of the Renaissance were commonly steeped in mystical philosophy. Renaissance mysticism itself can be classified under the broader heading of Neoplatonism, a modern term used by scholars today to describe a group of early Western philosophies that synthesized the mystical side of Plato's writings as they emerged in the 15th century. The goal of life was seen as the mystical journey, and man's innate talents would develop through magical practices.[5]

Although the first Neoplatonists were Classical pagans, their views were incorporated into the mystical teachings of Judaism, Christianity, and Islam. *Neoplatonism,* as such, refers to most of the Western mystical traditions, including Hermeticism, Gnosticism, Kabalah, Sufi mysticism, and Christian mysticism. Place notes that modern scholars believe Plato to have been not so much the source, but the transmitter, of these ideas dating back to the teachings of Pythagoras, the Greek philosopher of the 6th century BC. In brief, Pythagoras taught the doctrine of reincarnation and a method of purification through contemplation, which allowed the soul to free itself from the wheel of rebirth, remarkably Eastern in this view.[6]

As for karma, the Eastern term (from the Sanskrit *karman*) means "action, effect, fate." In Hinduism and Buddhism, karma is defined as the sum of a person's actions in this and previous states of existence, and viewed as deciding their fate in future existences. Karma, therefore, implies reincarnation, soul, and continuation after death. It is through

---

5.   Robert M. Place, *The Alchemical Tarot.*
6.   Robert M. Place, *The Tarot: History, Symbolism and Divination.*

karma that most "why questions" are answered. Why did 9/11 occur? What brought me to read this book? Why did these cards come up now, and not other cards? The answer is due to the sum of one's previous actions, one's karma, according to this understanding. Further explanation as to the specifics may, or may not, be available at this time (due to karma), and often will have only secondary relevance anyway, to the questions percolating before us now.

The acausal dimension, where in effect, "things arise of their own accord," stands alongside karma, and is given greater emphasis in Far Eastern beliefs, such as Taoism. Such views can seem terribly counterintuitive and discordant to the Western mind, and accounts for much of the resistance the West has traditionally had towards synchronistic practices such as the Tarot, as well as Eastern philosophies. The ten ox-herding pictures known in Zen, depict the stages of practice leading to the enlightenment at which Zen (Chan) Buddhism aims. They dramatize the fact that enlightenment reveals the true self, showing it to be the ordinary self, doing ordinary things, in the most extraordinary way.

The story of the ox and oxherd, was actually an old Taoist story, updated and modified by a twelfth century Chinese Buddhist master to explain the path to enlightenment. The ox symbolizes the ultimate, undivided reality, the Buddha-nature, which is the ground of all existence. The oxherd symbolizes the self, who initially identifies with the individuated ego, separate from the ox, but who, with progressive enlightenment, comes to realize the fundamental identity with the ultimate reality which transcends all distinctions. When this happens, the oxherd realizes the ultimate nature of all existence; there is nothing that is not the Buddha-nature. He now understands the preciousness and profundity of the most ordinary things of life, illuminating ordinary living with his enlightenment. In Appendix D (pages 292-293), you will find a modern execution of these illustrations, which I have turned into a Tarot spread, and invite the Zenist within you to experiment with it.

As we move to discover what it means to be a traveler on the Tarot path, the Eastern doctrine of karma will be explored as a contributing driver of "inner travel," as will be the Western doctrine of linkages by a system of correspondences and assimilations that inform its template, the Major Arcana. Paradigm shift is never easy, and the reader is commended for his or her willingness to explore radically these new and very old ideas.

IMPERMANENCE

Perennial truths that have stood the test of Time and remain unbowed by the intellectual winds of conjecture, theory, and controversy, or shifting paradigms, deconstruction, redescription, or remodeling, are themselves timeless agencies of wisdom, and apply without exception in any age or quarter. As we have discussed, another such timeless truth at the foundation of this work is the doctrine of impermanence. It accounts for why, in a manner of speaking, we are all Travelers, whether or not we realize it. On this point, Ven. Bhikkhu Bodhi, a contemporary Theravada Buddhist monk who now lives at Chuang Yen Monastery in Carmel, New York, writes:

> The notion of impermanence (*anicca*) forms the bedrock for the Buddha's teaching, having been the initial insight that impelled the Bodhisattva to leave the palace in search of a path to enlightenment. Impermanence, in the Buddhist view, comprises the totality of conditioned existence, ranging in scale from the cosmic to the microscopic. At the far end of the spectrum the Buddha's vision reveals a universe of immense dimensions evolving and disintegrating in repetitive cycles throughout beginning-less time. (*Tricycle*, Volume XXVII, Number 2, Winter 2016.)

The practice of mindfulness meditation, a technique of present-centered awareness found in many ancient schools of Buddhist teachings, and becoming widely incorporated into Western psychology today, for instance, brings the meditator to observe the ceaseless impermanence operating within his own mind. When the American psychologist William James introduced the phrase "stream of consciousness" in 1890, he was pointing to what the worldviews of Indic origin, including Hinduism, Buddhism, Jainism, and Sikhism, for thousands of years have known as "the mindstream" (*citta-santāna*). Understood through the wider lens of Eastern travel, the mindstream is "the moment-to-moment continuum of awareness which provides a continuity from one life to another."[7] *Citta-saṃtāna* in Sanskrit means literally "the stream of mind," and as such, it is the stream of succeeding moments of awareness. It provides a continuity of the personality in the absence of a permanently abiding "self" (ātman), which, in particular, Buddhism denies.

Eastern teachings visualize the continuity from one life to another via the mindstream as akin to the flame of a candle which may be passed from one candle to another, with karma the causal mechanism whereby transformations are transmitted from one lifetime to the next. In Buddhist practice, awareness, at the deepest levels, is always the goal. Not simply practicing or even resting in awareness, but more profoundly, resting *as* awareness, the final stage, where travel virtually stops, ego-identication dissolves, and as it is said in Zen, the final result is attained, where "Nothing to do, nowhere to go" means nothing other than pure, abiding, momentary awareness.

But it is not necessary for the Westerner, perhaps unfamiliar or uncomfortable with the notion of karma, reincarnation, or enlightenment, to subscribe to a kind of "mind travel" between lifetimes in a karmically-driven, beginningless, universe ala the Buddhist view, in order to directly observe the mindstream in action. Daily life provides sufficient evidence alone, for as another Zen slogan popularized by author Jon Kabat-Zinn reminds us, "Wherever you go, there you are."

Going Further Eastward

As for the philosophical concerns in Far Eastern thinking with respect to the ancient Chinese "Book of Changes" the *I Ching,* and the Classical Taoism of Lao Tzu-Chuang Tzu, central among them pertains to the origination of mental images, including visual, cognitive, linguistic, imaginal, and sense images. Where do they come from? It is a mystery. The relevance here pertains not so much to *"where"* we are going, as *who* or even *"what"* we are in the final analysis, and what is the nature of our perception of

---

7. http://chinabuddhismencyclopedia.com/en/index.php/mindstream.

reality? This too has great relevance to our topic as we are dealing with a map of wisdom-images to assist a Traveler of consciousness. The distinguished Japanese Professor of Religion, Toshihiko Izutsu writes:

> The Far Eastern way of thinking regarding the problem of mental images is that they are attributed to a particular activity of the Imageless or No-Image itself. Images, in this view, ultimately originate in the No-Image. All images that emerge into the daylight brightness of consciousness are first incubated and formed in the darkness of the sphere of No-Image."[8]

Out of nothing, comes something. The idea appears manageable enough at first glance, but upon closer inspection, it is the kind of puzzle that keeps one up past their bedtime. Whether we are speaking of rational or automatic thoughts, day dreams, the contents of our daily activities, physical destinations, or divinely-inspired tarot images, all mental content, accordingly, is first attributed to the Imageless or No-Image (mind) itself. In other words, the Void. Images that then emerge into the daylight of consciousness, that we can see and know, whether semantic (words and ideas) or perceptual (pictures, feelings, intuitions, etc.), rather curiously and paradoxically, are accordingly first incubated and formed in the darkness of the unconscious, the sphere of No-Image. This, as we will discuss later, is an expression of an unseen, unmanifest, and ubiquitous aspect of Nature.

One further revelation according to Izutsu deserves mentioning here. The images arise, ironically, through the process of our interpreting the abstract forms originally given, for the purpose of obtaining relevant oracles from them. In a sense, we ourselves co-create them out of our undying passion to awaken. It would seem that this is all part of a program hard-wired into our brains. That is to say, the images are generated unconsciously as we try to interpret or find meanings relevant to our experience in those abstract combinations of broken and unbroken lines (I Ching) or unblemished Number/Glyphs in Tarot. The first designers, therefore, are ourselves!

---

8. Toshihiko Izutsu, *Eranos Lecture Series, No. 7,* Spring Publication, 1988.

I Ching

In the divination process, whether East or West, symbols act heuristically to enable a person to discover, or learn something, for themselves, by inciting the native mind to find meanings hidden under a seemingly vacant or random presence. Images become coherent and meaningful as a result of our interpretative act, motivated by the desire to find out what is really meant by their abstract, at times obscure, magical, even counter-intuitive appearances in readings, in dreams, in art and so forth. This, in fact, is the great paradox of oracle work, we might say. They are at once meaningful and meaningless, foreign and domestic to our souls.

For our discussion of "Eastern travel," however, the most relevant parallel is with the ancient Chinese Book of Changes, the *I Ching*, a divinatory system with roots extending back over three thousand years. The symbolic system of the *I Ching* consists of the sixty-four Hexagrams, which themselves are formally nothing but the sixty-four mathematically possible combinations of the two primary symbols of this system: known respectively as Yin (the feminine principle) and Yang (the masculine principle).

Yin is graphically represented by a broken line, and Yang by an unbroken line. In themselves, the *I Ching* symbols are purely abstract or vacant forms having nothing to do with concrete imagery. Six such lines form a hexagram, which are randomly determined by the tossing of three coins, or more traditionally, the stalks of a yarrow plant. [From the diagram below, note that the hexagram is comprised of two trigrams]. Yet out of this imageless system based on two abstract principles (Yin and Yang), a profusion of differentiated images arise, replete with sages, mountains, marketplace, thunder, etc., ironically, from the labors of our own interpretations. Much as with Tarot, the images are generated, according to Izutsu, as we try to find meanings relevant to our purposes of divination. Out of the No-Image, images arise. If for no other reason than this, readings are always relevant.

One further note bears mentioning here. The realm we are leading up to in detail, namely, the Major Arcana of the Tarot, does not, theoretically, resolve in the ultimate state of pure mysticism, Final Liberation, Nirvana, Void, No-Mind, Tao, Enlightenment, Samadhi, Grace, Christ-Consciousness, Pure Awareness, Open Space, or any of the other terms used in both Eastern and Western spiritual traditions to describe Enlightenment. Nor does Tarot claim to take us to enlightenment as such. Rather, the world of Tarot is an intermediate realm of higher levels of human consciousness, accessible to the ordinary, rational, ego-driven mind of our time; it is an evolutionary "transfer" realm, if you will, operating beyond (above, below) the self/object perceptions of conventional rational-ego identity.

TRIGRAMS UPPER ▶ LOWER ▼	Ch'ien	Chên	K'an	Kên	K'un	Sun	Li	Tui
Ch'ien	1	34	5	26	11	9	14	43
Chên	25	51	3	27	24	42	21	17
K'an	6	40	29	4	7	59	64	47
Kên	33	62	39	52	15	53	56	31
K'un	12	16	8	23	2	20	35	45
Sun	44	32	48	18	46	57	50	28
Li	13	55	63	22	36	37	30	49
Tui	10	54	60	41	19	61	38	58

Key for Identifying the Hexagrams

This provides a gateway to the universal levels of higher consciousness that reside at far subtler and deeper regions of the human mind, as it was presumably designed by its unknown and mysterious creators, perhaps unconsciously, to prepare spiritual travelers on their way to final liberation, which apparently, like everything else, can only occur in stages.

The closest Tarot comes to liberation, we may speculate, is Key 0, The Fool, an agent of pure Possibility. This is why Tarot, as a map, should be thought of in a larger sense as an intermediate, liminal, transpersonal, "transfer realm," existing between ordinary consciousness and enlightenment. Properly placed, this is the meaning of "The Fool's Journey" which is discussed further in Chapter 12.

The common places we travel to as rational ego-driven adults in the mindstream of consciousness occur mostly in thoughts, feelings, and sensations. More subtly, we travel in intuitions and mental pictures as well as "felt senses" and symbolic imagery, often overlooked or devalued by conventional behavioral norms, organized religions, and modern science. Though less common perhaps, they are hailed as treasures in the Eastern view, occurring spontaneously and abundantly within the flow. They are the mindstream of imaginal travel. But we must keep in mind that all mental contents and processes, including the imaginal, are forever changing, mostly non-volitionally, and occur only partially within our general field of awareness. From the very tiniest sensation of a summer breeze to the widest conceptualization of mathematical perfection, all remain subject to the invariant condition of existence: impermanence.

THE INTERMEDIATE TERRITORY
The Realms of Tarot of the Nine Paths

THE CAUSAL LEVEL
The Unmanifest Source;
The Abyss (Gnosticism); The Void (Mahayana);
The Formless (Vedanta);
Effortless Insight culminating in nirvana
(Vipassana).

THE SUBTLE LEVEL
Seat of the archetypes. Platonic Forms.
Subtle sounds and audible illuminations.
Transcendent insight and absorption.
Home to personal deity-forms.

THE PSYCHIC LEVEL
When power of inner sight is
more direct than power of thought.
The 6th chakra or "3rd eye."
Marks beginning of transpersonal insights and
subtler level of self-reflection.

VISION LOGIC
The "higher mind" (Aurobindo).
Dialectical, integrative, synthetic.
Establishes networks of relationships.
Highest structure of the personal realm.
Synchronistic, non-linear, systemic.

Neither Fish Nor Fowl

Uniquely, the Major Keys of Tarot are sourced in an intermediate region of the mind operating between ego-driven rationality and pure Being. In readings, divination opens us to a liminal "rainbow realm" or twilight consciousness spoken of in Tibetan, Norse, and Native American practices, an experience that is at once exquisite, numinous, serene, colorful, seen by multiple observers, magical, and supra-mundane, yet also, impermanent, delicate, short-lived, and mysterious! Access to this dream-like imaginary land can be profoundly meaningful, blissful, creative, and revitalizing.

As outlined in the research and writings of transpersonal philosopher Ken Wilber (1992), mystics through the ages have accessed these advanced levels of consciousness on quests for liberation. Tarot, given its strong non-linear and synchronistic methodology, unquestionably activates the "higher mind" (Sri Aurobindo) or "vision-logic" that Wilber describes, and may lead to subtler and deeper meditative states and abilities as well.

Specifically, Wilber's term "vision-logic" is directly applicable to Tarot, perhaps more than other methods. According to Wilber, it is with vision-logic that consciousness first becomes aware of its fundamental structures and finds its own operations increasingly transparent to itself. Such transparency is inaccessible to "thinking" in common formal operations, i.e. the rational ego-based thought processes we are accustomed to, but instead is revealed in "seeing."

The direct "seeing" that begins with vision-logic should not be confused with rational self-reflection, which is also capable of taking its own operations as its object, commonly thought of as "introspection." Their difference lies in the fact that self-reflection and introspection are limited by the basic subject-object structure (i.e. duality) of all rational thinking. This limits its ability to penetrate the basis of its own operations. Though our rational minds can reflect on objects of perception, and uncover their presuppositions, they suffer a critical blind spot which distorts full awareness. Ordinary self-reflection cannot uncover its own presuppositions (or biases) it shares with the object. In other words, the underlying opera-tions that constitute dualistic thinking—the subject-object polarity—are not accessible to rational self-reflection.

By contrast, "seeing" is not bound to the subject-object structure. Indeed, in "seeing," this structure tends to soften, loosen up, and in some instances it may altogether dissolve. The problem is much as the Talmudic saying, "We do not see things as they are but as we are." The shift from "thinking" to "seeing" is seen in each of Wilber's higher developmental stages (see chart). Beginning with vision-logic, and moving through the psychic, subtle, and causal stages, "seeing" appears to become increasingly prominent and of greater luminosity and depth. Transpersonal psycholo-gist Kaisa Puhakka comments:

> The transition to "seeing" entails a freeing from being imprisoned in a subject that stands in a certain qualified relationship to all the objects of awareness. When this happens the contents of awareness are free. You can apprehend them without putting labels on them, without immediately having opinions about them, without directly having dedicated feelings in relation to them. It is a form of aware-ness in which "light touch" is a key quality.[9]

Though Wilber does not directly address it, oracle work, and partic-ularly cartomancy, carries the requisite conditions that activate this ele-vated shift in perception quite naturally. One is invited during a reading to directly apprehend the press of a card's imagery first, before interpre-tative conversation begins. Out of No Image comes Images. Their purely random appearances through blind selection further lightens the "formal-reflexive" response that habitually reacts to information from the dualistic ego-reservoir of subject/object. There is less urgency to locate meanings within the familiar frameworks of reason and problem solving, those "higher order" cognitions that otherwise organize things in our accus-tomed ways of receiving and digesting information. As Wilber suggests,

---

9. Kaisa Puhakka "Call To Play," *Ken Wilber in Dialogue: Conversations with Leading Transpersonal Thinkers*; p. 396-399. Edited by Donald Jay Rothberg, Sean M. Kelly, Theosophical Publishing House, 1998.

through the stage of Vision-Logic, perception naturally evolves to even deeper ground, such as the Psychic Realm, for instance, when the power of inner sight is more direct that the power of thought, and so forth.

WESTERN DENIAL

Freud observed that the single greatest defense against the feelings of deep humiliation is denial. One tendency, therefore, in Western culture today, perhaps more insidious than ever, is to approach the important question "Where am I really going?" (with respect to the bigger picture) with as little thought as possible, far more reflexively, risk-aversively, and avoidant than one might otherwise expect given the weight of the question.

To them, it seems like a stupid, obscure, or irrelevant question. It makes no sense. "Just chill, dude." In so many words, they attempt through a blasé form of denial to reset the investigation. They are being asked to disclose something about which they may have little knowledge or control over. They are being asked to disclose something that has been scientifically debunked as "neuronal nonsense" bubbling in our heads, a "mindstream," if you like, of randomly chattering tree monkeys on the vine. They have likely stopped paying attention to it, or listening at all. There is no point. They have perhaps medicated it away with pills, drugs, and alcohol, or buried its silent murmurs beneath their fascination and addiction to "virtual travel" with its "redescripted" content and speedy, exotic gadgetry.

Millennials and their descendants take notice: high speed internet, curiously, in the collateral damage of its own shadow, may actually serve to lessen awareness and observance of the middle phase, the crucial transfer phase, where so-called *gaps* may occur *inconveniently* between starts and finishes, in something formerly perceived and accommodated (though uncomfortably) as *waiting*. Take heart, as the poet Gregory Corso reminds us, "Standing on a street corner waiting for no one is power!" For all its wonders, this may actually be another unrecognized shortcoming and danger embedded in the Information Age itself. The lost power and virtue of waiting. In a timeless state, it carries no problem at all.

The appreciation of *process,* which, structurally-speaking, always bears a beginning, middle, and ending phase, is known and honored throughout nature, and is the hallmark of all levels of travel, though some now eagerly seek to eliminate it entirely with each faster-generation operating system. Knowing full well that technological progress is unlikely to be reversed, it is still necessary to recall that "as the crow flies" no longer shapes the calculus of our "travel" as it has since man first walked on the Earth, when today the bird family itself is computer-generated, and information bits can arrive instantaneously around the globe from any direction at the click of a mouse. The impressive stopgaps (i.e. contrivances) of postmodern human invention in the name of "technological progress," may psychologically, spiritually, (and quite literally) be signaling "stop gaps" to our souls, that is, eliminating the middle phase, with respect to self-observation, understanding, and awareness, a kind of metaphysical bypass few have noticed or commented on. As J.R.R. Tolkien, author of the beloved *The Fellowship of the Ring,* wrote, "Short cuts make long delays."

In the American denial of our time (in contradistinction to the American Idol of our time), glibness seems the veneer most often utilized to cover the vacuum of discomfort that is awakened when the question is asked: "So where are you really going?" A random imagined sampling: *"Wish the hell I knew..."* one might quip back, without another thought on the subject. *"To hell in a handbasket,"* another will say, not so humorously. *"Who says I'm going anywhere, dude?"* says a tough guy. *"I'll tell you when I get there,"* says the better humored one. *"I honestly never think about it,"* a thoughtful young lady admits. *"Nowhere in particular,"* a smug man answers, as if he has come to terms with his underlying existential confusion, and walks off. If pressed, one often becomes uncharacteristically defensive, concrete, even doctrinaire, reverting back to the PD level, *"To a place where people stopping asking me meaningless questions!"* An important premise of this book, however, recognizes this denial tendency as a serious problem of our times.

Closer to the truth, however, lies another sobering realization: I don't really know. *"I don't know where I am really going in my consciousness. In fact, I have no idea. There, I said it."* This may be a stark admission for some, even a source of fear, shame, or worry, given at least half the lifespan may be spent in this condition of ignorance! (It is hard to say definitively the extent of the problem, as mindstream activity is simply not studied in Western universities as far as I know). While "not knowing" in its purest sense can be a sign of deep introspection, what generally passes for it more likely falls into the basket of denial.

Still, some might ask for the first time, *"Am I supposed to be going somewhere?"* because when they survey their life for a moment, they quickly discover they are indeed going somewhere or another all the time, even when they are dreaming. It is so for all but the fully enlightened and the brain dead. Some find comfort in the scientific view that the mind just switches off at the time of their demise like their computers. "I'm going to turn off now" and that will be that. But beyond the PDs of ordinary life, stripped down to their most rudimentary structures (work, family, food, sex, education, entertainment, and sleep), we generally remain, to put it kindly, traveling aimlessly unaware in our minds, directionless to the bigger picture (if there is a bigger picture), and curiously, too busy, too unmotivated, or too unable to fix this. In the mindstream, we are, in a manner of speaking, no more than lost travelers adrift at sea, rudderless, unconscious, and indifferent to our destiny much of the time.

Or Maybe Not

Perhaps, the takeaway here can be something else entirely when it is learned there is actually a comprehensive map of this territory called Tarot! A means of navigation which has existed at least 600 years, and resonates with the ancient wisdom teachings that once upon a time deep, introspecting, wise sages have discovered throughout history. The Tarot map, among others, points to the places that you should not want to miss. Perhaps you didn't even realize there were such destinations to go to, so different than the physical places and activities you participate in outwardly, or even the "higher level cognitions" from books that you have been conditioned to follow inwardly and outwardly, to comprise the only destinations of travel that have value, relevance, and meaning?

Are you satisfied with this?

Now let me be clear. Much as the celebrated moral philosopher of American letters, Martha Nussbaum, citing Nietzche warns:

> When a philosopher harps very insistently on a theme, that shows us that there is a danger that something else is about to "play the master."

I confess openly, therefore, that as the title of this book makes plain, something else is indeed about to "play master." But I respect my readers far too greatly to ever say the "something else" prescribed to heal our travel blindness was exclusively found in the tarot cards or the *I Ching*, ancient wisdom, or any thing else; to the contrary, imaginative instruments like Tarot are simply symbol tools meant for another order of reflection. It is this other order of reflection that I play master to, not the tools that may get us there. Let me go on record now that I certainly do not wish this big hat hung exclusively on the head of Tarot; Tarot is not, and never will be a, religion, a new science, a psychological school, an ultimate metaphysics, or any other perfect bromide for the human condition, nothing of the sort. But neither is comedy a complete answer to entertainment, though without it the world would not laugh as much. Tarot is not "the answer" by a longshot, but if it were, it would likely be to the question, *"Is there an imaginative tool that can quickly let us to see through the spiritual eyes of higher consciousness?"* In this vein, Tarot does enable such a voice and vision of deep wisdom to pass casually over our kitchen tables, it is a sage whose medium is the curious symbolic images embedded in laminated card stock, which whisper the subtle tones of our essential identity and destination.

If you meditate, you have certainly glimpsed into the stream of mental arisings, gaps, and fallings away that are unfolding in your mind, ceaselessly. This will be helpful when working with the *Tarot of the Nine Paths,* as you will see later when we experiment. Traveling East or West, some reading this book no doubt have experienced more than just glimpses of awareness. For them, these are the materials that can serve as archetypal roadsigns and metaphysical markers on the road to finding out. They will be apprehended easily, and facilitate navigation on the long journey.

Imaginal Travel

There lives within all of us a very quiet corner of self-knowing that recognizes the fundamental truth: we basically don't know who we really are or where we're really going at all. We really only know who we think we are, where we are now physically, and where we are heading next, though even this is a bit sketchy. We are here (wherever "here" is at the moment), and we are moving from one place to another: we are traveling. How we know this remains an open question. The physical destinations and activities of our outer lives are reasonably clear and volitional, and they present no real problem at all, unless they do. The rational destinations of our mental life, those "higher order cognitions," our beliefs and values, our ideas, problem-solving and thinking styles, and all our "infinite wisdom," can be named, categorized, directed, and even changed and upgraded to better models of the same sometimes. But at the deeper levels, "This and $2.75," as the saying goes (during inflationary times), "gets you a cup of coffee."

But what of the so-called "right side" of our brains? The non-rational, more intuitive dimension of cognition, the deep images, the silence, felt-senses, psychic impressions, hunches, dreams and fantasies issuing forth spontaneously? The parts of ourselves that may be soothed by listening to The Beatles or Bach, or touched by a poem, or inspired by a great film, the parts that can imagine the future as if it were real, a moon made of cream cheese, or a city overtaken by zombies, and can sense danger before it occurs, visualize new possibilities, and even impossibilities? They are the sensations that often guide our bigger choices without recourse to logic, self-reference, planning, problem-solving, or the practical data that our evaluative centers provide. They are the place in our being where what we call "spirit," "awe," and "beauty" are found. They too are essential tributaries of the mindstream, are they not? And they too, like all things, are constantly in motion, arising and passing away, from moment to moment.

Shakespeare wrote in his final play, The Tempest, "We are such stuff as dreams are made on, and our little life is rounded with a sleep." It is through traveling in the imaginal realm that we access the stuff that dreams are made of, the deeper layers and wellspring of our creativity, and also the subtler dimensions of consciousness that guide the highest destinies of our human journey. Odd, therefore, that they should take backseat in our age to the power centers of the rational, the sensational, and the material.

"Love," said Voltaire, "is a canvas furnished by nature and embroidered by imagination." Imagination, therefore, is the driving force. The recognition, on the one hand, of our underlying confusion and suffering born of impermance and constant change, and on the other hand, the undertapped waters of the imaginal realms, marks the very starting point of the Way of the Nine Paths. It is here that we enter the Tarot. In the *Travel Guide* that comes with TNP, I describe an added 28th card called The Traveler, meant as the deck's significator and shown in the beginning of Chapter 2.

We Are All Travelers
The Traveler (+9) of Spiritual Indivduation

The 28th card (existing outside the matrix) represents **the personhood of postmodern man, woman, and child** pursuing beyond sense-fulfillment and material survival the many challenges of their lives.

+9 (above)
Signifies the unlimited potential for Spiritual Travelers to enter The Nine Paths at any point, as all situations, challenges, and mental states are accepted as fundamentally workable and amenable to this approach.

The Traveler

INDIVIDUATION

The Traveler's mind is over-run with images, ideas, memories, attractions, repulsions, habits, passions, goals, pain, pleasure, fears, emotions, fixations, fantasies, and other constructions. In effect, **if you have experienced change, pain, or conditionality** in your life, you are (by definition) a traveler. This card may be used as a "significator" (agent of present identity, openness, or circumstance) or be included in divinations.

CHAPTER 4

The Terminal

A terminal is any location whereby a passenger (or freight) departs, transfers, or arrives (or else is handled) in the transportation process. Well-known terminals in the US include: Grand Central Station in New York (train), the Port of Los Angeles (ship), and O'Hare Airport (plane) outside Chicago. Each serves a different type of *physical* destination (PD) transport. Experienced terminal managers will tell you unequivocally that three major attributes are nearly always linked to a terminal's importance, performance, and success: location, accessibility, and infrastructure. No matter its other fine qualities or endowments—classic or ultramodern architecture, the latest in technology, a long tradition of historical interest, aggressive marketing and corporate sponsorship, even high-ranking endorsements from local politicians, invariably, its long-term success, functionality, and endurance will depend upon the "Holy Trinity of Terminality": location, accessibility, and infrastructure. The same holds true for inner space.

According to the Oxford Dictionary, the word *terminal* originated in the early 19th century from the Latin *terminus* meaning "end or boundary." As a noun, it suggests "an end or extremity of something." Exceptions are always found, naturally, as with my current hometown of San Diego's fine International Airport Terminal standing smack-dab in the center of the city, albeit alongside the many yachts and sailboats of its sunny harbor. In this chapter, we shall explore differing dimensions of the word "terminal," and all usages will find a place of significance to our final destination.

Regarding its connotation of endpoint, one might think of the remarkable science fiction series *The Foundation* begun in the early 1950s by the late Isaac Asimov, in which a small forgotten, though critical, planet in outer space named *Terminus* is chosen for its unique location— namely, being the sole body orbiting an isolated star at the very edge of the galaxy, which had been uninhabited for five centuries. A *terminus par excellence!* The story takes place far into the distant future (50,000 years from now) when the entire Milky Way Galaxy is teeming with human civilizations. Most ironically, planet Earth has become all but a forgotten memory, a thing of arcane, even mythic, speculation bandied about by the fringe intelligentsia of the day, not unlike say Atlantis or Lemuria is today, whose ancient existence beyond obscure and pithy fable is left for the archaeologists, mythologists, conspiracy theorists, and historians of the thirty-five million worlds to debate and argue. Most citizens, in fact, had never heard of it.

Before we examine *The Foundation* in greater detail for its relevance to our discussion, it is well to remember that Man, above all else, is a storyteller, and lest we forget, the very book you are reading now is itself no more than a story I am telling you. But like the author of *Ender's Game,* Orson Scott Card, reminds us in his own classic science fiction:

> The story is one that you and I will construct together in your memory. If the story means anything to you at all, then when you remember it afterward, think of it, not as something I created, but rather as something that we made together.

In *The Foundation* narrative, planet Terminus was chosen precisely because of its utter obscurity and endpoint, that is, to serve as a hidden outpost where a meager 100,000 of the most gifted scientists in the universe were chosen to prepare secretly for a vast and immanent cycle of galactic decline, as foreseen in the work of its greatest mathematician, Professor Hari Seldon. Under the cover of researching and writing the first Galactic Encyclopedia, the scientists would work in secrecy to preserve and expand upon humanity's voluminous collective knowledge, but more importantly, they would develop new technologies of extremely high efficiency to serve as a positive counterforce during a future Seldon foresaw that would carry ten thousand years of a barbaric Dark Age, as predicted mathematically by his invincible prophecy machinery called simply "The Seldon Plan."

Seldon called his extraordinary method of analysis *psychohistory*, and knowledge of its power spread rapidly throughout the entire universe as utterly infallible; psychohistory was an extraordinary algorithm that yielded dauntingly accurate predictions concerning complex social and political turns of events affecting the masses and, invariably, it anticipated and demonstrated correctly its predictions down to the minute. Not surprisingly, The Seldon Plan became the most respected and coveted discovery of all time, as what could be more desired and useful than to know with precision and certainty exactly what would happen next, everywhere![1]

Seldon's psychohistory utilized a rather simple mathematical construct to achieve its amazing results, centered on the massive collection of data, but not collected simply from our single planetary sample base as we might today, where indexing several hundreds of thousands of individuals, or even many millions would more than suffice for data collection; this was a future of myriads of planetary civilizations, exceeding thirty five million worlds, and Professor Seldon had devised a method to mathematically capitalize on an unimaginably gargantuan data set. The effect rapidly increased the power of his analysis and accuracy in prediction. Interestingly, the statistical approach implemented was based upon a long-established mathematical law well known in Probability Theory today, namely, the Law of Large Numbers, first proved by the Swiss mathematician Jakob Bernoulli in 1713 CE! The Law states for all of time: *As a sample size grows in size, its mean will get closer and closer to the average of the whole population.* A regression to the mean.

Though this was fictional science imagined by the great Russian-born Isaac Asimov, a brilliant professor of biochemistry at Boston University in his own right, the impact of Asimov's fictional vision continues to this

---

1. Paul Krugman, "Asimov's Foundation novels grounded my economics," *The Guardian*, December 4, 2012.

day. Economist Paul Krugman, for instance, another Nobel prize winner, and a fan of *The Foundation* since a teenager, writes:

> There are wonderful, insightful political scientists and sociologists working today, but their fields have yet to develop even the (very limited) degree of intellectual integration that makes doing economics sometimes feel like we're living in at least the very early dawn of Hari Seldon's psychohistory....[2]

Asimov's *psychohistory* method combined science, history, sociology, and statistics to make extraordinarily accurate predictions about the whole of humanity, even throughout the vast galaxy. In this vision, one does well to remember the sheer size of the Galactic Empire that had soared in population by that time to include millions of inhabited planets, each populated by throngs of human beings with genotypes the same as ours [note: with not an insectoid, wookie, or reptilian overlord among them], and a full estimated census upward of 500 quadrillion residents![3] These truly are large numbers to predict from statistically.

Moreover, each single independent world had evolved with its own distinctive history and cultural permutations, including local traditions, language, governmental structures, economy, etc... but on a "galactic scale" of unimaginable size. And much as today we witness global populations continue to explode in size, it is owing to the Law of Large Numbers and the regression to the mean that counter-intuitively the world is getting smaller every year (qualitatively), more homogeneous, less differentiated, more the same everywhere. As we grow bigger in number, our "mean gets closer to the average of the whole population." One need look no farther today than the presence of smart phones in sub-Saharan huts, Subway wrappers in Eskimo igloos, and *Game of Thrones* on Ukrainian TV.

So what does this suggest here? One thing certainly is the rather fascinating irony that for the Seldon formula to work, enormously large numbers of very ordinary and average human subjects are required in the

---

2. Ibid.
3. That is, 500 (10^{15}) or five hundred times one thousand million million residents.

sample. Here is a clear instance where quantity bests quality, such that outliers, minorities, the exceptional, the artist, the unique etc. are quickly dissolved in a sea of mediocrity. For Seldon's equations to yield reliable results in *The Foundation,* a sample size of at least 50 billion human beings *minimally* would be necessary to reliably generalize from the average. In other words, approximately seven times the entire world population on Earth in 2018. A major logistical challenge, no doubt, even for the psychohistory graduate students in 12,069 GE (Galactic Era), the year of Hari Seldon's death.

Secondly, it seems odd at first that the immense basket of subjects in his database, despite their considerable cultural and planetary differences, and despite also their access to remarkable technological advances of their age in outer space—with easy and affordable space travel to physical destinations anywhere in the Galaxy at near light speeds, for example—these were samples, nonetheless, comprised by design of quite ordinary, unremarkable citizens, that is, human beings of the future fundamentally unaware of who they really were, and where they were really going. Sound familiar? True, they make life much easier for predictors, but this calls into question whether prediction of the future is even a good thing? Do we truly wish to be homogenized?

Asimov later wrote, "Humanity has the stars in its future, and that future is too important to be lost under the burden of juvenile folly and ignorant superstition," and this no doubt is as true today as it was when he wrote it late in the last century. But the future he foresaw, we must remember, though astounding with respect to the technological advances envisioned thousands of years in the future, with human beings spanning outwards to comprise millions of new civilizations, psychologically-speaking, that increase in size and distance of humanity nevertheless remained as frozen and ego-bound as it is today. In fact, from the gargantuan pool of half-conscious human subjects, scientists could exploit their limitations seamlessly, yielding extraordinary historical predictions throughout their many worlds with near certainty. Imagine it!

But we must be mindful of Orwell's omen, noted in the introduction: "Who controls the past controls the future. Who controls the present controls the past." If nothing more, sadly, *The Foundation* should further warn us about the remarkably predictable (and controllable) status we carry in the present—through our ignorance, and despite our sexy outer space technologies (PDs), information gadgetry, and their seductive gifts. Asimov himself was well aware of the danger, and for that reason, he had the foresight to create The Second Foundation, also founded by the seer Hari Seldon, as a budding colony of mentalics, people with extraordinary telepathic abilities, and direct access and mastery of inner space.

Located at Star's End, its purpose was to be hidden from the first Foundation to help insure success in his master plan to save the galaxy. The Second Foundation was a competing, and equally formidable, counter-force of highly gifted intuitive "speakers," whose location and membership remained mysterious and secretive from the dominant inter-galactic ruling powers of The Foundation. The series' main plot involves the internecine struggles and interactions between the two powerful factions, structurally no different than today's struggle between science and metaphysics.

The good news of Asimov's classic trilogy is not just the intellectual brilliance and effectiveness of clever scientists of the future using basic mathematical laws to produce highly accurate, world-changing, predictions. It is also the wisdom and necessity for a counter-balancing interior science built upon a profound knowledge of psychological and metaphysical principles as advanced in the mysterious Second Foundation. The bad news, however, must be with Seldon's woeful findings themselves: an entire galaxy of quadrillions of sentient beings (just like us) heading irreversibly towards a 10, 000 year cycle of barbarous Dark Ages. Asimov was well aware of the potential dangers posed by an advanced, run-away techno-logical science capable of both controlling past, present, and future, even if only as an unintended consequence of their well-meaning endeavors.

One final thought regarding *The Foundation* that is relevant to our discussion. Krugman, draws the following conclusion:

> If there eventually is a true, integrated social science [as found in psychohistory], it will still be a science of complex, nonlinear sys-tems—systems that are chaotic in the technical sense, and hence not

susceptible to detailed long-run forecasts. Think of weather forecasting: no matter how good the models get, we're never going to be able to predict that a particular storm will hit Philadelphia in a particular week 20 years from now.

Though Asimov's *Foundation* is "merely" science fiction, of course, we do well here to review Giles' earlier observation regarding the too-often undervalued impact that is made possible by the freedoms granted in imaginal travel. Because all that we know, and, in fact, that *can* be known, is a narrative mediated through the mind, including history, science, and even mathematics. Giles further reminds us that we necessarily experience the natural world and the passage of time in specific anthropocentric ways under normal circumstances, through our conditioning. These perceptual limitations may be altered under what Giles calls "abnormal circumstances," by changes in brain chemistry and/or brain function. I would also add, during imaginal travel as well, and by way of one of its most stunning catalysts, oracular divination, which will be examined in the next section.

TERMINALITY: 'SPIRITUM CONTRA SPIRITUS'

In quite another scale and context all together, as an adjective, the word *terminal* means "leading to death," especially a slow, often painful, and incurable death. Like many forms of cancer, terminal illness is a disease that cannot be cured or adequately treated, and is reasonably expected to result in the demise of the patient within a short period of time. Cancers, advanced heart disease, at one time AIDS, among others, are all thought to be terminal illnesses. Alcoholism, is also regarded by many as a terminal disease (with psychological markers), primarily because its course when left untreated will invariably lead to death, either directly, or through indirect (e.g. suicide, homicide, car accidents etc.) alcohol-related causes. To be "terminal," therefore, means to be in the throes of death. Informally, the word may also connote extreme, and usually "beyond cure or alteration" behaviors born from very bad, ill-fated, or unfortunate decisions, conditions, or judgment, as in *"You're making a terminal ass of yourself."*

For our purposes, *terminal* speaks to the human condition itself as encountered by The Traveler, unaware of who he really is, or where he's really going; he is saddled to the PDs of his outer life owing to his cultural conditioning, habits, role-modeling and, at times, for simple convenience sake. In a sense, all of these limitations become a kind of generalized *alcoholism of life*. The Traveler has been limited largely due to the rational functions of his mind and the addictions of his life, as he struggles to navigate an impermanent and ever-changing world and self. People, jobs, health, relationships, bills, social and political events, children, spouses, and friends are constantly changing (though often imperceptibly) on a yearly, monthly, weekly, daily, hourly, and momentary basis it seems, right before his eyes. Of course this is not a new phenomenon, we are just more aware of the nature of reality now.

The rapidity of change in our era is only equaled by the speed and reach of The Traveler's constantly expanding information terminals. His visions, fantasies, dreams, and other imaginings are generally regarded as impractical, one step above dreamless sleep, or "just" entertainment, the kind of stuff children are made of. Like the addict or alcoholic, The Traveler has cloaked his underlying confusion, despair, feelings of absurdity, and powerlessness, beneath a mask of denial (including, minimization, distortion, and projection), often unconsciously or with intermittent awareness only, until (and unless) he breaks free of the "habit."

Interestingly, the most effective treatment for the alcoholic or addictive personality, as research continually demonstrates, is the very low-tech infusion of spiritual intervention. Spiritual medicine, a "turning it over to a higher power" in the parlance of Alcoholics Anonymous, is proven the best medicine for this disease, including the timeless wisdom that lives in AA's Serenity Prayer:

> God, grant me the serenity to accept the things I cannot change,
> Courage to change the things I can,
> And wisdom to know the difference.

Spiritual medicine was certainly in keeping with Jung's early advice to an American alcoholic named Rowland Howard, at the encouragement of AA's founders Bill W. and Dr. Bob, who first traveled to Zurich, Switzerland to Dr. Jung's clinic in 1932. After about a year, Jung told Rowland that since they had been unable to bring about a psychic change in him, he would be discharged. No doubt startled, Rowland asked, "Is there no hope, then?" Dr. Jung's answer, an astonishing one for a man of science, was, "No, there is none—except that some people with your problem have recovered if they have had a transforming experience of the spirit." In a letter to Bill Wilson decades later in 1961, at age 86 and six months before he died, Jung wrote about Roland's case:

> What I really thought was the result of experiences with many men of his kind. His craving for alcohol was the equivalent for a spiritual thirst of our being for wholeness, expressed in medieval language as the union with God ("As the heart panteth after the water brooks, so panteth my soul after thee, O God." (Psalm 42:1)... You see, Alcohol in Latin is "spiritus," and you use the same word for the highest religious experience as well as for the most depraving poison, the helpful formula is: 'spiritum contra spiritus' [Higher Power opposes alcoholism].

The terminal habit of all addictions, we may say, is rooted in attachment, spiritual thirst, and ignorance. In the larger sense, of course, who could doubt that we are all addicts and alcoholics of some variety, ignorant of the root causes of our condition, and thirsty for spiritual direction.

A Point of Connection

In still quite another sense, a *terminal* can also mean a point of connection, for instance, in closing an electric circuit, where any device at which a user enters data or commands for a computer system, the received output is displayed. In data communications, a terminal is usually applied only to the extended end points in a network, not to central or intermediate devices. But more broadly, if you can send signals to it, it's a terminal. Terminal data typically is utilized for rational and organizational functions such as recording, tracking, calculations, billing, categorization, prediction, planning, and problem-solving purposes, serving complex systems requiring the highly efficient and accurate processing of information.

Metaphorically, however, a terminal as such may be thought of as a station that facilitates "hooking up with" or "plugging into" the flow of a powerful energy system of information. Here we are speaking of a special type of data transfer collected deliberately from intuitive and imaginal reservoirs of mind, used for navigation through the subtler and higher regions of consciousness. The Tarot itself is such a powerful energy system of information, comprised of a special set of archetypal keys—the archetypes of transformation—representing critical agents and agencies for growth and transformation of the human mind. In TNP, these regions are generally termed The Intermediate Territory, comprising a bandwidth of consciousness that is post-rational-egoic (thinking) and pre-nondual pure awareness (No Mind, Void, or Enlightenment) on your dial, comprising what theorists today commonly call Transpersonal Psychology, or "the transpersonal band" (Wilber).

As points of connection, terminals are not limited to electronic technology. In late August of 1993, for example, I had the good fortune to travel to Chicago to attend the auspicious five-day Parliament of World Religions. This was a terminal of a different sort, and by all measures was to be an extraordinary spiritual bonanza, commemorating the 100th anniversary of the great Indian saint, Swami Vivekananda, and his epic journey to America in August of 1893, for the express purpose of initiating the first major "interfaith conference" in recorded history.

The centennial celebration was truly a marvelous event to behold, with every emanation of guru, spiritual ambassador, captain of consciousness, priest and priestess imaginable. The colorful opening ceremony was a procession of Hindus, Buddhists, Native Americans, Sikhs, Jains, Moslems, Rastafarians, B'hais, Yorubans, and Zoroastrians, with women participating on a par with men, and, all in all, creating a truly overwhelming, joyous, point of human connection in spiritual diversity and community. With more than five thousand attendees filling the luxurious ballrooms of the Palmer Hotel in downtown Chicago, we all were free to pick and choose from various talks and instructions given by a virtual smorgasbord of "spiritual bridgemakers" at any given hour (it was worth surrendering your lunch ticket for).

Yet for so impressive a mandala of spiritual diversity, I don't believe any speaker throughout the entire convention once mentioned the incomparable deck of human possibility, that is, *the Tarot*. I believe there is an important reason for this notable omission: Tarot is not a religion, but a sacred tool. Nor is the Tarot a spiritual movement or a school of consciousness, but a catalyst of imagination, and a creator (some may prefer *inventor*) of consciousness. As such, it carries little traction in the official world dialogue of spirit or consciousness to date.

Though in terms of animating, and indeed, advancing the vision and vitality of organizations of any kind, including those purportedly dedicated to the spiritual growth and expansion of consciousness, the Tarot is an unparalleled terminal of metaphysical connection, and might be utilized as a gauge of vitality and health, a transpersonal thermometer of sorts. The medical thermometer, of course, with its insertion into one of several small physical openings, is a diagnostic instrument designed to measure body temperature. Its feedback alerts the patient, nurse, or physician to a preliminary and non-specific assessment of multiple, simultaneous, and interrelated systems operating within the physical organism either in health or in sickness.

Curiously, this useful instrument's scientific precursors, mechanics, composition and components, internal structure, place of manufacture etc. are entirely secondary if not irrelevant to its function. Such technicalities are left to the physicians, producers, and distributors of the product. As users, to put it plainly, we simply stick it in, pull it out, read, and wash—without concern for such irrelevancies. Its utility nonetheless remains unrivaled in common medical practice. Proper placement and correct interpretation are the sole challenges in application and, for most users, easily achieved. Quite succinctly, and utterly low-tech, the medical thermometer's long-term success, functionality, and endurance is a prime example of what we have called the "Holy Trinity of Terminality": location, accessibility, and infrastructure. Historically, change and innovation in the thermometer has come mainly in its manufacturing and distributing sectors, though its purpose, utility, and validity have remained largely unquestioned, at least within the parameters of modern Western medicine.

So, too, we might say, is the Tarot a kind of thermometer. Its insertion also is placed into one of several small *metaphysical* openings—for example, a context of exhausted rationality, the invocation of a higher power, or perhaps, a moment of compelling uncertainty that calls out for guidance. Similarly, its feedback alerts one to a non-specific, generalized assessment of structures operating within the whole personality. Though interestingly, unlike the medical thermometer, owing to its great versatility in applications, depending on its user's need, the Tarot can also be directed to specific systems and subsystems throughout multiple levels of experience, and is nearly without limit is this regard.

THE MATRIX

Generally-speaking, a system is a set of interacting or interdependent component parts forming a complex and intricate whole. At Terminal 9, as we shall see, The Traveler enters a *meta*physical system whose intricacy is seen in a set of interdependent "wisdom agents" illustrated in a deck of cards, and forming a complex/intricate whole called the Major Arcana, Higher Keys, Tarot Canon, or Matrix.

In both traditional and modern Tarot decks alike, there reside 22 Higher Keys in total (including The Fool), but in TNP there are 27. Mathematicians circling the globe may therefore, without need of a calculator, deduce a simple difference of 5! Yet unlike presumably the rest of the universe with few exceptions, numbers are *never* arbitrary or random in Tarot, even in divinations. We shall examine in some detail in the second and third sections of this book exactly how the addition of these particular 5 cards was determined in *Tarot of the Nine Paths,* and precisely why they are named "The Five Emerging Archetypes of Finality." We will see how they close the circuit of this powerful energy system of information, and by so doing, in effect, bring a full functioning, complete system to Tarot. Taken then as a fully closed and complete circuit, the

Major Arcana will be shown as a map of higher psychological agencies believed to comprise the blueprints to human wholeness, a highly inter-woven matrix of archetypal principles concerning psychospiritual trans-formation, The TNP Matrix. This is not only the stuff that dreams are made of; it's is the very air through which The Traveler makes his journey in search of who he really is and of where he is going.

The TNP Matrix, as such, must *not* be confused with the popular 1989 science fiction film by the Wachowski Brothers called *The Matrix,* a story about a dystopian future in which reality as perceived by most humans is actually a simulated world created by sentient machines to sub-due the human population, while their bodies' heat and electrical activity are used as an energy source. The film has been lauded for its compelling philosophical deconstructions of the evolving postmodern world, and there are some parallels here worth exploring.

In the film, Morpheus tells Neo that human existence is merely a facade. In reality, humans are being "farmed" as a source of energy by a race of sentient, malevolent machines. People actually live their entire lives in pods, with their brains being fed sensory stimuli that gives them the illusion of leading "ordinary" lives. To this point, it seems a perfectly apt allusion to the delusional filters that envelop man's (mis)perception of who and *what* he really is. From our perspective, however, there is no malevolent intent or conspiracy theory necessarily at play. No Agent Smiths or Satanic conspiracies, etc., it is more simply a contour of evo-lution. The movie *The Matrix,* I believe, sells popcorn but points fingers in the wrong direction, and little else, as the true "evil agent" invariably reveals itself on the bottom-rung of the many-storied ladder of human ignorance itself. Rather, it seems more telling to me that what we are encountering in this transitional stage of awareness today quite simply is the collective ignorance at this phase of our evolution, perhaps it is even a developmental necessity, in our long march to full consciousness.

At the outset of the film, Neo is offered the choice between a red pill and a blue pill. The blue pill would allow him to remain in the fabricated reality of the Matrix, therefore living the "ignorance of illusion," while the red pill would lead to his escape from the Matrix and into the real world, to finally live and breath the "truth of reality" even though it is a harsher, more difficult life. Freedom and liberation are thus conceived as mature rational-egoic acceptance of the natural reality, which humanity must come to terms with. But both blue- and red-pill worlds, by degree, remain imprisoned in dualistic illusions born of rational/ego-based perceptions, tragic as that may seem.

Escaping to become a responsible, disillusioned adult now breathing real air beneath sun and sky—out of the pod, so to speak—seems closer to achieving the status of The Traveler, but in our story that goal is merely the prerequisite for Essential Travel. TNP, on the other hand, begins with the red-pill condition itself, and passage through its "rabbit hole" offers direct contact with new territory on a timeless map of innate spiritual guidance and wisdom. But here again, perhaps the more relevant agreement these two "matrices" share is namely, the compelling potency of the creative imagination in philosophical matters of ultimate concern, whether or not they resonate with our metaphysics, in ways that ordinary prose and scientific proofs cannot. "A cannonball travels only two thousand miles an hour; light travels two hundred thousand miles a second," the celebrated 19th century French writer Victor Hugo wrote in his time. "Such is the superiority of Jesus Christ over Napoleon."

A Rectangular Arrangement of Rows and Columns

The term "matrix" for our purposes means simply a rectangular arrangement of elements into rows and columns that reveals the inner logic of a map. Its true origin in Tarot, as we shall learn, comes not from any first designer of the deck (an authorship, that appropriately remains a mystery to this day); were a lone first designer/creator historically cleared for the honor, they undoubtedly would be nothing more or less esteemed than a conduit or channel of a heritage more profound. Ultimately, it can be nothing other than the deepest, most timeless recesses of the human mind itself, made manifest in the archetypal imagery of spontaneous dreams, creative fantasies, intuitions, and visions, that is the Tarot's true author. As Jung observed: "The collective unconscious contains the whole spiritual heritage of mankind's evolution born anew in the brain structure of every individual." We may henceforth imagine this invisible source as nothing more than a draftsman's cabinet containing the sacred blueprints outlining the higher reaches of the human mind.

In the TNP Matrix, much as those of the Marseilles and Waite decks, Number plays a significant role in both card ordering and number-assignments. Numbers, in fact, are never arbitrary in Tarot, but rather based on "symbolic mathematics" (i.e. numerology) which emphasizes the ancient Pythagorean "meaning-dimensions" of number quality (not quantity), plus the simple operation of addition, that play a parallel role to the illustrations (or image-narratives) themselves, along with their long-established correspondences to parallel systems such as astrology, numerology, and the Kabbala, in the precise mapping of these subtler and higher bands of consciousness.

The Matrix of The Nine Paths is used to visually display a hidden but "perfect" magic square of sorts (it's actually just a rectangle), showing embedded inter-relationships between the archetypes pertaining to psychological transformation, and moreover, revealing nine distinct pathways leading to completion ("finality") all within the Major Arcana of the Tarot. A hidden code of sorts, based on the "magical properties of number 9," will be shown to reveal that the Major Arcana, in its current construction since the Rider Waite tarot deck (1909), now cries out for a handful of missing pieces; it is our hypothesis then, that five new cards be added to the 600-year-old set of Higher Keys, in order to achieve the full elegance and symmetry incumbent upon a map of consciousness for the future.

I should add that, in all likelihood, this small expansion will not be undertaken without some controversy for the many loyal holders of the existent work whom I refer to as The Keepers of the Past. This is only to be expected, and I take no offense from my detractors. While I applaud their fealty to the original, I must remind them that not even the incomparable deck of possibility can escape the relentless forces of change and the demands of evolution. The proof, however, will be shown in the numbers themselves in concert with their corresponding principles. I firmly believe the time for this correction is upon us, and my chosen task is to expand the classic wisdom-edifice philosophically without disturbing its sacred architecture. You can be the judge for yourself by trying it, and seeing what is learned.

CHAPTER 5

TERMINAL 9

An airport terminal is a building where passengers transfer between ground transportation and the facilities that allow them to board and disembark from aircraft. Within the terminal, passengers purchase tickets, transfer their luggage, and go through security. The buildings that provide access to the airplanes (via gates) are typically called concourses. The terms "terminal" and "concourse" are sometimes used interchangeably, depending on the configuration of the airport. At small airports like Terminal 9, an extended single terminal building typically serves all of the functions of a terminal and a concourse.

Terminal 9, of course, is not an airport for physical destinations (PDs) and exists primarily for the mental realms of travel. More specifically, it is a portal or gateway into higher levels of consciousness that facilitates exploration of The Intermediate Territory, an imaginal space between ego-driven awareness and enlightenment, that will also help us better grasp and visualize the metaphysical workings of Tarot.

Terminal 9 was designed for Spiritual Travelers of all levels and persuasions, even complete novices unfamiliar with Tarot, and, doubtless, if you are still reading this book you are very likely a Traveler yourself. Like all Travelers, you have struggled for better or worse with the challenges of modern life through the trials and tribulations of your human conditioning, born as it is of ignorance regarding your essential self and its true destination, and subject to an ever-changing, impermanent world. You have likely encountered many of the existential realities of your fate, the certainty of death, though its time be unknown, the freedom to make choices to varying degrees, and some underlying confusion

WELCOME TRAVELERS

TERMINAL 9

THE FOUR ELEMENTS

Quaternity

1 - Intuition   S - Sensation
T - Thinking   F - Feeling

DOMESTIC USE GTE 28 →

	Gate 1-9 Departures
X	Gate 1-9 Departures
Y	Gate 10-18 Transfer
Z	Gate 19-0 Arrivals
⊘ Ego	NO ENTRY Baggage

+9

The Traveler

INDIVIDUATION

E N T E R ←

The 9 PATHWAYS: **TNP MATRIX**

X	1	2	3	4	5	6	7	8	9
Y	10	11	12	13	14	15	16	17	18
Z	19	20	21	22	23	24	25	26	0

DEPARTURES X
1 The Magician/Intention
2 The Priestess/Intuition
3 The Empress/Passion
4 The Emperor/Dominion
5 The Hierophant/Spirit
6 The Lovers/Union
7 The Chariot/Challenge
8 Strength/Life Force
9 The Hermit/Wisdom

TRANSFERS Y
10 Wheel of Fortune/Synchronicity
11 Justice/Balance
12 The Hanged Man/Surrender
13 Death/Dissolution
14 Temperance/Synergy
15 The Devil/Separation
16 The Tower/Upheaval
17 The Star/Essence
18 The Moon/Imagination

ARRIVALS Z
19 The Sun/Consciousness
20 Judgement/Awakening
21 The World/Integration
22 The Well/Renewal
23 The River/Flow
24 The Ring/Wholeness
25 The Dragon/Initiation
26 The Great Web/Interbeing
0 The Fool/Possibility

and dissatisfaction about the purpose and meaning of your life on Earth. Some may have achieved many positive things in their conventional life, but still believe there is something more to learn.

You have come here to enter a spiritual path, as you sensed something valuable may be discovered. By *spiritual path* is meant a direction that is centered on the deepest values and meanings by which people live, embraces the idea of an ultimate immaterial reality, and envisions an inner pathway that enables a person to discover the essence of being.

Perhaps wisdom advisors, teachers, or friends have recommended it, or you have stumbled upon it by accident, and are now drawn simply by curiosity, though you are not exactly sure what this is about, whether you will like it, or where it is leading you. Nonetheless, you are now feeling reasonably open to learning more and, understandably, it may be a little nerve-racking at times, a little more than you expected from a book about tarot cards and such... And so the journey begins.

WELCOME TO TERMINAL 9

Ahead is the concourse where you will be greeted by preliminary travel information, and given instructions to leave your baggage behind. You are advised that it will be cumbersome and a distraction for this type of travel. You are also encouraged to "suspend your disbelief" once you enter through the gates. This is not to make a "believer" out of you in something else, but rather that you learn to travel with "beginner's mind," a phrase borrowed from Zen that means empty of thought, open and curious, present to the moment, and being in the Now. A single carry-on will be allowed if needed, which may include your identification information (current residence, age, birthdate, and place of birth); occupation, relationship status, health, present emotional state, and economic circumstance are strictly optional and your choice to share.

Stories will be discouraged onboard, as will all previous knowledge, personal beliefs, achievements and credentials which should be stored in lockers and collected at your return. As previously stated, such things are regarded as baggage here and will interfere with your travel from Terminal 9. Alcohol, and other mind or mood-altering drugs are discouraged, and will not be served in flight. You may bring questions pertaining to who you are and where you are going, but these must be sincerely held and honestly disclosed. Questions of this nature are often encouraged in oracle travel, even if they cannot be put in words. Intellectual gamesmanship, however, is unacceptable and will not be tolerated. Some Traveler's find meditation, centering, and other mind-clearing techniques valuable before and during passage through the gates, but this also is optional.

Finally, you must only enter the gates with the aforementioned guidelines taken voluntarily, otherwise your trip will be a waste of time, and you are likely to experience discomfort, dizziness, even nausea. Essential travel is not recommended for those currently experiencing emotional or mental agitation, circumstantial crises, major mental disorders, children without parental supervision, religious fundamentalists, professional skeptics, and others unprepared or ill-suited for spiritual travel. Note: For those seeking insights and solutions to specific worldly concerns alone, for example, relational questions and career-related direction, proceed directly to Gate 28, for Domestic Flights only. Although Terminal 9 is primarily designed for Spiritual Travelers wishing to visit Essential Destinations, Domestic Travel is available on a limited basis. May your journey be fruitful. Bon voyage!

Beyond the Gates

It seems as if we are finally going somewhere now. We have passed through preliminary checkpoints, and are getting ready to depart. Though up ahead stands something obstructing us. There are signs and what looks to be a travel station or podium of some kind. This is the Main Gateway at the rear of the Concourse. As *traveling* means moving from one place to another, purely speaking, (and yes, we are clearly doing so even now), let it be understood also that *gates* and gateways are mostly non-physical, and defined as specific *places or points of transition* occurring during travel which must be passed through. The word originates from the Old English "*geat*" meaning "opening." Gates provide entry or exit; they are portals or transfer stations standing between here and there, this and that, known and unknown.

At Terminal 9, three Main Gates provide the specific openings necessary for Essential Travel; Gate X (Departures), Gate Y (Transfers), and Gate Z (Arrivals). A smaller Fourth Gate around the corner, Gate 28, remains technically outside The Matrix Proper, and is used exclusively for "local" or Domestic Travel.

At a psychological level, gates are found between inner and outer worlds, as between sleeping and waking when one labors to bring a half-remembered dream *through* the gateway of sleep into daylight. Gates, it may be noted, are related to but distinct from gaps (as discussed in Chapter 2) in that gates carry a specific purpose in facilitating passage, and are more akin to doors. Gaps, on the other hand, are purposeless. They, ostensibly, just are. Meditators attempt to apprehend them as formless, empty phenomena existing between breaths. The famed British writer Aldous Huxley in his classic book *The Doors of Perception* (1954) spoke of the search for "doors in the wall," that is, openings or gates from everyday consciousness to the transcendent—through ecstatic states, meditation, and hallucinogens. I would add through oracle travel with Tarot.

A mother's body may be seen as the gateway opening to this world, a tomb the gateway to what comes after death. In ancient Egypt, a "doorway" in the tomb was literally built to allow free passage—in and out—to our soul. Jung described The Virgin Mary symbolically as having long been considered a Christian personification of the holy gateway, closed in virginity but open as the channel for Christ's crossing from heaven to earth. A twelfth-century hymn goes:

> Sancta Maria
> Closed gate
> Opened at God's command—
> Sealed fountain,
> Locked garden,
> Gate of paradise. (Jung, CG, CW 5; 577)

Openings from everyday consciousness to the transcendent is precisely the purpose behind our travel here, and as we look closer we shall understand why and how the *Tarot of the Nine Paths* (TNP) was designed for precisely this. By no means the only vehicle or doorway to do this, TNP nevertheless is a gateway to higher consciousness. As The Traveler passes now to the end of the Concourse, he beholds another large sign ahead, and must recognize that beyond this point, there is no going back:

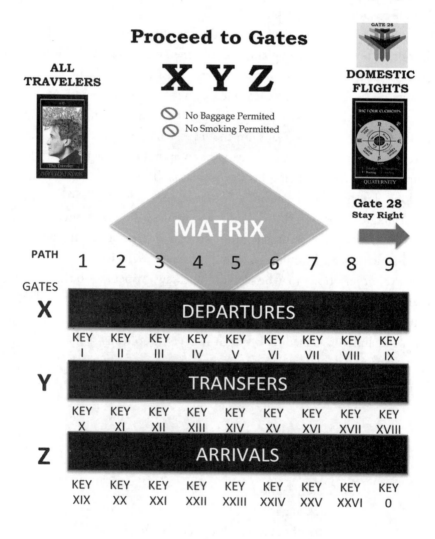

Proceed to Gates

GATE 26

ALL TRAVELERS

X Y Z

DOMESTIC FLIGHTS

🚫 No Baggage Permited
🚫 No Smoking Permitted

THE FOUR CLOROTHS

QUATERNITY

The Traveler

Gate 28
Stay Right

MATRIX

PATH	1	2	3	4	5	6	7	8	9
GATES									
X				DEPARTURES					
	KEY I	KEY II	KEY III	KEY IV	KEY V	KEY VI	KEY VII	KEY VIII	KEY IX
Y				TRANSFERS					
	KEY X	KEY XI	KEY XII	KEY XIII	KEY XIV	KEY XV	KEY XVI	KEY XVII	KEY XVIII
Z				ARRIVALS					
	KEY XIX	KEY XX	KEY XXI	KEY XXII	KEY XXIII	KEY XXIV	KEY XXV	KEY XXVI	KEY 0

On the walls, a series of informational signs are further presented for The Traveler to familiarize himself:

No Baggage Policy

Baggage is defined as personal effects of ego identity, including long-held beliefs about who you are and where you are going. This includes hidden agendas, magical and escapist fantasies, and other ulterior motives which may interfere with your travel experience. Travel from Terminal 9 is not recommended for casual interest or entertainment, and is not advised. Violators run the risk of missing the point, and may experience adverse effects, including confusion, anxiety, as well as emotional and physical discomfort. Tofu potato chips and other such horrible things may be provided to help quell cravings should they arise.

Main Gates: Three Stages of Essential Transit (X, Y, Z)

The Traveler +9, is an agent of spiritual Individuation. He represents the personhood of postmodern man, woman and child pursuing beyond sense-fulfillment and material survival the many challenges of their lives. His mind is overrun with images, ideas, memories, attractions, repulsions, habits, passions, goals, pain, pleasure, fears, boredom, emotions, fixations, fantasies and other constructions. Sound familiar? In effect, if you have experienced change, pain, or conditionality in your life, and seek deeper understanding, you are (by definition) a traveler.

The +9 (above) signifies *in the service of spiritual individuation* (ITSOSI), which means not only "becoming one's true psychological self" as Jung defined individuation, but more deeply, becoming one's true spiritual self. +9 also signals the unlimited potential for all Spiritual Travelers to enter The Nine Paths at any point and circumstance, as all situations, challenges, orientations, and mental states are fundamentally workable and amenable to this approach (provided the No Baggage Policy is observed).

TERMINAL 9: MAIN GATES

DEPARTURES (X): Gates 1-9 Magician to Hermit
Agencies:

(1)	(2)	(3)	(4)	(5)	(6)	(7)	(8)	(9)
INTENTION	INTUITION	PASSION	DOMINION	SPIRIT	UNION	CHALLENGE	LIFE FORCE	WISDOM

TRANSFERS (Y): Gates 10-18 Wheel of Fortune to Moon
Agencies:

(10)	(11)	(12)	(13)	(14)	(15)	(16)	(17)	(18)
SYNCHRONICITY	BALANCE	SURRENDER	DISSOLUTION	SYNERGY	SEPARATION	UPHEAVAL	ESSENCE	IMAGINATION

ARRIVALS (Z): Gates 19-0 Sun to Fool
Agencies:

(19)	(20)	(21)	(22)	(23)	(24)	(25)	(26)	(0)
CONSCIOUSNESS	AWAKENING	INTEGRATION	RENEWAL	FLOW	WHOLENESS	INITIATION	INTERBEING	POSSIBILITY

GATE 28: DOMESTIC TRAVEL ONLY

For travel within the known borders of everyday life, Domestic travel is a common and useful divinatory realm, excellent for personal problem-solving, sorting out complex situations and circumstances, as well as expanding one's knowledge and understanding of the structure and probabilities contained in personal development, and all challenges of worldly existence. It occurs, for the most part, "off-grid," that is, outside of The Matrix of Transformation and The Nine Paths.

Many cultures of the ancient world used a set of primary archetypal elements as metaphors to explain recurrent patterns in nature, and also, differences in perception and human typology. This "doctrine of the elements" i.e. the manifestations of Fire, Water, Air, and Earth, is added to TNP to account for ordinary surface realities and the experiential sensations of the natural world. All things derivative (of The 27 Principles), and which can be further reduced into opposites, polarities, and quaternities (i.e. systems), are found in this card. The card is reminiscent of T.S. Eliot's immortal poem *The Four Quartets* (1944) and its sanguine reminder to all Spiritual Travelers:

> When we get to the end of our seeking
> We will find out where we've always been
> And know it for the first time.

In both traditional and modern Tarot decks, this region of universal experience is commonly termed the "Minor Arcana," and is structurally akin to playing cards, divided into four suits (Pentacles, Swords, Cups, Wands), and associated respectively with the four classical elements (Earth, Air, Water, and Fire respectively). It also includes four court cards for each suit (Page, Knight, Queen, and King)[11]. As Jung observed, the structures of existential reality are regularly perceived and represented by a tendency of the rational mind to construct the world in breakdowns of four, such as the four seasons, functions, elements, directions, Noble Truths, stages of life, Zodiacal Elements, Qabalistic Worlds, Hindu Yugas, Beatles, and so forth: hence the

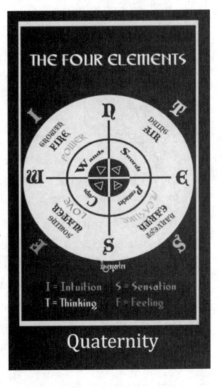

THE FOUR ELEMENTS

I = Intuition   S = Sensation
T = Thinking   F = Feeling

Quaternity

---

1. Tarot adds Knights to standard playing card courts of Jack, Queen, and King.

subtitle "Quaternity." In TNP, the entire 56 Minor Arcanum are reduced into one single card bearing the mark of manifest "fourness," entitled: The Four Elements (see above), an agent of Quaternity, in a very general sense. A clue to the symbolism of 4 is often given in Key 4/The Emperor with his leg folded across his knee in formation of the 4. It corresponds to bringing structure (four-fold reality) to his dominion, and law and order to the land and its people.

Such being the case, obviously TNP is not typical of a full tarot deck, in this and other ways as will be shown. As the deck's subtitle suggests, TNP is uniquely an "Advanced Tarot for the Spiritual Traveler." Though some tarot readers apply TNP for domestic (i.e. practical) questions and concerns as well, they will invariably discover with TNP in particular a far deeper spiritual dimension underlying their original inquiry comes to the fore, touched inconsistently at best by standard decks. Perhaps the distinction is made clearer by the distinguished American author and psychologist, the late James Hillman, who wrote:

> Rather than developmental psychology, we should study essential psychology, the structure of character, the innate endowment of talent, the unalterable psychopathologies.[2]

Within this purview, we may attribute to the Minor Arcana the structure of character as illustrated in the Court Cards, which carry a perfect correspondence to the sixteen personality types of the Myers-Briggs Type Indicator (MBTI), and the "unalterable psychopathologies" (i.e. the universal challenges and struggles of being human) in the Pips; in the higher Keys of the Major Arcana, the focus of this study, we ascribe the innate endowment of talent, as Hillman calls it, that is, "the innate talents!" It is this dimension of the human mind that we refer to as

---

2.   James Hillman and Michael Ventura, *We've Had A Hundred Years of Psychotherapy and the World's Getting Worse,* 1992, p. 61.

"Essential Travel" as it speaks of our essences.

There can be no question, however, that without the full Minor Arcana differentiated into 56 parts, much can be found wanting with respect to the structure of character (i.e. ego preferences), and the travails of ordinary life. The author himself is a great fan of the Minor Arcana, and finds it invaluable when exploring human drama, and the nuances and complexity of human relationships, fates, and fortunes. I believe there is a time and place for both deck levels, and often will follow-up a standard Tarot deck reading with a TNP divination to get a deeper understanding and bigger picture. Minors focus on mundane matters, for the most part, things impingent upon personal karma, conditioning, and worldly circumstance.

Arguably, it can even be said that the single most important and enduring development in all of 20th century Tarot has been the full illustration of the Minor Arcana in telling imagery first launched by the English occult scholar Arthur E. Waite and his American artist, Pamela Coleman Smith in 1909. Nevertheless, the Rider Waite Tarot, and its offshoots, as many of the myriad decks to follow with illustrated Pips (including the tarot-related Lenormand which proceeded them), are best approached when traveling is intended exclusively for domestic problems, insights, and destinations. Gate 28, therefore, can be taken as a preliminary shuttle ride helpful before entering the Main Gates. It can provide a useful review and clearing stage for The Traveler before parting with his baggage, in preparation for Essential Travel, a place he may identify and then set aside ("bracket") the loose ends of his present life that may otherwise interfere with deeper excursions.

In divination, however, The Four Elements of Quaternity card is shuffled into the full mix, as we shall see in the next section, and should it appears in a reading one takes it broadly to point to unfinished outer challenges and solutions in general, and perhaps to identified "systemic" or psychological concerns of the querent relevant to Essential Travel.

But from the perspective of Essential Travel, the Minors are viewed merely as derivative of archetypal reality, shorn from The Great Matrix like handicraft from fine art, that is to say, human manifestations and expressions on the mandala of timeless universal forms. Jung believed that the spontaneous production of quaternary images (including mandalas), whether consciously or in dreams and fantasies, often indicate the ego's capacity to assimilate unconscious material. But they may also be essentially *apotropaic*, an attempt by the psyche to prevent itself from disintegrating.

> These images are naturally only anticipations of a wholeness which is, in principle, always just beyond our reach. Also, they do not invariably indicate a subliminal readiness on the part of the patient to realize that wholeness consciously, at a later stage; often they mean no more than a temporary compensation of chaotic confusion.[3]

In the next chapter we will look more closely inside the Main Gates of Essential Travel before taking our first official Departure. Essential Travel is soul travel. The Traveler temporarily suspends his beliefs and disbeliefs, checks his baggage, and empties his mind for this level of experience. He may be reminded of the vision of the early 20th century Austrian psychoanalyst Otto Rank (1884-1931), who proclaimed almost a hundred years ago:

> The new meaning of soul is creativity and mysticism. These will become the foundation of the psychological type and with him or her will come the new civilization.[4]

---

3. C. G. Jung, *The Psychology of the Transference,* CW 16, par. 536.
4. "Otto Rank Quotes," https://www.brainyquote.com/quotes/quotes/o/otto-rank195619.html.

CHAPTER 6

Beyond the Gates

Agents and Agencies

The Magician

INTENTION

As we enter into this very different kind of spacecraft, allow me to introduce your first mate, The Magician. He is number 1 of the 27 travel agents you will be working with, and his general identifying archetypal principal is Intention. He is known by many expressions, "magician in the lab of life," "transformer of dark into light, difficulty into ease, chaos into form, ideal into real," and so forth. He embodies the ancient metaphysical formula, "As above, so below."

Like all cards on The Matrix, The Magician is a Wisdom Agent. In divination, he could appear at any time, and any place but on the map, He is the first. He is a master of inspired communication, right speech, and skillful means. The Magus is associated with gods Hermes and Mercury for his quickness of mind and adroit skillful actions. Moreover, as Tarot's agent of Intentionality, He represents the human will, the faculty by which a person decides on and initiates action. He creates by choice and intention. As we will learn on The Matrix, he represents Departure on the Path of Mastery. The Wheel behind him, we will learn, points to his numeric correspondence to Key 10, The Wheel of Fortune, where Intention transfers to Synchronicity. The owl above his right shoulder suggests the wisdom that informs his creative actions. For now, we will leave aside the astrological and Kabbalistic glyphs[1] included in the composition of the card that further connect him to other ancient metaphysical systems.

In modern conventional travel (PDs), say from Boston to Miami Beach during the Christmas holidays, it's not uncommon to consult a travel agency to reserve the best fares, receive travel information, etc. A travel agency's main function is to act as a liaison, selling travel products and the services of a supplier. Individuals who are sales personnel represent the agency in behalf of direct service to customers and related operational transactions. Agents, in any line of work, are inextricably tied to their agencies, and tasked to represent the agency's policies and operations faithfully and professionally.

With imaginal travel, we find many similarities and some differences in this regard. In TNP, for instance, travel agents are "wisdom agents" tasked to faithfully represent the wisdom principle of its particular agency (as given at the bottom of each card). The Magician, therefore, is an agent of Intention in the argot of TNP, though his "Keyword," like all others, is a generalized umbrella-term chosen to quickly identify the particular spectrum of wisdom teachings associated with the agency represented. Some agencies, in fact, may seem to overlap or duplicate a theme, as for instance, Integration (The World) and Wholeness (The Ring); but in actual terms, as a rule of thumb, no agency can be exactly duplicated, redundant, or narrowly provincial in scope, on The Matrix.

But what does the word "agency" actually mean in this context? Psychologically, agency is defined as "the experience of personal causation, authorship of action, and the intention behind that action." As such, "Intention"—the given agency of The Magician—suggests Key 1's unique talent for "skillful means," for focusing one's mind intensively towards a specific outcome, change, or effect. These special talents are the

---

1. Author's note: all kabbalistic and astrological glyphs can be found in the Appendix, under Hermetic Correspondences.

drivers of its agency, the author and justification of its actions, and the definer of its purpose.

There are 27 unique agencies in TNP (22 in standard decks), and each is tied to an archetypal principle concerning spiritual transformation, in keeping with Jung's general observation regarding the Major Arcana, as "distantly descending from the archetypes of transformation." In practice, therefore, the proper way of identifying a TNP card begins with the card's agency, or purpose, as stated above. One might say, "Strength is *an agent of* Life Force," or perhaps, "Life Force is *the agency of* Strength." "Death is *an agent of* Dissolution" or "Dissolution is Death's agency" both perfectly proper in the parlance of TNP.

Keep in mind, however, that this is not an aberration or change from what has evolved over Tarot's six hundred year history, only an elaboration and etiquette. By design, TNP retains Tarot's essential infrastructure with respect to long established naming and ordering conventions, pictorial motifs, and esoteric correspondences, while expanding only in size, depth, and scope from 22 to 27 "Keys" by the addition of 5.[2] The rationale for this expansion, based on several compelling factors, including Tarot's innate numerology itself, will continue to be explained as we go along. As it says in the deck's *Travel Guide*, "TNP was undertaken to 're-tune' the tarot map, but with unswerving respect for all that has gone before. In effect, TNP adds a final wing to the 'edifice' without disturbing the sacred architecture."

The correction has been made, if you will, largely with respect to the unstainable fealty of meaningful numbers as we will learn in the next section—that is, number archetypes appreciated from the perspective of *qualia* not *quanta*—as a means by which since pre-Socratic times, the world has been philosophically and psychologically grasped and understood (see Pythagoras, ca. 571– ca. 497 BCE). We have discussed this so far in the magic and supreme relevance of number 9 in the Major Arcana; to a lesser degree, the symbolic meanings laden in all root numbers (1-9)

---

2. Due to recent linguistic contamination in the political culture, the author has elected to substitute the word "key" for what has been previously called "trump."

are also compelling. As one courses through the mysterious map's underground springs, its transcendent intelligence and insights thus revealed become elegant and obvious to all who can see them. There is some inner tapestry at work in the Tarot, and the implications for consciousness are highly relevant to these times, and not to be ignored. We shall be guided, therefore, with the helpful assistance of highly qualified travel agencies, and their agents, who have weighed in for centuries with their expertise and experience, for our great benefit. I refer here, naturally, to the *imaginal* travel agencies that lie at the heart of each and every archetype, according to many Jungian scholars.

The Archetype

By no means the first but, over the past century, the most important and respected advocate of archetypal psychology was Carl Jung (1876-1961), the Swiss psychologist and unsurpassed giant of 20th century psychological development. Jung's critics, and there have been many, have tended to over-mystify Jung's notion of archetypes incorrectly, but conceptually, so-called "Jungian archetypes" represent, as Jung himself said, the operation of natural law as it expresses itself in the psyche, analogous to the laws of matter and biological instinct. Jung believed that archetypes are not subject to debate; they are empirical facts, and here we will take him at his word. Cirlot further elucidates:

> Jung uses the word "archetype" to designate those universal symbols which possess the greatest constancy and efficiency, the greatest potentiality for psychic evolution, and which point away from the inferior towards the superior.[3]

In *Tarot and Psychology* (p. 148), I discussed the constructivist perspectives of post-Jungian author/analysts Polly Young-Eisendrath and James A. Hall in regard to Jung's self psychology, wherein the authors have isolated four "invariant principles" believed to be present in all archetypal contents. Drawing from the philosophical works of Jung,

---

3.　Cirlot, J.E., A Dictionary of Symbols (Second Edition); Routledge & Keegan Paul Ltd., London, 1962.

R. Harre, Piaget, and many developmental, psychoanalytic, and constructivist theorists, the authors list the following four necessary and sufficient conditions that structure every archetype (and Tarot card). It bears repeating for our purposes here, as we draw this map of a Tarot of the Future. With my own added brackets, these, therefore, are the four conditions which structure every archetype, the first being "agency" as we have just discussed, according to this research:

Invariants of Archetypal Reality

1. *Agency:* the experience of personal causation, authorship of action, intentionality. [If they could speak to us, they might say: "I am an agent of_____. My intention is _____."]

2. *Coherence:* the experience of unity or "core being"; the collusion of body/psyche; the location of oneself as a point of view with an immediate knowledge of psychical boundaries and discrete bodily organization. ["I am organized around_____"]

3. *Continuity:* the experience of "going on being" over time that provides the functional connections that eventually result in foresight and nonverbal and verbal memory as the bases of self narratives that permit us to connect to the present with past and future. ["I am in the process of_____. I am becoming_____."]

4.*Emotional arousal:* the instinctual patterns of arousal, expression, and motivational readiness that are relatively fixed systems of subjective relating between persons, and with organisms and things, throughout the lifespan. ["I am aroused and motivated by_____"].[4]

---

4. Young-Eisendrath, Polly, and Hall, James A, *Jung's Self Psychology: A Constructivist Perspective;* The Guilford Press, New York, 1991, p.5. [As cited in *Tarot and Psychology: Spectrums of Possibility,* Rosengarten, Arthur, p. 148.]

Examples of Archetypal Images in TNP

Keywords given in TNP, as previously stated, are merely umbrella terms or generalized headings, selected by the author after long study and research not simply of highly qualified tarot commentators over centuries, but perhaps as importantly, psychological and spiritual masters East and West, as well as his own personal experience, and the oral transmission teachings received from many remarkable teachers over his forty years as a student and practitioner of the sacred art. They are, however, necessarily imperfect and inexact, and do not claim to be otherwise. But one must keep in mind that it is virtually impossible for any keyword to fully and exhaustively eclipse an entire archetype, as Joseph Campbell made abundantly clear in his seminal text in comparative mythology written in 1949, *The Hero with a Thousand Faces*. The truth is, rather delightfully, there can be no last word here.

In TNP I have taken the liberty to use a handful of "upgraded" Keywords which in my opinion better capture the flavor of a deck of the future, as given for the aforementioned "Life Force" for Strength (I was tempted to use Chi), "Synchronicity" for The Wheel of Fortune (a term invented by Jung himself in his Foreword to the Wilhelm/Baynes *I Ching*, in 1939), and "Interbeing" for the new card The Great Web, an invented word by the Vietnamese Zen master, Thich Nhat Hanh to suggest interdependency. Certainly, the observant reader has by now noticed that, philosophically-speaking, the two dominant "faces of the hero" providing this deck's distinctive flavoring are unapologetically Jungian and Eastern, owing to the author's personal background, training, and proclivities. I make no bones regarding what I lightly call my *"Tabugian"* orientation (i.e. Tarot-based Buddhist Jungian) pronounced "tá-boo-ghe-en". But I am quick to admit "a rose by any other name would smell just as sweet."

It should be restated also that this work may be approached from any and all theoretical perspectives, whether traditional Tarot, Christian, Hermetic, Hopi, Yoga, Humanistic, Shamanic, Psychoanalytic, Thelemic, Cognitive, Scientific, New Age, Post-modern, Integral, and so forth, as such philosophic constructions have only secondary bearing in this world. One only need check his or her own experience of its workings. Make an experiment of it, as Maslow suggested, and see what you find.

The 27 Archetypal Principles

With the addition of five new cards, TNP expands from the traditional 22 to 27 Greater Keys, along with their corresponding archetypal agencies, to form an integrated map of higher consciousness (this is, we must always remember, according to Tarot). The map is comprised of 27 archetypal principles. While some of these principles can be seen to overlap at times, each maintains its own unique spectrum of meanings, all are universal and none redundant.

The 27 ARCHETYPAL PRINCIPLES
Embedded in The Canon (by sequence)

Path: X   (+9)   Y   (+9)   Z

	X	Y	Z
(1)	INTENTION	SYNCHRONICITY	CONSCIOUSNESS
(2)	INTUITION	BALANCE	AWAKENING
(3)	PASSION	SURRENDER	INTEGRATION
(4)	DOMINION	DISSOLUTION	RENEWAL
(5)	SPIRIT	SYNERGY	FLOW
(6)	UNION	SEPARATION	WHOLENESS
(7)	CHALLENGE	UPHEAVAL	INITIATION
(8)	LIFE FORCE	ESSENCE	INTERBEING
(9)	WISDOM	IMAGINATION	POSSIBILITY

The list makes no claim of special privilege or exclusivity, nor are the Keywords given sacrosanct, or immune to theoretical re-casting. But the principles themselves, *in principle,* are immovable, as well as indelible, in the human soul, and therefore inexhaustible in outer manifestations and associations. They are thought to be the complete and final collection of "The Archetypes of Transformation" as Jung suggested in his cursory study of the Major Arcana.

Archetypes, we repeat, should be understood as the operation of natural law as it expresses itself in the psyche, analogous to the laws of matter and biological instinct. Tarot presents these natural laws primarily by way of its imagery, but also linguistically and numerically, through card names, placement, and numbers. But the cards themselves should be appreciated merely as *archetypal images* (a first-grader could finger paint them just as well[5]) which may even carry these formless laws unwittingly, within imperfect, artistic interpretations, and expressions mediated by individual human imagination, historical context and tradition, cultural iconography, artistic endowment, and, individual preference and idiosyncrasy. Let me take this opportunity, however, to apologize for repeating myself. I have taught Tarot for over 25 years now, and find repetition can be a helpful way of mastering what otherwise can become an unwieldy immense body of information.

According to Jung, all archetypal contents share the following features: they are inherited patterns or blueprints expressed in images; they are capable of infinite variation; they are numinous (i.e. awe-inspiring), unconscious, and autonomous; they are usually clustered around basic universal experiences (such as birth, old age, marriage, death, initiation, good and evil, confronting the shadow, becoming an adult, etc.); and they carry strong, overpowering charges of energy, which is why a good reading can be electrifying. Jung adds, "The collective unconscious [i.e. dwelling place of the archetypes] contains the whole spiritual heritage of mankind's evolution born anew in the brain structure of every individual." In other words, they are hard-wired as well.

AFTER THE MAGICIAN...

We began this chapter with an introduction to The Magician, Key 1,

---

5. Speaking of children's art, see a marvelous (Waite-based) new deck that works perfectly for Domestic Travel (for all ages), called "The Gummy Bear Tarot" (Bittrich, 2005).

the agent of Intention, a perfect initial departure, I think, as it cannot be denied that Tarot is an innately magical place from the very start of this adventure, if magic be defined as "the power of apparently influencing events by using mysterious or supernatural forces" as in the Oxford English Dictionary. The dictionary, I find, is the perfect station from which to begin our understanding. From it, we will later address another of its overused and misplaced entries, namely, "supernatural," and begin to clear it from the contamination effects that popular culture has fastened upon it.

In the unconventional manner of travel for which The Magician is an instrument, we find a highly imaginal, creative, intuitive, focused, and yes, transformational set of movements. Dyed-in-the-wool tarotists will never, as they should not, sit by idly when the purveyors of "higher level functions of the brain" (i.e. scientists) attempt to modernize (sanitize) this timeless art with so-called "evidenced-based" conclusions curried from cognitive, neurological, or behavioral research. It will be like mixing oranges and pomegranates. Tools targeted for a mass scale to measure or alleviate psychological disorders, such as the sturdy Minnesota Multiphasic Personality Inventory (MMPI), I believe are best left to the psychologists and their kin, in the service of basic mental health issues and better social functioning, much in need for the society at large.

Tarot, in contrast, and Key 1, The Magician in particular, are charged specifically for the far rarer breed whom we may call "Spiritual Travelers." But as we have only begun the Departure, it is time we make our first acquaintance with the rest of the first row, albeit cursorily.

Below are the eight cards that follow Key 1, The Magician, of the first row, and form the points of Departure (X). Their agencies are listed below, and each is given a relatively short list of associations as can be found for each card of this deck in the Lexicon at the back of the book. Together, the first nine agents and agencies are the root cards of Tarot (1-9), and comprise what might be thought of as the mothers and fathers, primary teachers and spiritual friends, that initially greet us, solicit our interest, and perhaps seal our contract for learning on the first phase of the journey. In later chapters, when we delve into divination, the inner workings of The Matrix, and their completion stage in the final row, they will be visited again. For now, it is enough simply to make their acquaintance as we have done with The Magician.

(X) Departures

DEPARTURES BY PHRASE ONLY (See Lexicon for full descriptions of all Keys)
1-9 The Root Principles in Tarot

1 Magician/Intention	Magician in the lab of life; skillful means; lead to gold; as within/so without
2 Priestess/Intuition	Deep memory; subtle knowledge; keeper of the secrets; inner knowing, past lives
3 Empress/Passion	Anima or feminine principle; nature/nurture; the dancer; love is here; sensuality and trust
4 Emperor/Dominion	Structure and protection; formation, masculine leadership, father principle; sovereignty.
5 Hierophant/Spirit	Bridgemaker between truth and community; human ethics; teacher of the way
6 Lovers/Union	Integration of opposites; I/Thou; the loving relationship; divine love
7 Chariot/Challenge	Quest; victory over obstacles; emissary of the sacred; determination and purpose
8 Strength/Life Force	Vitality and health; chi; taming the beast; feminine firmness and power; energy medicine
9 Hermit/Wisdom	Individuation; following one's bliss; fierce independence and tenacity; self realization

AN IMAGE NET

Question: What do The Priestess, The Hierophant, and say, The Chariot, or Strength cards all share in common? Certainly, each are unique wisdom-agents of spiritual transformation, each has their own special multi-layered skill set, as well as number symbol, felt-sense, appearance, etc. The answer I am looking for, however, is this: they are all image-nets! All the cards are, in fact. Tarot itself is one large image-net, nothing more. Compared to other divinatory tools and maps of consciousness, Tarot uniquely captures The Principles primarily through the power of pictures, and unlike its closest rival and ancient Chinese ancestor. The *I Ching,* which often is thought by scholars to be a divinatory "word net" that transmits its wisdom linguistically through mythopoeic speech and allusions, Tarot, by contrast, is primarily a divinatory "image net." An *archetypal image* net at that! Notes Watts, "The ear cannot detect as many variables at the same time as the eye, for sound is a slower vibration than light." And so it is with Tarot. By comparison, alphabetic "sound-based" language structures, i.e. words on a page, tend to force one-sided divisions and more linear constructions that obscure the true nuances of human experience as it is felt and lived. Take a look.

Aquarian Tarot

For instance, we might respond "I felt happy" to the question *How did you feel on the morning of your 50th birthday?"* when, to be truly honest, a more accurate accounting would be something like, "I felt happy/sad," or perhaps "grateful/resentful," or both "proud/anxious/confused," and "happy/sad," etc. The Aquarian Tarot (right), as most good modern decks, suggest through direct illustration, its image-net, all these reactions occur simultaneously in a single image, and many other things besides.

Ideas that retain their intrinsic polarities (and also their ambiguities) are best captured not through words, but through visual representations, or pictures. As a picture is worth a thousand words, according to Confucius, it is well known that Chinese writing (not unlike Hebrew and Egyptian hieroglyphs) is unique in that it does not employ sound-based alphabets, but rather characters or ideograms that were originally pictures and (symbols) that may be apprehended directly, without need for interpretation or translation. The *I Ching,* we may concede, however, is a richly mythopoetic "word net," but even still, it lacks the immediacy and power found in the images of Tarot.

Triads

In *Tarot of the Nine Paths,* triads refer to the three vertical (top-to-bottom) consecutive cards that form each of the nine columns or pathways on The Matrix. As such, the triadic structure is set by three rows of nine, the central ordering pattern of this matrix. Triads can refer to the constituent Keys (cards), their agents and agencies (Keywords), their Principles (archetypes), or their pathways (Paths) on The TNP Matrix (such as Path 6, Relationship); they express the unique "process dimension" or pattern of unfoldment in terms of a beginning, middle, and ending phase, which in TNP is called XYZ, or Departure-Transfer-Arrival. Below, for example, are the first three triads on the map, namely Mastery, Insight, and Joy.

TRIADS 1-3

DEPARTURES	1	2	3
	Magician	Priestess	Empress
↓	+9	+9	+9
TRANSFERS	10	11	12
	Wheel of Fortune	Justice	Hanged Man
↓	+9	+9	+9
ARRIVALS	19	20	21
	Sun	Judgement	World

Example: **PATH ONE: MASTERY**
1→10→19
(Magician-Wheel of Fortune-Sun)

Note: All triadic descent originates in Departure (X), passes directly below through Transfer (Y), and culminates in Arrival (Z) by way of The Hermit Effect, that is, the addition of 9.

For example, Path 1 departs with Key 1 (The Magician), adding 9 transfers to Key 10 (Wheel of Fortune), and further adding 9 arrives in Key 19 (Sun).

In TNP, +9 is framed as "in the service of spiritual individuation" (The Hermit Effect). It runs similarly throughout The Matrix.

Rites of Passage

Imagine, for the moment, you lived in a powerful and respected country, one with longstanding laws and traditions, that have evolved over hundreds of years. They had been based on high principles of freedom and fairness as written in their constitution, though, naturally, many cycles of change over centuries came and went, adjustments made to social challenges over evolving generations, and absorbing new technologies, shifting alliances, and the like. Sometimes the country would swing to the left, and at other times to the right, yet through it all it maintained its core defining principles, values and identity, as set forth from the constitution that governed it. Then some unimaginably shocking event occurred and swept over the land, and could not be unturned. It threatened the very fabric of the nation to its core, and survival, as an enduring state, was seriously cast in doubt, as Orwell foresaw many decades ago, when "the very concept of objective truth is fading out of the world. Lies will pass into history." That, in effect, would be a sobering, full-bodied (and at times, terrifying) "rite of passage" to behold. Arguably, we are living in such a condition at the time of this writing, and if not now, then certainly we are growing more susceptible to such a scenario in the future.

We must retain access to our deepest human nature. With Tarot, in effect, each triad reveals an archetypal-level rite of passage, truly sobering in its own right, on the *inner* journey all human beings must face on their predetermined road to completion. Jung believed these rites were written in humanity's DNA and passed through the brain stem of every individual born anew. Whether one believes this or requires evidence for such a bold claim, imagine for the moment that something to this effect is really happening. There is little point in arguing over something that cannot be adequately proven either way, but the views of one of the great minds of our age can not be taken out of hand.

On the socio-cultural level, the celebration of passage that occurs when an individual leaves one group to enter another can be cast triumphantly or dire, but rarely without resistance. The formal concept of passage was first introduced by the French ethnographer Arnold van Gennep in his work *Les Rites de Passage* (1909). Van Gennep identified three phases of passage: separation (preliminal), liminality (threshold), and incorporation (post-liminal).[6]

In the domains of inner space, the processes of psychological individuation, becoming an authentic individual, the very same patterns likewise occur; they are timeless, cross-cultural, and universal phenomena, known even to prehistoric man and the animal kingdom. In the first phase of separation (TNP's "Departure"), people withdraw from their current status and prepare to move from one place or status to another; van Gennup concentrates on the rites individuals normally encounter in their outer lives: pregnancy, childbirth, initiation, betrothal, marriage, funerals and the like. He mentions others as well, such as territorial passage, and the crossing of borders into culturally-alien regions, where may prevail different customs, religion, language, etc.; this rite of passage today is becoming increasingly more common, either by choice, or

---

6. Arnold van Gennep, *The Rites of Passage*, Chicago: University of Chicago Press, 1960, p. 11.

sadly, by exile. In terms of our primary focus here—spiritual and imaginal travel—similar rules apply.

According to van Gennep, the first phase comprises symbolic behaviors that signify detachment from an earlier fixed point in the social structure. In TNP, when The Traveler elects to enter the spiritual path, he too detaches from his accustomed way to deal with and understand the patterns of his life. He can utilize Tarot either through contemplation of its teachings, or through divination with its symbols. In the former, with respect to the many layers and inter-relationships within The Matrix, The Traveler should properly begin with the nine Keys of Departure X. In divination, as we will see later, departure may occur at any point at all, often not initially of one's conscious choosing, via random card selection; the first row, so to speak, carries no privilege or loyalty at all. Reflection afterwards, however, on the divined set of cards may indeed be illuminating when referring back to The Matrix, and reflecting upon their natural resting places "on grid."

Van Gennep notes there is a detachment or "cutting away" from the former self in the departure phase, often signified in symbolic actions and rituals. We see this, accordingly, when The Traveler first enters Terminal 9, checks his baggage, empties his mind of unnecessary distraction, and commences to engage Tarot. This "cutting away" from normal routine commonly dominated by the physical and cognitive destinations of "business as usual," marks the early commencement or "pre-boarding" phase of the Tarot journey.

True to van Gennep's larger theory, what follows next in TNP is the middle, *liminal* or threshold phase of Transition, called Transfer (Y). We shall soon learn the value of "going liminal," and indeed, the madness as well, which means going "in between," to an intermediate threshold situated between two known states, conditions, or regions. It is not unlike the "stopover" experience we have discussed when travelling on longer plane rides. Arguably, it is here where the most challenging wisdom agents of Tarot are encountered, including the notorious Death and Devil cards, as we shall discover in Section II of this book.

Finally, in the third phase ("re-aggregation or incorporation"), van

Gennep notes "passage is consummated [by] the ritual subject." This is "The Return" phase that Campbell and others have described in the "hero's quest," equivalent in TNP to The Transfer Phase (Y). Having completed the rite (or ride), and assumed a "new" station, one re-enters society with a certain new status. I believe on a metaphysical scale, we are collectively only midway through the transfer phase in the current construction of the Tarot deck, and accordingly, the deck is incomplete, and in need of expansion. Campbell writes:

> The psychological dangers through which earlier generations were guided by the symbols and spiritual exercises of their mythological and religious inheritance, we today (in so far as we are unbelievers, or, if believers, in so far as our inherited beliefs fail to represent the real problems of contemporary life) must face alone, or, at best with only tentative, impromptu, and not often very effective guidance. This is our problem as modern, "enlightened" individuals, for whom all gods and devils have been rationalized out of existence.—Joseph Campbell, *The Hero With a Thousand Faces.*

This, quite succinctly stated, is the very reason why a new tool and map are needed so urgently today. They must have absorbed the timeless wisdom teachings of humanity, and be capable of guiding us forward. Without sounding terribly over-dramatic, it could be that our very survival as a race of beings we still can recognize is at stake. To steer clear of the fortresses of resistance embedded in the cultural structures around the globe, this precious map would necessarily be doctrinally unaffiliated, and intrinsically foundationless, timeless, cross-cultural, essential, archetypal, highly intuitive, and I would add, synchronistic. It would satisfy the requirements of successful terminality, namely, location, accessibility, and infrastructure. And with an eye out for the power elite of the scientific establishment, it must also provide a direct channel to the "nonrational" modes of perception as well. Science, who could argue otherwise, produces indispensably great marvels when it is at its best, but it alone cannot provide sufficient sustenance for the evolving human soul and imagination.

A completed body, therefore, of symbolic wisdom teachings assembled from the deepest insights of human knowing, accessible to anyone, and transmitted through images and numbers, anyone, that is, who would dare enter Terminal 9, to receive another type of learning and vision from the timeless oracle. A Tarot, we might call it, of the future.

SECTION 2

TRANSFER (Y)

CHAPTER 7

THE LiminaL

In the purest sense, as we have discussed, travel means movement from one place to another. Whether traveling to physical destinations (PDs) like the library or work, or the more layered dimensions of mental travel, including the "higher-level cognitive functions" of the brain travel (language, perception and planning), such as paying your taxes, reading the newspaper, or talking to your brother about football, but not just those regions alone. For Travelers, it is the more "right brained" movements witnessed in intuition, awareness practices, guided imagery, creative projects, listening to music, watching a sunset, and most spiritual and imaginal travel. Regardless of levels, all human travel that is subject to time, without exception, will have a middle "liminal" phase after departure.

In the previous chapters we have also begun discussing this middle phase as a stopover phase, a "transition" or "transfer." Regarding so-called "rites of passage" introduced in the last chapter, van Gennep notes that this triadic growth pattern differs only in detail from one culture to another, and in essence, rites of passage are universal, cross-cultural, and archetypally-bound processes innate to human development. They occur in individuals throughout the lifespan and collectively in families, organizations, societies, and nations. Additionally, this three-step shuffle of beginnings, middles, and endings, though seemingly obvious as water to the fish, contains the structural hallmark of all narratives as well, i.e. the stories we tell that give meaning to our lives. Owen Flanagan of Duke University, a leading consciousness researcher, writes:

Evidence strongly suggests that humans in all cultures come to cast their own identity in some sort of narrative form. We are inveterate storytellers." (*Consciousness Reconsidered,* Flanagan, Owen, MIT Press, 1992.)

We are now ready, therefore, to proceed to Stage 2, the middle row of the sacred canon's Major Arcana. Van Gennep calls this the "Liminal Stage of Transition," which we know well in the language of *Tarot of the Nine Paths* to be Transfer (Y).

Liminal means simply, "in between," the intermediate threshold between two stable states, conditions, or regions perhaps most dramatically characterized in "the liminal space between life or death" undergone during a major operation, an out-of-body, or near-death experience. Jungians describe self-realization in terms of "the individuation" process (denoting, in fact, the agency of The Traveler himself) as taking place within a liminal space. Individuation begins with a withdrawal from normal modes of socialization, epitomized by the breakdown of the persona and thus initiating a liminal dimension of awareness. Carl Rogers, one of the founders of Humanistic Psychology, describes "the 'out-of-this-world' quality that many therapists have remarked upon, a sort of trance-like feeling in the relationship that client and therapist emerge from at the end of the hour, as if from a deep well or tunnel. The French talk of how the analytic setting opens or forges the "intermediate space," "excluded middle," or "between" that figures importantly in psychoanalysis. In this work the term "intermediate territory" is used more extensively to designate the vast region of consciousness that exists beyond ego-centered awareness and before the ultimate state of pure nonduality, liberation, moksha, or as the Buddhists call it, "emptiness."

But liminal is by no means reserved for exceptional states of mind, crises, or rare events, and can be observed literally in everything we do and everywhere we go. In TNP, it is the phase in-between Departures (X) and Arrivals (Z), studiously developed in traditional and modern decks as well, where specific, purposeful "transfer" experiences are clearly designated for the growth of consciousness.

The nine Transfer (Y) stations of the middle row of the traditional Major Arcana (Keys 10-18) sequentially are shown below:

TRANSFER (Y) The Liminal Keys

10	11	12	13	14	15	16	17	18
WHEEL OF FORTUNE	JUSTICE	HANGED MAN	DEATH	TEMPERANCE	DEVIL	TOWER	STAR	MOON
Synchronicity	Balance	Surrender	Dissolution	Synergy	Separation	Upheaval	Essence	Imagination

Visually, of course, all tarot cards are creative expressions subject to the limitations of a particular artist's personal vision, talent, understanding, execution, etc., as in this case my own, bound to some extent by long established motifs and Tarot tradition, including num-

Sandplay scene

bering and naming, characters, etc., and as such, the cards do not so much contain the archetype *per say* (as Jung called it), which is unknowable, but rather, they point to this as an "archetypal image." There is nothing uniquely magical in the physical manifestation of the cards themselves, and little value in attempting to ingest them like witch's potion or manna from heaven. Tarots are simply symbol-information carriers "embossed in laminated card stock," as my colleague Lon Milo DuQuette would tell us, though it cannot be denied, that the information carried therein is profoundly mysterious and rich.

As far as construction, TNP, quite uniquely, was created intuitively through the medium of Jungian Sandplay Therapy[1]—a technique that takes from a menagerie of miniature objects collected from my travels, and set randomly on shelves beside an empty therapeutic sandbox in the author's own office. TNPs in their original state were actually "sandplay

---

1. Sandplay therapy is depth psychology approach of active imagination in which a therapist holds a safe and protected space for the patient to spontaneously create scenes made of miniature objects of his choosing in a therapeutic sandtray.

scenes" intuitively and spontaneously created, digitally photographed, and later crafted artistically on the computer into pictures, and layered with established corresponding astrological and Kabbalistic glyphs, in a project extending over many years. The making of a deck is itself a highly liminal undertaking, and admittedly, what has emerged is an imperfect, amateur work of art—but art was never the primary intention. The deck was created to graphically demonstrate why the author believes the Major Arcana in its current state though perfect, is unfinished, and how it can properly be completed for the future. While many secrets are revealed in TNP's interiors, their agencies (given in red letters) are perhaps of equal importance with respect to the deep principals the cards contain.

A Mystery Bundled Between Two Knowns

Not only are Travelers bundled in mystery between two baseline states of consciousness in the liminal condition when they first step into Terminal 9 to undertake a reading, they are extremely vulnerable as well. And after the divination procedure proper has begun, The Traveler is no longer at The Terminal from which he departed, nor has he arrived to his destination. In flight, as it were, the territory The Traveler now finds himself is temporary, unfamiliar, rapidly changing, and transitional, but this rite of passage is a required and necessary leg of the journey. Religiously-speaking, we are in limbo.

On The Tarot Matrix, the middle row called Transfer (Y) is Tarot's most liminal realm. Though like everything else on the map, it is integral to the larger rite of passage to higher consciousness. The Traveler has now entered the full force of the in-between stage of The Intermediate Territory, that is, the Tarot itself.

Van Gennup notes the attributes of liminality are by nature "necessarily ambiguous," and here in Tarot's labyrinth of transition too we encounter a wide array of instrumentation (agency) assembled on The Matrix's (Y) stage. A cursory run through suggests a certain "push-plunge" pattern repeated, beginning with (10) The Wheel of Fortune's initial burst of fortuitous harmony (Synchronicity), moving next to a recalibration in (11) Justice (Balance), then some deeper ego-shedding in (12) The Hanged Man (Surrender), followed by a disquieting descent and metamorphisis in (13) Death (Dissolution)... and one senses a darker entrainment in the psychic transfer process is now underway.

The Push-Plunge

Examining the procession more closely, at first we are heartened with the prospect of rare opportunity in The Wheel of Fortune, this agent of Synchronicity. It portends a magical zone of uncanny luck. The secrets of right timing—that bromide used to penetrate the incessant, invisible laws of change would seem to be now at our fingertips, and we think, "So far, so good." The Wheel is pasted, it should be noted, with the many fortunes found in the (Rider Waite) Minor Arcana, and where it stops, nobody knows. Possibility now looms large as the transfer begins; Tarot magic is in the air, though it remains mysterious.

We are soon reminded to remain alert and fasten the seat belts of our minds, as sequentially we rapidly move to another place, the more austere auspices of Key 11/Justice. In TNP, an American flag is shown, a symbol of "Truth, Justice, and the American Way" much as Superman would tell us. The flag we find (as shown on previous page) is frayed and dampened by the mist. It is much in need of restoration that now comes swiftly in the emerging wisdom of the owl. The Scales of Justice suggest a new equilibrium is needed, and the previous seen mask of The Priestess (2) from the early Departure phase (The Priestess being the root principle of Justice 11 = 1 + 1 = 2) has now been removed—unmasked, if you will, such that the Sun and Moon now fill its eyes, reinforcing the call in this correction for a deeper, more universal state of Balance, the card's given agency. Many critical teachings arise in the liminal realm, and we must not lose ourselves in the mire of imbalance during this otherwise foundationless operation underway.

When next we encounter the curious (12) The Hanged Man, we notice Sun and Moon have now eclipsed in closer proximity, and a fat Buddha is now leaping into the void. Stranger things have happened, we might remind ourselves. A chest of treasure with two attendants sits off to the side. It signals "divestment," that is, detachment from worldly things and accumulated frames of reference. The archetypal realms are indeed fantastic and alien, and surrender we must, but this is no simple dream world passing in the night like the wind whistling through our bedroom shutters; the images of Tarot are fully developed, paradoxically stable, and remain locked onto our screen.

We are here guided by The Hanged Man's wisdom agency to "surrender" to the travel process itself. The Laughing Buddha, Budai (Pu

Tai), embodies the crazy wisdom required in the liminal phase, a spiritual roller coaster ride of sorts, that is winding without control through our minds in mysterious travel. Budai also models for us the fearless, joyful, surrender of bodhisattvas when the liminal forces propel us downwards into the fabulous sectors of the unknown and in-between regions. He shows us, therefore, that it is good to retain a sense of humor during such times. Into the swirling vortex, The Traveler likewise takes the plunge, and encounters the transpersonal energies of higher consciousness washing over this strange, numinous land. The Traveler too must take this leap of faith with nothing to hold onto but direct experience.

But passage always continues and never stops for long, yet at the next stop not much in the way of ambivalence is easily apprehended—Death...or is there? We witness here in black and white shades only the bones and shells of what we were before; a death rider is stepping respectfully upon his horse past the last vestiges of our former selves. In time, the bones and shells too will dissolve into nothing, they are merely left as reminders. But we must remember again that this is the "in-between" realm of Tarot, and death here is primarily ego death, the dissolution of the formerly known, identified with, and conditioned. Rachel Pollack underscores Death as the "great democrat":

> Death strikes everyone, kings and commoners alike. This basic democracy of death was a favorite theme of medieval sermons. As an idea it goes back at least as far as the Jewish practice of burying everyone in the same style, a white shroud and a plain pine box, so that in death rich become level with the poor. (*Seventy-Eight Degrees of Wisdom*, Part 1, p. 91)

Something continues, we may be pleased to discover, beyond Death—an empty space of remnants and rubble, where all personal domains of limitation have suddenly dissolved into nothingness like water splashing over The Wicked Witch of the West *("I'm melting!")*, but then, it seems, a second push-plunge cycle begins anew, just when you thought the ride was over.

Thus we motor on, and the roller coaster now descends even further like a swooping Disney ghost ride downwards into the formless abyss, as if to recalibrate once again, deeper into Tarot's underworld, and to sweep away whatever still remains. Once again the push-plunge cycle begins fortuitously, as we saw with the Wheel of Fortune, but now we have entered a rather cooled and pleasing magical blue room of sorts, where we behold a surreal, feminine water ceremony is taking place beside a bridge.

This is (14) the Temperance card (Synergy), where a blending, alchemical, synthesis is occurring. In the magnificent *Thoth deck* of Aleister Crowley and Lady Frieda Harris, the card is called Art, underscoring the creative profusion it instills. In our version crafted in a box of sand, we see an allusion to the Arthurian legend of the storied Lady of the Lake, a goddess and enchantress of many Medieval tales whose pivotal resume includes giving King Arthur his sword, enchanting the wizard Merlin but refusing him love until he teaches her all his secrets, and raising Lancelot after the death of his father. As Temperance in Tarot, her synergizing talent for sifting and blending primary materials and color is classically revealed in the motif: "One foot on land, one foot in water."

On the rollercoaster ride through the psyche's archetypal realms (or collective unconscious), Key 14 is at the very midpoint of the journey, bearing 13 agents above her, and 13 below on The TNP Matrix.[2] Now at the centerpoint of a 27-card matrix, Temperance brightly signals to all Travelers what Buddhist teachings call The Middle Way, and what similarly in Advaita Vedanta is expressed as "neti-neti" *not this, not that*. We

---

2. Numerologically 13 reduces to 4 (i.e. 1+3=4), suggesting "structure above, structure below."

are therefore at once commencing on a second "push-plunge" cycle in the liminal phase immediately following Death, but also in the bigger picture smack dab at the very center of The TNP Matrix itself! Synergy, you may recall from the Introduction, means "the creative blending of a diverse set of contributors." The mandate from the center: blend the opposites synergistically! They may include, but are not limited to masculine/feminine, black/white, right/left, war/peace, above/below, etc.

But as you certainly must know by now, for Travelers, change is unceasing, not always comfortable, and so we move on. Here begins the second liminal "plunge," and it isn't pretty, let me warn you. Our Lady of the Lake, it would seem, for all her lovely alchemy and middle way magic, has deposited us on a fast track to hell! We are now sitting in the darkened chambers of The Devil himself. By what evil treachery could this happen? Please note: I must often remind Christian Travelers that Tarot is not simply *not a religion per se* but it is a sacred tool, and furthermore, it bears deep roots pre-dating Christianity itself. This devil, in fact, is often associated with Pan, the Greek god of merriment and sensuality, but here in *Tarot of the Nine Paths,* it leans most heavily on the devil of modern Depth Psychology, namely, the shadow.

In this vein, admittedly, it still is no bed of roses either, nor was it ever meant to be. The Devil (15) represents another universal part of our minds, albeit, its shadow side. The Swiss analyst Carl Jung coined a number of words that have entered the psychological lexicon of our time, and are highly incorporated into TNP as well. These would include the "collective unconscious" which is akin to "The Intermediate Territory," "synchronicity" which in the agency we have identified for the Wheel of Fortune, and the very mechanism by which divination is set in motion as we shall see later in this section, and here in The Devil card, the construct of "the shadow" which is implied in the Keyword, Separation.

In Jungian Psychology, the shadow or shadow aspect refers to an unconscious aspect of the personality with which the conscious ego does not identify, and mistakenly projects outwards onto other objects (people). Because one tends to reject or remain ignorant of the least desirable aspects of one's personality, the shadow, like The Devil, is largely negative.

Interestingly, according to Jungian author Anthony Stevens, the shadow is roughly equivalent to the whole of the Freudian unconscious.[3]

We are confronted psychically, therefore, with a kind of steam-cleaning, no holds barred, humiliation in the mirror, if you will, a necessary dress-down of the polarizing defilements of attachment and delusion that are typically projected onto other things and people. They can no longer be avoided on this ride, as The Devil knows, and is here to help us remember where we remain separate from our true natures, where we continue to split off, or fall into the trap of dualistic thinking. These are dream images, not evil entities of what we speak, voices hollering from deep inside us and we must listen, and learn from them. It is well to remember a haiku written by the beloved Zen Roshi of San Francisco, Shunryu Suzuki, author of the classic *Zen Mind, Beginner's Mind* (1970): "Hell is not punishment, it's training."

In the outer world, in general, we can observe parallel dynamics collectively in the events and circumstances of public record. More recently, usage of the term *liminal* has broadened to describe the external destinations of political and cultural change as well, quite aptly for the time of this writing, late in the year 2016. All quarters anxiously await the incipient commencement of a controversial new leader, our liminal king. During transitional periods of all kinds, it is believed, social hierarchies may be reversed or temporarily dissolved, continuity of tradition may become uncertain, and future outcomes once taken for granted may be thrown into doubt. Notes anthropologist Bjørn Thomassen, "The dissolution of order during liminality creates a fluid, malleable situation that enables new institutions and customs to become established."[4]

---

3. Anthony Stevens, *On Jung* (London 1990) p. 43.
4.   Bjørn Thomassen, *The Uses and Meanings of Liminality* (International Political Anthropology 2009) p. 51.

On this "joyride" through Tarot's liminal row, we might append Thomassen's list to include its opposite, namely, "a malleable situation that enables old institutions and customs to crumble and collapse" as well, particularly given what's next up. Yes, my friends, it could get much worse... We now find ourselves in a war torn battlefield surrounding a fortress under attack—the lightning-struck madness of Key 16, The Tower, agent of Upheaval! If there were a bottom to Tarot's terribly fraught and lonely descent, this arguably would be that bottom.

In the lexicon at the end of this book, (much as all TNPs are given a full paragraph of descriptive associations), of (16) The Tower it says this:

> Radical and immediate change; sudden awakening (satori); attack from outside, crumbling within; time to abandon ship; "ivory tower collapsing from decay"; war; terrorism; seeking safe harbor with laser intensity; (reversed) shake-up of core values, corruption, self-imprisonment, or inner breakthrough. Spectrum: Destruction, Upheaval, Evacuation, Liberation. (Mars).

Judging by the tenor and range represented within this card's spectrum of meanings, one quickly grasps this will be no cakewalk in the park. Things will fall apart rapidly and irreversibly. Humpty Dumpty now sits on the precipice of his great fall and, as every child by the age of five knows, there will be immense futility suffered by all the king's horses, and all the king's men, to try and put the somber-eyed egg Humpty back together again!

Certainly, on a subtler level, this is the predictable result for any Traveler who dares enter Terminal 9, rolls through the Main Gates, and comfortably departs with the kindly mothers and fathers, teachers and spiritual friends of the first row and then find themselves plunging downward into the liminal spiral. "Radical change NOW!", screams The Tower, like a first responder in an immanent Category 4 disaster. "Get to safe ground immediately if you can." This is not simply advised, it is required. But where should I go? What must I radically change? And how? The answer is glaringly obvious in the one positive symbol within the card's composition, the lightning bolt!

Witnessing lightning is well known to churn up a whole slew of internal reactions. In essence, lightning ignites our deeper selves. These bolts of pure energy can potentially tap our most primal, basic emotions, and are power symbols in many of the great traditions, including Norse and Tibetan. In Native American wisdom, lightning is closely aligned with the thunderbird, associated with honesty, truth and morality. According to tribal legends, the thunderbird emits lightning bolts from its eyes that strike down those who misguide, mislead, or withhold the truth. The Tower's bolts of lightning can be seen as both destructive and creative. They heed us to evacuate completely and immediately from the decay of the old order, the "ivory tower," and do so with the laser light intensity necessary in the chaos of wartime, through plunderous assaults that struggle to protect a dying regime, as suggested in the ninja skateboarder rolling over the head of a fallen defender of the past. Pollack suggests when this card is reversed, it means we are locked below in the Tower's dungeon and cannot escape, amongst the most unfortunate places to be stuck in the entire arcana unless, of course, we can find the special key that unlocks the dungeon's steel bars.

THE LIMINAL DOORS OPEN

At the conclusion of the middle row—finally—a far more expansive and numinous result comes, just in time. It begins with an opening to the luminous gates of the greater cosmos—Star Essence (Key 17)—where a portal to the radiant galaxies of the imagination now glistens in the starlight of bliss-consciousness. "Gods in the heavens," we cry out, "Oh, how I do need thee now!" The Tarot oracle only smiles. The liminal realm to this point has been no picnic by any stretch, but it has prepared us for something larger than we can even imagine. And now, seeing that the laser-packed lightning bolt from The Tower has done its job, swiftly and magnificently, we may take a deep, self-soothing breath, and relax.

In TNP, The Star card features the Tibetan goddess Green Tara, Mother of All the Buddhas, an emanation of the "Buddha of enlightened activity." She is seen now giving transmission and healing through a meditative practice known as *guru yoga* to us, the transiting, "human, all too human," Travelers (who are agents of ourselves) in colored beams of wisdom-light radiating through her sacred mantra:

> *"Oṃ Tāre Tuttāre Ture Svāhā"* (OM! O Tara! I entreat you, O Tara! O swift one! Hail!).

Kathleen McDonald, a Western nun in the Tibetan Buddhist tradition further elucidates the image of Green Tara sending us her unconditional love:

> Visualize in the space before you Tara, manifestation of all that is positive. Her body is emerald-green light, translucent and radiant. Her left leg is drawn up, signifying complete control over sexual energy, and her right leg extended, indicating that she is ready to rise to the aid of all beings...In each hand she holds the stem of a blue flower, a symbol of the unblocking of the central channel. She is exquisitely beautiful and smiles lovingly at you. Her clothing is of celestial silk and her ornaments of precious gems.[5]

Non-Buddhists may take this simply as the exchange of essential healing-light channeled down from the heavens above and reflected off a cool Earthly pool below, providing water nurturance for the transmission to occur, a foreshadowing of the Arrival (Z) phase to come. The Keyword "Essence" refers to the elemental purity and universal intelligence embodied in starlight. We begin now to sense a purpose behind the intense pushing-plunging cycles we have thus far endured, we have deposited our former self like dirty laundry into some cosmic, liminal, washing machine necessary for preparation, cleansing, and purification.

---

5. McDonald, Kathleen, *How To Meditate: A Practical Guide* (1984), p. 118.

But only one card remains in the middle row. Has this all been for this last transition?

The answer is "Yes." In effect, the roller coaster ride beginning with Key 10 The Wheel of Fortune, and push-plunging through two intensive cycles followed the fresh liberating skies of Key 17, The Star, according to the Tarot oracle, has all been in preparation for the final plunge—Key 18, The Moon. How perfectly mysterious, you may be scratching your head, remembering the sobering Death experience you encountered, or the magical water ceremony in the blue room beside the bridge, or perhaps, the stunning gravity of the Devil's chamber, and the fires blazing wildly around The Lightning-Struck Tower are still resonating in your insides. Especially as you discover that Key 18 in this deck is subscribed as an agent of Imagination! After all we have been through, what can be the meaning of this now? It may be time to reflect upon the oracle's wisdom and alien ways.

Crossing The Abyss That Separates Us From Ourselves

"Three things cannot be hidden," said the Buddha. "The sun, the moon, and the truth." And if for the moment, we can say that The Sun (discussed later) captures all that is light, all that is seen, and all that is known in its symbology, The Moon, we can also say, captures all that is dark, all that is unseen, and all that is unknown, by the same methodology. Perhaps more telling, however, at this denouement of our travels through the liminal stage, is the question posed by Thomas Merton, the 20th century American Catholic writer and mystic, pondering the value of traveling to the moon, and in a larger sense, The Moon of Tarot:

> What can we gain by sailing to the moon if we are not able to cross the abyss that separates us from ourselves? This is the most important of all voyages of discovery, and without it, all the rest are not only useless, but disastrous.

As a cardinal symbol in all world mythologies including Tarot's, it should not be surprising that there are many symbolic meanings attached to it. The Moon, psychologically speaking, is a symbol of the psyche, the

unconscious, and the collective unconscious itself. It is known for its fluc-
tuating nature, its hold on instinctive emotions, and hence the "lunacy"
it can sometimes produce. The Moon is the source of dreams and the
dream world, and the deep feminine in her many manifestations. It can
also serve as a harbinger of romance, sexual passion, as well as menstrual
cycles, moods and emotions; it is often home to supernatural activity,
mysteries, phantoms and fantastic creatures, and the list goes on and on.
As the symbolic repository of the buried and for-
gotten, the unknown, the instinctive, the unseen,
the shamanic, the occult, the mystical, magical, and mysterious... and the great secrets. The
Moon, finally, is tied to the "left-hand path," the
irrational, the intuitive, memory, secrets, and of
course, the imaginal.

We may recall in Chapter 3 on the subject
of "Eastern Travels," the Far Eastern philosophical
concern regarding the origination of images, that
is, where do they come from? And more immediately, where do all Tarot images first arise, came
with the arcane formula: "Image from No-Image."
Izutsu writes:

> All images that emerge into the daylight brightness of conscious-
> ness are first incubated and formed in the darkness of the sphere of
> No-Image."[6]

That dark sphere where consciousness is first formulated, that sits
at the base of the collective unconscious itself, and where all images are
first incubated and formed, finds its home in The Moon. It is a place
where images are born from no-image. "Imagination," defined as "The
act or power of forming a mental image" (*Merriam-Webster*) rightly
serves, therefore, as The Moon's agency, including even, paradoxically, its
"no-image" source. This is precisely where the Tarot oracle wants to bring
us by the conclusion of the great transition: pure imagination. Why?

---

6. Toshihiko Izutsu, *Eranos Lecture Series, No. 7,* Spring Publication, 1988.

Because quite simply, as Einstein said: "Imagination is more important than knowledge. Knowledge is limited. Imagination encircles the world."

PATH 9 *Path of the Sage*
Hermit-Moon-Fool

Key 9 Hermit/Wisdom

Key 18 Moon/ Imagination

Key 0 Fool/Possibility

One last note regarding Key18. The Moon, and its given agency, Imagination, recall that within the schema of TNP The Moon/ Imagination is positioned alluringly in the Y Phase (i.e. liminal) stage, that is, sandwiched between Wisdom (The Hermit) and Possibility (The Fool). These three cards form the 9th and final Path on The TNP Matrix, the Path of the Sage. Could there be any more natural intelligence or poetic justice? As one examines, and fully comprehends, the elegance with which agencies coalesce in TNP, that expanded logic becomes clear as running waters are.

But to gain a full understanding of how TNP "pathways" were formed, we must now look more closely into the hidden numerology within the Major Arcana based on meaningful number archetypes which have resided in the canon since its ordering system stabilized around three hundred years ago, was first made available in our time in so-called "Tarot Constellations" (see A. Arrien 1987, and M.K. Greer, 1987), and then made conscious by TNP's most compelling formula, The Hermit Effect, or +9. We will revisit this final Path in the last section.

CHAPTER 8

Meaningful Numbers

Mindless Digits

We fight the impersonality of them when manipulated like a raw statistic, or when left scrambling to meet our quotas, or being scored on performance, or reduced like a prisoner of war to simply a name, a rank, and a serial number. Increasingly, we fall dependent upon them and adjust to their wishes. In impossibly long invisible strings they are etched into the gray matter of our digital alter egos. And more than they can ever know, our fate rests on their keyboard.

But, take heart people—these noiseless, virus-prone brainchildren of the Information Age cannot even wipe their own noses, change a light bulb, or count to three! They are built merely of brittle, geek-spawned, non-metalic chips of sand. Though they can perform seemingly infinite calculations in a matter of moments, they cannot think for themselves and possess less real intelligence than the Guatemalan banana slug. But, unlike the slug, when squashed beneath your boot, all that oozes is their mindless, meaningless number circuits.

Modern digits depersonalize and reduce; they are the new minions of the postmodern world. For our government, they tabulate us by our driver's license, zip code, age, date of birth, Tax I.D., and Social Security; to our friends, they insure that we are contacted and catalogued by street, phone, fax, Facebook page, and cell numbers. To ourselves, they orient us to the world by our clock, calendar, thermostat, speed limit, paycheck, credit card, bankbook, passwords, and smart devices. They put us in our place, structure, protect, and monitor our lives, and stifle our (sometimes preferred) irrationality. For this we regard them as useful poison. They help simplify, reason, and organize, but in the end they may kill us.

Just Doing Their Job

Tempting though it may be, blaming the guileless digit is an exercise in misplaced rancor. In fairness, we should forgive them for they are just doing their jobs; number digits, including the binary zero and one, are merely functionaries, and practical organizers, of systems and things that come in larger quantities than we have fingers to count upon or greater complexities than we have brains to decipher. They must be shown the proper respect, and admired as the "meta-fingers and brain surrogates" of extended reality. Sure they can hypnotize with their endless continuity, minisculity, ingenuity, and grandeur, not to mention their impeccable consistency and accuracy in operations. Indeed, they can fragment and fractionalize any quantity and reduce the very complicated to the very basic. But at their lowest common denominator they work for *us*—like our internet technicians from Bangalore—they solve functional problems that far exceed our capacity, but they don't really make us happy or intelligent in themselves and, more importantly, they tell us little about who we really are or where we are really going.

In essence, "quants" are merely "bean counters," that is, signs of quantification hobbled to the datum of life. In themselves they are empty and meaningless beyond the defined parameters, base-sets, and applications that we assign them. They are the unpaid accountants of size and quantity who work on the weekends, though we human beings, in the final reckoning, are their lords and masters. (Though if truth be told, not for very much longer thanks to those traitorous AI wizards bent on giving them real brains...at which point, we may have trouble, and this is a really bad idea when you think of it, in my opinion, despite the alluring potential "upside" that wets the technologist's dreams). Luckily, in their current generation, they are too stupid to plan ahead for their future.

Innocent or not, we defer to them far too often, particularly when making choices concerning where to park our being in the world. They bring efficiency to our physical destinations (PDs) in the language of meters and measures, denominations and actuarials, statistics and algorithms, and we rely on them today more that we care to admit. Based on the Law of Large Numbers, in shockingly enormous quantities, we too often elect to find our answers in *them,* not in ourselves. Scientific polls, surveys, focus groups, voting booths, demographics, and Vegas odds-makers implore us more than ever to place their carts of probability *before* our horses of possibility—and in so doing, decisions based on numbers only lower the bar for self-fulfilling prophecy and data-driven decisions, not internally-channeled choices funneled through the sacred interiors of our humanity. We become ever more predictable, ever less imaginative. Tacitly, we contribute to validating our own statistical probabilities whenever we surrender to their control, and sadly, we are becoming more like them, than ourselves.

As we saw in The Seldon Plan of Asimov's *The Foundation* (in Chapter 4), decisions that are largely data-driven bring not only less individuality and conviction to our choices, they remove human responsibility for their outcome in our lemmingesque collective regressions to the mean. Popularity, much like in high school, rules the roost, and the virtues of "groupthink" are reinforced as numbers (not individuals) become the choice-makers. The hidden agenda behind a data-driven world, and this is ominous, is to eliminate the non-rational from its equation.

But polls can be immensely deceptive as we have learned from presidential elections, and we must remember the dreaded nonrational dimension (which polls tellingly bracket out) includes not only the vast chaos, instincts, randomness, anomalies, base emotions, and eccentricities of the natural world, but also the vital processes of intuition, creativity, and imagination that drive spiritual and imaginal travel, and open the gates to vision-logic, a liminal shift in perception where the subtler realms of human consciousness may be apprehended and nourished. Taken to the extreme, therefore, digit-based societies become a sort of rote, paint-by-the-numbers, preschool activity, more easily supervised and controlled, eventually graduating an adult class of robot-like clones—dry technicians of logic unpracticed in creativity or wisdom. In the current trajectory, this is where we are going.

Naked Truth

One may concede a certain raw and elegant "signature of being" gets revealed in the reduction of a thing to its essential *name, rank, and number*. At least for the inorganic among us, uncomplicated by a brain, heart, or soul. Peel away the outer layers of any object's sheathing, however, until simply its most fundamental *suchness* remains, devoid of particulars, and behold what is meant by number *quality*! It holds the essence of any object (or being's) energy, purpose, pattern, structure, and destiny. Should we in fact be dealing with organic matter, a number may in fact reveal universal fundaments of the brain, heart, and soul, though in man, they are not limited to zero and one.

The prideful numerologist may sneeringly demote what are mistakenly called "numbers" to their more vulgar and proper class of mere "figures," hoping by this distinction to erase any further misconception that mindless "arithmetic entities" be confused for his beloved and intelligent true *numbers*. And he is not wrong to do so. Even quantum computing, with its surreal capacities to calculate, quantify, predict, and reduce multiple universes through the end of time, is over-quantified for admission to this dance. The pre-schooler is perhaps more able to behold the richness of character in the pure number *two*, for instance, or the splendor of the magnificent *seven*, if only for a moment's pause before the mystery they foretell. But this is not just child's play.

And one needn't be a numerologist to appreciate the essential beauty of a number's naked truth. Without metaphysical association, an object's most primary quality, wrote Carl Jung, is whether it adheres to the "one" or the "many." By fifteen months of age, adventuress toddlers first behold a profound sense of "the many" when stacking a tower of four rubber Barney blocks onto the living room carpet and delighting in the primitive magic of multiples (well before their rational faculties will instantaneously override these animistic perceptions of the world).

Thereafter numbers begin to amass a parallel and private soul of their own, one rich in poetic allusion and emotion as found in the fabled *three* blind mice, and the *seven* dwarfs of the pre-Oedipal years, where *threes* and *sevens* become indelibly merged with the narrative itself, marking more than a mere counting of myopic rodents or bearded little people. To the conscious mind, numbers are symbols of the interior world.

Numerically-Challenged

Some years later this more primitive vestige of number magic, and the numinosum it inspires, gathers a certain adolescent ambiguity which *"once upon a time"* was transfixed to the ballfields and backyard games of latency (though naturally, now in watered down versions, due to the cruel intrusion of social awareness and hormonal change). The roar of "Strike three!" means far more to a little leaguer than the termination of his batting turn. It rings of humiliation, and dismissal, and will resound through his entire being if only for a moment as the fateful vibration of defeat. Indeed, these numbers have emotions and associations rooted in the primary experiences of our maturation. Yet today one worries whether boys and girls are not robbed of this mythic outlet in their epidemic *electronic* programming, so limited by its binary options, over-buttoned, over-pushed, and divorced as it is from the traditional number magic of childhood? The Tarot, however, as a game, retains the dignity and importance that number traditionally has played in childhood narratives. We don't just speak of The Empress, for example, we speak of her "three-ness" as well.

Sooner or later, for all generations, primitive numbers must recede altogether behind the blinding sunlight of maturing ego consciousness and its more calculated and successive arrays of rational numbers. Algebra replaces the primary numbers of our minds. Only later (during sudden lapses of adulthood) will their numinous qualities occasionally reappear via regression (in the service of imagination) as sub-text in altered or non-waking states of consciousness, in dreams, visions, and creative imaginings, in divination practices, synchronicities, or else in the serious study of ancient Indian, Greek, Chinese, Buddhist, Hebrew, Hermetic, Gnostic, Neoplatonic, Shamanic, Fourth Way, New Age, Thelemic, Transpersonal, or other Perennial Philosophy and its many derivatives, who have through such means approached the awesome splendor of "The One."

Popular culture too plays upon the universality of living integers lost to the oppression of just numbers, as even feckless adults prefer the older system when describing the metaphors of lived experience, no matter that "A bird in the hand is worth two in the bush," "*one*" remains "*the loneliest number,*" "*two is company*" and unquestionably "*three's a crowd.*" The old system in fact, becomes the stuff of proverbs, love songs, lullabies, lucky numbers, and magic spells. *But why count backwards in time?* Are we not a postmodern, tech-savvy, forward-looking, algorthmic new people? Because the old system better captures what we feel and intuit to be true, that is, before our conditioning to know more is sealed within our psychological make-up. It speaks the quasi-logical "feeling-tones of mathematics," the roots from which we have evolved, and remains intimately tied to who we really are, and where we're really going. Number digits, including the binary zero and one, are merely functionaries, and practical organizers, of systems and things that come in larger quantities than we have fingers to count upon or greater complexities than we have brains to decipher, that is, should we suspend pretending to be singularly rational quantities.

TIMELESS NUMBERS

Some five hundred years before Jesus of Nazareth, the man considered "the fountainhead of Greek philosophy"—Pythagoras of Samos—believed that numbers were the foundation of the universe, and the very "essences of the gods" were defined and divined by them. Timeless numbers are inherently liminal unlike mere digits, because we never know precisely what precedes or follows them naturally, as they bear no primary allegiance to succession and order. They may be classified as root principles, and though highly inter-connected via correspondences to time-worn archetypal principles, each stands alone from its own side. In absolute terms, *one* is not simply the first number, it is the *only number.* In self-reflection, *two* is grasped. In love, a *third is born—the us! Hallelujah!* And from these *three* (with allowances for the babysitter) emerge the 10,000 manifest forms. The Hopi remind us of a number's discrete limitations as well, as "One finger cannot lift a pebble."

The Jungian analyst and author Marie-Louise von Franz in her study of ancient Chinese divination recounts the following true story:

> There were once eleven generals who had to decide whether to attack or retreat in battle. They held a meeting and some were for attacking and others for retreat. They had a long strategic discussion, and finally took a vote: three were for attacking, and eight were for retreating, and they therefore decided to attack, because three is the number of unanimity!

Von Franz explains:

> You see, in China three has the quality of unanimity, and by the chance effect that three people were for attacking they hit the quality of the number three, therefore that opinion was the right one. A Chinese might say perhaps that underneath, unconsciously, there was unanimity for attack, despite the fact that only three were consciously for it, while eight were only unconsciously for it and consciously for another decision. Therefore they attacked—and successfully, according to the story![1]

This twist to our logical Western assumption of number *quantity* and "majority rule," exemplifies the often paradoxical meaning-dimension that opens when working with numbers qualitatively. The intuitive mind looks more for qualitative, feeling-toned relationships and anomalies, often oblivious to strictly quantitative factors. But the vignette also shows a magical aspect of numbers as well—magical in the sense of revealing information existing beneath the veil, or what in psychological usage we'd term today "the unconscious." Number magic is common but not exclusive to divinatory practices, including the *I Ching* and Tarot, but it can be found as well simply in special properties that natural integers display in computations, that is, arithmetically.

---

1. Von Franz, Marie-Louise, *On Divination And Synchronicity,* p. 83.

Modern theoretical physicists, corporate CEOs, and prison inmates alike are identified by their long strings of numbers, and (for very different reasons) each prays for *"the one that sets them free"* as it's in their genes and they cannot help themselves. Theologians and football coaches rhapsodize in pre-second grade numerologies that enumerate their respective highest canons, from the *"ten* commandments," the *"eightfold path,* " and the *"seven deadly sins,"* to the *"six* point touchdown," *"three*-point field goal," and strategically, the life-altering *"two*-point conversion." The emotions that this order of number touch are not simply quaint or subcultural—they carry information that we have lost as a society—they are about our primary make-up. Another fundamental attribute of Tarot is that it brings meaningful numbers back into consciousness, and returns us to our forgotten selves.

Natural numbers best capture the fundamental energy, purpose, pattern, structure, and destiny of things regarded sacred, that is, when used symbolically and qualitatively (as opposed to literally and quantitatively). By "sacred" we may think beyond religiously sacred alone, to ascribe anything that is too valuable to be interfered with; that which is *sacrosanct*. Sacred numbers, as such, provide a kind of shorthand for the deepest regions of human discovery. At such times they are universally recognized for pointing beyond the immediate and actual, to the mythic world of the human soul. That is to say, they add a second dimension of bright and ponderous meaning to our otherwise linear self-contained existence.

Root Numbers in the Tarot

In Tarot, meaningful numbers, located in the upper or lower margins of each card, express a timeless and special set of universal themes and principles that correspond to the spectrums of human possibility. It should be noted that Eastern cultures too have a deep tradition of number meaning, as we saw with the Chinese generals and in the *I Ching*, but owing perhaps to their differing physical, cultural, historical, and mental landscapes, Eastern associations are a bit different to those of the Italian Renaissance-born Tarot.

The Tarot is a multi-layered symbol system, and includes more than just the fertile ground of meaningful numbers. Each card is a collage of symbolic images, colors, glyphs, magical tools, elements, activities, spatial relations, social interactions, titles, animal and human figures, dwellings, landscapes, clothing, background environments and more. While certain imagistic conventions by tradition are typically acknowledged in each Tarot artists' execution of a new deck—for instance, Strength regularly portrays some form of a woman opening or closing the jowls of a lion—creative artistry, emphasis, and style

have shown great variation. As part of the beauty and freedom unique to the Tarot tradition, no rigid standards of expression have ever been established for the design and execution of a deck. The unspoken rule, as Campbell made clear in his classic study *The Hero with a Thousand Faces,* is that universal symbols may be expressed in inexhaustibly varied and original forms.

Meaningful numbers are also different than other symbolic images in this regard: they operate within the precise and invariant laws of naked truth. Since the early 18th century, when the deck's numbering assignments and sequence pretty much stabilized with the classic Tarot De Marseilles with few exceptions, all Tarot decks have adhered to these essential numeric constants.

On the next page, I've made a short list of meaningful root numbers with respect to the timeless deck of Tarot. For the symbolically inclined and spiritually hungry, I recommend putting these to memory as on many occasions they will help to lift the veil, reminding us that there is far more to the number than a calculator can reveal. We may now turn to the special properties and magic of the single number that most gives sustenance and coherency to the Major Arcana in general, and in the particular, masterfully weaves the metaphysical fabric that consciously adorns the TNP Matrix. I speak, of course, of the Number 9.

Root Number Meanings in Tarot

ZERO FOOL	No-thing, Emptiness, Open Field, Possibility, The Void, The Unmanifest
ONE MAGICIAN	Unity, Singularity, Thesis, Primacy, Solitude, Point
TWO PRIESTESS	Relation, Polarity, Duality, Pair, Antithesis, Counterpoint, Line
THREE EMPRESS	Process, Synthesis, Divinity, Trinity, Growth, Progeny, The "Us," Triangle
FOUR EMPEROR	Form, Structure, Earth, Elements, Order, Body, Quaternity, Family, Square
FIVE HIEROPHANT	Complexity, Man, Spirit, Ethics, Quintessence, Pentagram
SIX LOVERS	Harmony, Equilibrium, Union, Choice, Love, Hexagram
SEVEN CHARIOT	Pursuit, Perfection, Quest, Mysticism, Victory, Spectrum
EIGHT STRENGTH	Balance, Regeneration, Strength, Solidity, Vitality, Infinity
NINE HERMIT	Completion, Individuation, Truth, Soul, Triangle of the Ternary, Fulfillment
TEN FORTUNE	Perfection, Mastery, Cycle, Reunification, Return

CHAPTER 9

The Hermit Effect (+9)

The Tarot of the Nine Paths (TNP) is a perfect matrix of twenty-seven principles believed to be instrumental in all processes of psychospiritual development. "Perfection" here refers to something complete or whole unto itself like a living organism, ecosystem, enlightened being, or true work of art. TNP marks a crucial departure from traditional tarot in its exclusive concern with the trump cards or higher keys of the Major Arcana. One needs no previous knowledge or special abilities to find great benefit from working with this original divinatory system. Its life-blood is built upon meaningful numbers.

TNP catalogues timeless teachings of humanity's higher purpose, destination, and spiritual completion, echoing C.G. Jung's view that the Keys of the Major Arcana embody the "archetypes of transformation," that is, those universal symbols possessing the greatest constancy, efficiency, and potentiality for psychic evolution, and which point away from the inferior and towards the superior. By design, TNP retains Tarot's essential infrastructure with respect to long-established naming and ordering conventions, pictorial motifs, and esoteric correspondences, while expanding in size, depth, and scope from 22 to 27 in number. TNP was undertaken to "re-tune" the Tarot map, but with unswerving respect for what has gone before. In effect, TNP adds a final wing to the "edifice" without disturbing the sacred architecture.

Expanding the Wisdom Map

Approaching Tarot's higher keys as a matrix of consciousness places critical significance on the sequential ordering and boundaries of the territory. This is because nothing in Tarot is arbitrary, accidental, or superfluous. Below, the "problem" with the modern system is obvious: mid-way through the 3rd row, the matrix unaccountably stops short. TNP, in essence, is the solution to this mystery:

Figure 1: Classic 17th Century Matrix of 22 Keys

1	2	3	4	5	6	7	8	9
Magician	Priestess	Empress	Emperor	Hierophant	Lovers	Chariot	Justice	Hermit
10	11	12	13	14	15	16	17	18
Wheel of Fortune	Strength	Hanged Man	Death	Temperance	Devil	Tower	Star	Moon
19	20	21	0	?	?	?	?	?
Sun	Judgement	World	Fool					

Note: In all Marseilles decks of the classic tarot era the third row is missing 5 cards to form a symetrical canon when presented in rows of 9.

Figure 2: Standard 20th Century Matrix of 22 Keys

1	2	3	4	5	6	7	8	9
Magician	Priestess	Empress	Emperor	Hierophant	Lovers	Chariot	Strength	Hermit
10	11	12	13	14	15	16	17	18
Wheel of Fortune	Justice	Hanged Man	Death	Temperance	Devil	Tower	Star	Moon
19	20	21	0	?	?	?	?	?
Sun	Judgement	World	Fool					

Note: Strength and Justice have traded positions by Waite, the rest is consistent with Marseilles. The third row still missing 5 cards necessary for 3 completed rows of 9. In TNP, Key 0 is placed in the final 27th position, and Keys 22-26 are sandwiched between The World (21) and The Fool (0) to form a completed 27 card matrix.

It is as if the original designer(s) ran out of ideas at 21 (The World), covered it with The Fool, the Great Zero, which can go anywhere with out disturbance, so they simply placed it at the end and let that be that! The Fool, if one examines the fourth triad, rather cryptically became the destination phase of The Emperor! The result, one imagines, is a preponderance of "Emperor-Fools" which in their shadow-aspect, history has certainly born out on occasion. This can be forgiven in view of Tarot's historical linkage with astrology, as its late 14th century creation predates the invention of the modern telescope, and accordingly, the "transpersonal planets" Neptune, Uranus, and Pluto had yet to be discovered and integrated into the map. But the history of Man is not a static affair, nor is his evolution of consciousness. Though many would still argue the logic of The Emperor/Fool connection, esoterically showcasing the conjunction between form (4) and formlessness (0), and certainly in a political sense, the assimilation portends for either an ideal or aberration of leadership and power.

Perhaps the most obvious clue as to why the matrix should be laid out in rows of 9 (rather than say, three rows of 7 plus 1) is seen most glaringly in the 6th Path (Relationships) bearing cards (6) The Lovers and (15) The Devil. The two cards are nearly identical in composition, reflecting the bright and dark sides of the relationship archetype, and split dualistically to illustrate its thesis (Lover/Union) and antithesis (Devil/Separation). Unfortunately, a synthesis remains unknown on the third row, and perhaps tellingly, the relationship archetype terminates in in The Devil's grip of bondage, addiction, anger, deception, attachment, and separation.

Outwardly, it points to the marriage/divorce dichotomy, which in the present day in America is nearing 60 percent, and certainly has begun fraying at the seams. Surely a deeper resolution must reside somewhere in the sacred canon? But it cannot be found in its current unfinished state. The same is true regarding the other missing syntheses (Arrivals) in four other "missing places" on the third row. Because we are purportedly talking about a perfect map of human consciousness, these omissions can no longer be easily excused, denied, rationalized, or dismissed. Nor will clever justifications for the existent order stand the test of time.

FROM MARSEILLE THROUGH POST-WAITE

Interestingly, O'Neill (1986) and other scholars have shown early variance in membership, sequencing, size, order, and naming conventions of earliest tarots. In first known decks, Major Keys were actually not numbered; structural consistency, in fact, is not fully solidified until the mid-17th century's "French school" Tarot de Marseille, at least several hundred years after tarot's mysterious arrival in Europe (circa the late 14th century). The authenticity of early Italian decks has been challenged for their Christian revisioning as a pandering to the Church's catholicism of the Italian culture, and modern researchers have generally concluded the Marseilles template most closely carries structural vision of the map's original designer(s). Of course, with more recent interest in Tarot as a divinatory tool, even seemingly minor structural discrepancies can carry a ripple effect of cosmic proportions for practitioners who find profound metaphysical significance in the precision of such designations.

Since Marseilles, however, the canon has congealed remarkably in its constitution save for a slight transposition of Keys 8 and 11 (Justice and Strength) by A. E. Waite, in the famed Waite-Smith Rider Tarot (1909), the modern standard bearer even today.[1] Yet despite a vibrant flurry of creativity that has characterized the profusion of late 20th century decks, it is not until *Tarot of the Nine Paths* that the canon itself has been challenged with respect to structural and conceptual assumptions. In this careful "re-tuning" endeavor, Tarot's own guidance has been sought and tapped with special regard for the magical properties of Number 9.

---

1. Waite determined this shift for astrological consistency.

Nine-ness

Investigations into the fertile sub-terrain of number symbolism, and specifically the special role Number 9 plays as Tarot's hidden "signature," was first discussed seriously by modern scholars in essays by Richard Roberts and Joseph Campbell in *Tarot Revelations* (1983). Roberts writes: "Nine may very well be called a magical number because it always returns to itself. Like the elusive Hermes/Mercurius it may take many forms while yet retains its essential identity."

The late Tarot master, author, cultural anthropologist, and one of my own primary teachers of Tarot, Angeles Arrien, in her book *The Nine Muses,* further amplifies:

> When the number "nine" comes up in our speech, the Muses announce their presence: "a cat has nine lives, dressed to the nines; go the whole nine yards; to be on cloud nine; a stitch in time saves nine." All are ways of reminding us that the Muses are there to assist us in bringing our gifts and talents forward to the world and to become more whole. In a more subtle way, they live within and through us... [In science] there are nine openings in the body; it takes nine months to be born; and nine rings comprise the centriole of the human cell. Cultural uses of nine are found in China, with nine-story pagodas; Native American, Aztec, and Mayan myths speak of nine cosmic levels; and in Christian symbolism we find nine orders of angel choirs in nine circles of heaven, and nine devils within nine rings of hell. The Greek poet Hesiod, in his Theogony, describes the Muses as "all of one mind" and describes how their nine voices tend to unite into one creative song.[2]

In *Tarot of the Nine Paths,* the Number 9 is the very signature of the deck itself as it forms the basis of the pathways, and animates what I have called *The Hermit Effect,* based on Key 9, The Hermit card. As will be explained shortly, The Hermit Effect accounts for the inner logic

---

2. Angeles Arrien, *The Nine Muses: A Mythological Path to Creativity* (2000); N.Y.: Tarcher, p. 14.

of the entire Major Arcana in all tarot decks, and upon closer examination, it is through The Hermit Effect that it can be clearly demonstrated why Tarot's Higher Canon, in its present form, remains unfinished and incomplete, owing to what I call "The Overbite" (see Figures 1 and 2) which points glaringly to the lack of symmetry in the third row. By the time we are finished, a full orthodontic intervention shall bring a beautifully smiling face to the map, if you will. This will be made as clear as pearls and diaphanous gems as we explore the treasure chest of Tarot.

The Overbite

But the *Tarot of the Nine Paths* is not meant to interfere with The Keepers of the Past, nor their artifacts; it is expressly a Tarot for the future. We shall see that Number 9 and "nine-ness" runs through every Tarot, though more consciously through TNP at every turn, and this even explains why this deck for the future is assembled comfortably around 9 discreet Pathways. Symbolically in Tarot, 9 is numeric shorthand for the production of transformational wisdom as confirmed by Tarot's own Ninth Key, The Hermit card.

The Hermit (IX) and The Hermit Effect (+9)

Tarot historian and scholar Robert V. O'Neill, Ph.D. writes:

> Whereas seven symbolizes the completion of the material man, nine symbolizes the completion of the spiritual man."[3]

Not surprisingly, therefore, do we find The Keepers of the Past content to conceptualize the current Matrix as a Magic Square of 7, that is, three rows of 7 cards, with a remainder of one, that often is placed as the

---

3. Robert V. O'Neill, *Tarot Symbolism* (1986), p. 292.

22nd card—(Key Zero) The Fool, but can theoretically belong anywhere on the map. In this, The Fool assumes a similar role to The Joker, in standard playing cards, typically dismissed when the game begins. We might speculate that the base 7 Arcana, perhaps unconsciously, has served its time in the completion of the material man, and in this, it has been quite successful. But here our intent is expressly different and, in keeping with the forecasts of the future laid out in the introduction, TNP is specifically oriented to the spiritual person, and his completion. The future, at this turn, remains an idea that by our study's completion will be articulated from the perspective of oracular and imaginal travel. Completion and finality, however, are the very rationales behind this deck's creation; exploration of inner space and the sacred interior of our mind is our objective. And Wisdom will serve as our modus operandi.

The Lexicon of The Hermit

In the TNP Lexicon [see Appendix], Key 9, The Hermit is described:

> Wisdom and tenacity in pursuit of true self; "spiritual individuation" i.e. "the process by which a person becomes a [psychospiritual] individual" (Jung); self-realization. Fiercely independent and self-directed; a master of the invisible; philosopher-artist; cares little for outside approval, values aloneness, independence; He "seeks his own salvation with diligence" (as advised the Buddha).

If, as we have discussed, The Traveler (+9) is the agent of Individuation, the wisdom agent of Wisdom itself—Key (9) The Hermit—addresses what is more precisely termed "psychospiritual" individuation. "Psychospiritual," we define simply as "of or pertaining to the relationship between spirituality and the mind." Spiritual individuation, accordingly, is "the process by which a person becomes a whole *psychospiritual* individual." The distinction may seem a matter of semantics,

but Jungian individuation alone does not require the spiritual dimension explicitly as does TNP. Moreover, The Hermit's traditional accou-
terments shown consistently for centuries, being The Lamp (symbolic
of clarity), The Mantle (universal fabric), and Staff (direct experience),
inspire Travelers with His timeless incentive:

> To be... Of clarity and light
> Within the fabric of universal spirit
> As revealed in immediate experience.

The eminent Spanish symbolist J. E. Cirlot further explicates nine's
esoteric uniqueness (both symbolically and arithmetically), including its
implicit relation to the numerology of The Three (as found in the three
stages X, Y, and Z):

> "The triangle of the ternary, and the triplication of the triple. Nine
> is therefore a complete image of the three worlds. It is the end-limit
> of the numerical series before its return to unity. For the Hebrews,
> it was the symbol of truth, being characterized by the fact that when
> multiplied it reproduces itself (in mystic addition)."

In *Tarot of the Nine Paths,* there are:

9 Points of Departure (X)
9 Transfers (Y)
9 Arrivals (Z)
9 Triads (Rites of Passage)
9 Direct Paths (Mastery-Sage)
9 The Hermit's number
+9 The Traveler's Number
3 Stages of Transit (9/3)
27 Archetypal Principles (9 X 3)
27 Wisdom Agents (9 X 3)

In essence, The Hermit Effect is the conscious embrace of the innate
wisdom associated with number nine and denoted as "+9." It can therefore be translated as *"in the service of psychospiritual individuation,"* or

with fewer syllables, *"in the service of spiritual individuation"* [wherein *"psycho-spiritual"* is implied]. Its related "ternary" or triadic structure becomes obvious when the canon is sequenced as a magical table of three rows of 9, thereby revealing nine distinct Rites of Passage (Triads) leading to higher levels of awareness, or consciousness. In nine-ness, we are given a compass for imaginal travel. Insofar as TNP is concerned, these properties are demonstrated first in numeric equations, and then in The TNP Matrix itself, from which the five additional cards were inferred and the Major Arcana completed.

The Hermit Effect or +9 in *Tarot of the Nine Paths* means re-conceptualizing and re-tuning all 27 Principles through the prism of The Hermit's Wisdom and the magical properties of number nine. In this way, each tarot takes on its own unique nine-based character. Key 11, Justice, for instance, becomes "Justice in the service of psychospiritual individuation." One reflects, therefore, less so on the card's outward effects—as found in the legal, transactional, or political sense—and more exclusively, to a kind of "poetic justice" and equanimity which furthers one's journey with regard to wholeness and completion as a human being. It is a liminal, "hermitized," brand of Justice, if you will, and the same goes for every card in the deck.

Figure 3: The TNP Matrix of 27 Keys

1	2	3	4	5	6	7	8	9
Magician	Priestess	Empress	Emperor	Hierophant	Lovers	Chariot	Strength	Hermit
10	11	12	13	14	15	16	17	18
Wheel of Fortune	Justice	Hanged Man	Death	Temperance	Devil	Tower	Star	Moon
19	20	21	22	23	24	25	26	0
Sun	Judgement	World	Well	River	Ring	Dragon	Great Web	Fool

The Hermit Effect itself is liminal because its workings are invisible. Something shifts in perspective when it's activated, though initial cause and effect may remain unchanged. That something is the subtle hand of wisdom. In TNP, The Hermit Effect is like an underground stream of consciousness flowing beneath the higher matrix of spiritual potentials, a river of final destinations on the return journey to the unconditioned mind, all guided, if you will, by the invisible hand of Wisdom. In Figure 3 the first step of the re-tuning process which begins with the hermitizing of the final Key, 0 The Fool, which now slides to the 9th place on the third row. The significance of this adjustment will be examined in the third section.

The Magical Properties of Nine

Nine may be considered a magical number, as noted earlier, *because it always returns to itself*, and though it may take many forms, it retains its essential identity. This is easily demonstrated by applying what is some-times referred to as "mystic addition" to otherwise normal and simple arithmetic operations which is the *sine qua non* of numerology in gen-eral, and *Tarot Constellations*, which in effect populate and structure the Major Arcana itself (Arrien, 1987; Greer, 1987).

To understand how this works, let's take Key 19/The Sun, for exam-ple. Using "mystic addition" (also known as numeric reduction, natural or Fadic addition in numerology), one must always *add multi-digit num-bers across until reducing to a single digit* (e.g. 19 = 1 + 9 = 10). Then further reducing, 10 = 1+ 0 = *1* (i.e. The Magician). Another example, Key 17 (The Star): 17= 1+7 = *8* (Strength). To be more precise, I prefer using the symbol "≅" to mean *corresponds to* rather than "equals" as Eliade spoke of symbolism generally:

> Nothing is isolated inside its own existence: every-thing is linked by a system of correspondences and assimilations.

The Sun

XIX

CONSCIOUSNESS

In this vein, numerically, Key 19, The Sun (Consciousness) *corresponds to* Key 10, The Wheel of Fortune (Synchronicity), which further is reduced (i.e. *corresponds to)* Key 1, The Magician (Intention); what separates and interlinks them numerically is Number 9 (i.e. 19 - *9* = 10, much as

1 + 9 = 10). The Star (17), our second example, likewise corresponds to the Strength (8) card (8 + 9 = 17). The significance of these correspondences is revealed in The Matrix itself.

Contemplating the significance of such linkages via agencies, as for example with Key (19) The Sun: (19) Consciousness » (10) Synchronicity » (1) Intention is really where the deep teachings of this system come alive. Were we to stage this by triad, or rite of passage, we might say, departing with Intention, transfers to Synchronicity, and arrives at Consciousness. What we are describing, in any event, is Path 1, Mastery. Thus, in Tarot, we begin to see that meaningful linkages between 27 transformational archetypes occur throughout The Matrix via Number patterns, not simply garden-variety quantification and arithmetic operations (17 = 1+7= 8), but more tellingly, "at the taproots" of *qualification,* that is, the qualia of human experience.

We might even go a step further and call this qualia "wisdom teachings" as they are all made possible through Key 9, The Hermit, the agent of Wisdom. As one therefore plunges deeper into Tarot soil, one soon discovers an extraordinary "energy system of information" lies teeming beneath! A virtual Grand Central Station of the mind. When, for instance, our rollercoaster ride through the liminal phase brought us, perhaps unthankfully, to (13) Death, (15) The Devil, and (16) The Tower, to name a few of the more memorable stops, this was not some random funhouse tour of Tarot's darkened underworld, but more telling, a systemic by-product of highly linked, purposeful, steps ordained by the deep numeric logic of this metaphysical terminal.

But what does this all have to do with Number 9? The answer quite plainly is: everything! As Arrien suggests, the qualia of *Nine* should remind us that the Nine Muses are energetically here to assist in bringing our gifts and talents forward to the world and to become more whole. Magically, (not supernaturally), any number that is multiplied by 9 reduces to 9 again! (See chart on next page). Shown in the center is one example—the human genome—of how 9 always returns to itself, and also, how in primary matters (i.e. 1-9 matters), a root card may take many forms when 9 is added to it while retaining its essential identity, extended infinitely out in all directions into the Universe, theoretically. Suppose then, we return to planet Terminus of *The Foundation*—fifty thousand years in the future—to learn that a new galactic census had revealed say another meager four billion six hundred and fifty-eight million, seven hundred and forty-three thousand, nine hundred and fifty-two MORE citizens had been added to the 500 quadrillion estimated residents last taken, for a whopping 1,000,004,658,743,952 in total.

The Magical Properties of Nine

By using the operation of numeric reduction, any number multiplied by 9 reduces to 9 again:

Multiply by 9 Reduces to 9

$2 \times 9 = 18.\ 18 = 1 + 8 = \mathbf{9}$
$3 \times 9 = 27.\ 27 = 2 + 7 = \mathbf{9}$
$4 \times 9 = 36.\ 36 = 3 + 6 = \mathbf{9}$
$5 \times 9 = 45.\ 45 = 4 + 5 = \mathbf{9}$

The effect is virtually limitless and applies to large numbers equally, as for instance the estimated number of genes in the Human Genome: **62,598:**

$$62,598 \times 9 = 563,382 = 5 + 6 + 3 + 3 + 8 + 2 = 27$$
$$= 2 + 7 = \mathbf{9}$$

When 9 is added to any of the primary digits, numeric reduction restores the original number.

Examples:
Add 9 Reduces to Original
$1 + \mathbf{9} = 10.\ 10 = 1 + 0 = 1$
$2 + \mathbf{9} = 11.\ 11 = 1 + 1 = 2$
$3 + \mathbf{9} = 12.\ 12 = 1 + 2 = 3$ (etc.)

Thus in primary matters (by the magic of nine):
(1). A something behaves like a nothing.
(2). Through increase, one returns to "essence."
(3). Expansion occurs with conscious retention of root value, or origins.

Witness what happens to this example when we multiply by 9:

Population: 1,000,004,658,743,952 X 9 = 9,000,041,928,695,568.

Now using mystic addition, add and reduce across:

9+0+0+0+0+4+1+9+2+8+6+9+5+5+6+8 = 72 = 9.

You see, it's inescapable!

A second magical property also is evidenced as well. When 9 is added to any primary or (single) digit (i.e. 1-9), *numeric reduction restores the original number.* For example: 5 + 9 = 14. 14 = 1 + 4 = 5 (the original number). There are no other numbers possessing such magic, but what does this suggest for our study? The answer is that Trump 9, The Hermit, is *9ness* in action!

In the second capacity, concerning the "primary" matters we face in existence—the Law of Impermanence, the certainty of death, confusion about who we really are and where we are really going, or even, in dealings with our essential mothers and fathers, teachers, and spiritual friends (i.e. Departures X) in Tarot—9 reveals profound lessons as well. The first is that, mysteriously, when 9 is added "a something behaves like a nothing" as in the 5 +9 = 14 and 14 = 1 +4 = 5 example above, thus returning us back to where we started. Something significant happened, but we seem to be right back where we began with echoes of Lao Tzu ("Without leaving my house, I know the whole universe"). Or are we? We departed at 5, an invisible, liminal intervention occurred, and by golly, we're right back at 5 again...? That invisible something is another manifestation of The Hermit Effect (+9). We've been "hermitized!"

Suppose we substituted any other primary whole number, say 8, and tried the same operation: 5 +8 = 13? But here as any first grader can see, no luck! 13 = 1+ 3, which sadly returns us to 4 (not the original number at all!). What then might this suggest for human consciousness? The answer to this rhetorical question is a cornerstone of this study, and will be developed in the chapters to follow.

The effect, we can say, is very Zen-like. To begin with, something gets added to an original condition—say, for example, a broken heart. Something expansive occurs, (namely, the hermitizing effect of 9 added to it), and a kind of psychological space is expanded in the subject's experience, yet by mystic addition, it doesn't go away so much as we return to the original love-sick condition...but something qualitatively (i.e. experientially) has changed. Something non-intrusive and subtle has interceded, leaving no visible signs. The heart may still feel hurt, but it has been touched by the Hermit's wisdom, if invisibly, though by outward appearances the condition remains untouched, yet nevertheless, The Hermit Effect has lightened our understanding, and made it more spacious and acceptable, with the added layer *in the service of spiritual individuation.* The broken heart remains, but its deeper meaning and purpose has been elevated to soul work. This by example is how the craft of Tarot in general brings its light touch of guidance through the gentle vision-logic of The Tarot Oracle. Inner space is expanded.

Subsequent corollaries may also be drawn from this example. By the magic of 9 (that is, in primary matters), "through increase, one returns to essence." It is as if adding on and getting bigger by increasing one's awareness on a particular issue, accessing more information—in this case, regarding the complexity of love—the added information is deconstructive; it returns us to our original condition, but with a far simpler, less elaborated, level of understanding.

This leads to our third corollary, namely, "Expansion occurs with conscious retention of root values, or origins." We have expanded in our interpretative understanding of the situation, but its meaning now takes on new significance rooted in timeless wisdom. Our pain, in this case, is now seen as a vehicle of growth.

In TNP, The Hermit card is the wisdom agent of Wisdom itself, contrary to popular misconceptions of a lonely, isolated guy with antisocial tendencies. The Hermit may be personified as a person living in solitude, though by modern Western standards, he could even by your boss, husband, wife, daughter, or your self. Whether introverted or extraverted by nature, The Hermit is associated with spiritual individuation, the process by which a person becomes a psychospiritual individual.

On the Kabbalistic Tree of Life, the 9th sephirah is Yesod (יסוד), the foundation. It is understood as the vehicle, and the power, of connection between the lower and the higher realms. Yesod is associated with The Moon and also the sexual organs, collects the vital forces of the sephirot above, and transmits these creative and vital energies into the feminine Malkuth below such that the earthly Kingdom of Man may interact with divinity. In this correspondence we see the number 9 at play in the transformation of sexual energy as found in ancient Eastern Tantric practices and modern *kareeza*,[4] where orgasmic abstinence is the preferred method, in favor of more intimate, lasting, and loving pleasure relations between the sexes, without release, thereby tapping the powerful and satisfying spiritual centers of the human body. We might call this as well a Hermit Effect!

By The Hermit's mercurial, magical, and unique set of principles and special talents, the entire Matrix of Tarot has been built, and now completed. Each triad, each rite of passage, and indeed, each of the 9 Paths of the TNP Matrix, are perfectly connected, re-tuned, and inter-related by dint of the magical properties of 9 in The Hermit Effect (+9), and in total, they coalesce into a completed map of consciousness for Travelers in the service of spiritual individuation.

It is time now to explore the mysterious way this potent map is set in motion during readings, an operation that fully and deliberately capitalizes on the liminal dimension we call "randomness," and offers new "space craft" for the interior dimension.

---

4. See Marnia Robinson, *Cupid's Poisoned Arrow: From Habit to Harmony in Sexual Relations* (2009).

CHAPTER 10

Divination

Intend to see the hidden beauty of all that exists—it then reveals itself.

—David R. Hawkins, M.D.

Fate, Fortune, and Destiny

The liminal realm of Tarot does not simply apply to the middle row of The Matrix—it is also intimately tied to the mysterious methodology of the oracle itself, namely, *divination.* Casting one's fate, whether to the wind, the stars, leaves of tea, or palms of hands is a deliberate liminal act. In cartomancy (divination by cards), we best begin with its antiquated terminology, and differentiate these three intertwining concepts: Fate, Fortune, and Destiny in accordance with their long traditions of significance.

Fate, we will then say, is a concept based on the belief in a fixed natural order to the universe, and in some conceptions, the *cosmos,* stemming from the ancient Greeks who believed the world to be perfectly harmonious and impeccably put in order. Each person's destiny was thought of as a thread spun, measured, and cut by the three Fates: Clotho, Lachesis, and Atropos, who preside over the birth and life of humans. Traditional usage through the ages defines Fate as a power or agency that predetermines and orders the course of events. Fate is often conceived of as being divinely inspired. In our model, Fate would most correspond with Departure (X), the perfectly ordered world in which our journey begins.

Fortune, the second of the trio, differs from Destiny and Fate by having more to do with the bumps in the road, if you will, the specific occurrences, interfaces, and developments in the human story we call "our life." Fortune tells what may come on the way to Destiny; it is conceived of as a hypothetical force or personified power that unpredictably determines events and issues favorably or unfavorably, whereas Destiny is more finalizing in the particular, and ultimately revolves around death or the completion of a cycle, rather than the particular events that comprise the chapters of one's narrative. Fortune-telling, therefore, technically speaking, should be about the bumps in the road, not the final results, and is most akin to the liminal middle stage on The Matrix, Transfer. But I suggest, at this point in our study, we do well to remain agnostic regarding this storied trio, though usage of these concepts will serve us to better understand the phenomenon of divination, and as well, our meditation on Tarot and the future.

Destiny, quite different still, is used with regard to the finality of events as they have worked themselves out; how the flow of Fate and Fortune will come to resolution at completion, or terminus. Destiny upholds the events that will necessarily happen to a particular person or thing at their conclusion, and claims the hidden power believed to control what will happen in the future, much in contrast to the modern scientific view, which relativizes not only the future, but the past as well, as expressed by the contemporary physicist Stephen Hawking: "The past, like the future, is indefinite and exists only as a spectrum of possibilities." At this juncture, we may remain comfortably ambivalent about what in fact the so-called "future" entails; in our model, the third stage on The Matrix called Arrival (Z) best corresponds to this traditional notion of Destiny.

Fortune-telling

In Tarot, this refers simply to the reading of the cards in divination. The common definition given for *divination* is "the practice of seeking knowledge of the future or the unknown by supernatural means." Modern lovers of dreams, by contrast, including the romantic, the sleep-deprived, and the psychoanalyst, may be chastened to learn that divination outscores their beloved nocturnal outpourings both with respect to its acuity in future-viewing, possibility-spinning, and, I'd argue, truth-telling, and therefore we might think of dreaming per say as a kind of unconscious realm of divination. Though dreaming and divining both appear liminally, that is, betwixt and between two ordinary conscious baseline states, in divination, the "traveler" remains fully awake and in possession of his faculties unlike the sleeper, and in this sense, we might even think of divination as a kind of waking lucid dream. Hypnosis, by comparison, cannot make this claim unless exceedingly light, as under it our normal faculties ("higher-order cognitions") are subsumed in trance.

I take issue, however, mostly with the definition's term "supernatural" as the causative agency through which the purported future (or unknown) supposedly arises, for two reasons. Firstly, the word *supernatural* has gathered so much dust and vast emotional coloring, often in the darkest and silliest of night shades, due primarily, one suspects, to the popular folklore forever shadowing it viscerally, and thenceforth, this thing called "supernatural," under certain inexplicable "threshold" circumstances, tends naively (and wrongly) to be projected onto the unknown as if we are standing outside a dark cave and imagining what might lurk within its darkness, done generally with dimensionless and predictable results. In fact, it is not truly "the unknown" one projects inside the dark cave, but rather things that are quite familiar to the subject, and usually dark, alien, and sinister. Jung had a term for this: shadow projection.

The result has degraded the connotative significance of the term supernatural to literally comic book proportions, further propelled by its self-serving purveyors of Hollywood, such that the so-called supernatural today correlates most highly with popcorn sales, misguided fascinations with "powers," unsubtle phantoms and psychopaths of creepiness, and Halloween costumes that children adore. Oh, for the love of popular culture! But for all its beauty as children's literature, sadly, what we've seen in *Harry Potterism* primarily survives for entertainment, not enlightenment.

For our purposes then, we shall revert back to *supernatural's* true meaning, defined a second time in the Oxford English Dictionary, as "a manifestation or event attributed to some force beyond scientific understanding or the laws of nature." This we can work with, though the proposed qualifier "beyond" in this definition too runs counter to scientific discoveries made, admittedly though, only in the first half of the last century, within the fields of Parapsychology, New Physics, and Analytical Psychology, to say nothing of the timeless insights from "Eastern travels," as discussed in previous chapters.

One must remember that up-to date scientific understanding often is gridlocked between old and new models much like politics, and not surprisingly, cutting-edge discoveries are often given short shrift by the definition-makers who tell us what things mean. This, I suppose, should be forgiven as the findings and implications of quantum physics for instance, are, after all, but one hundred years old, and never easy to digest or visualize. As for the second "beyond" of the definition—where the self-evident "laws of nature" have been invoked, albeit loosely, I must again take issue. To this point, Jung keenly observed: "Science comes to a stop at the frontiers of logic, but nature does not—she thrives on ground as yet untrodden by theory." At the historic Terry Lectures (1937) in New Haven, where he was invited to speak about Psychology's interface with Religion, he told the Yale audience: "The shortcoming of Western religious rituals is the emphasis that is placed on highly structured, as opposed to spontaneous, religious experience." What is now needed, he said, is a new approach that opens the door to a direct, spontaneous religious encounter with nature, by which for Jung means a direct, spontaneous encounter with the living symbols of the unconscious psyche.

Nature, in the broader view, is that which occurs of its own accord. Emily Dickenson, who has been called "perhaps the greatest poet to write on American soil" and in particular, "a scholar of passing time,"[1] wrote:

---

1. "Emily Dickenson's Singular Scrap Poetry," Dan Chiasson, *The New Yorker,* December 5, 2016, p. 79.

Nature is what we know
Yet have not art to say
So impotent our wisdom is
To her simplicity.

Later a cartomantic approach I call "natural divination" will be offered which expressly allows the freedom for things to arise of their own accord in all their natural simplicity. Our position will be that divination, purely understood, is no less natural than a virgin forest, REM sleep, or for that matter, the archetypal layers of the mind and their universal laws that govern psychological growth and development, including "rites of passage." What we are essentially describing in this larger conception of the natural is perhaps most succinctly put by no more postmodern a philosopher than the 4th century BCE Chinese sage Chuang Tzu, in his formulation of the Tao (The Way) as: "That which is so of itself." What arises in divination is a natural revelation, in *that which is so of itself.* The distinguished British critic and fantasy writer Charles Williams in *The Greater Trumps* (1932) writes:

> It's said that the shuffling of the cards is the earth, and the pattering of the cards is the rain, and the beating of the cards is the wind, and the pointing of the cards is the fire. That's of the four suits. But the Greater Trumps, it's said, are the meaning of all process and the measure of the everlasting dance.

But for now, let's simply imagine divination as a courageous invitation (call it "an experiment") to the natural world. We ask Her to tell us a story about our lives (or ourselves), that is, of *Her* choosing (not our own). Because no thunder clouds, lily ferns, or rattlesnakes have yet been given direct access to human language that we can easily interpret, the natural vehicle we will utilize will be a purely random offering from the Tarot gods (though tea leaves would work as well!). Preparation will entail an exhaustive, and mathematically-verified (for its randomness) shuffling of the cards, such that a wholly blind selection of a small subset set of tarots may be had with eyes closed, though I prefer to call this natural vehicle "empowered randomness." The empowerment is found in the degree of sincerity inside the shuffler's heart. What we are seeking for is a fully natural (or "accidental") condition—natural intelligence, if you will—from which a "tarot dream" can be consciously spun without the trappings of human interference. Though quite rare in ordinary travels, in divination, this is viewed as a very good thing indeed.

A hero within us is thus called forth to enter a quest in the forest, or perhaps, it is a *"quest-ion"* as both words derive from the Latin *quaerere*—"to ask or seek." And like the knights of old, it is a matter of bravery and simple pride for Traveler-knights of this wood to likewise enter the forest alone, "off the beaten path," and "at the darkest hour of night" which suffices in metaphor perfectly for the curious practice of consulting the Tarot oracle. If our knight were not so brave, he might simply wait for the morning and talk it over with his therapist. But a divinatory procedure requires a modicum of blind faith and supreme trust placed in the oracle's wisdom, and the great unknown is seen as a virtuous teacher when navigating this territory. He, The Oracle, arises of his own accord (though in many circles "He" might be more properly personified as "She").

In truth, it is more a matter of *blind trust* than blind faith, trust, that is, in the divinatory process itself, when mediated by a competent interpreter and qualified source. The skeptic will have great difficulty making this necessary leap, which is most likely why his own questionable experiments testing the art invariably fail to produce results. Though a cautionary note for believers must here be sounded as well, regrettably, regarding the well-known abuses of counterfeit, self-serving, or unqualified readers of the smoke-and-mirror variety now circulating like flies on the internet. Requesting references, and a pre-screening interview, may be a wise precaution when going in cold for such supernal travel adventures, though sometimes one is left simply to their own intuitive judgment as to the reader's credibility, which is oftentimes correct. Like when investing in all precious things of great value, whether sparkling jewels, miracle cures, love at first sight etc., one must guard against the fakery and bold promises dealt, in this case, with what may be called the "misscleofication" of Tarot, in reference to the felonious Jamaican hotline psychic of that name. Otherwise, when a solid decision is made, and properly entered with a reliable intermediary, it is not a problem should one's nerves be frayed by the potential magnitude of the experiment, nor even that one should attempt to lighten the intensity by pretending "it's really just a game," only that one bravely summons one's courage, and goes.

The Jigsaw Puzzle Is Dropped

With *Tarot of the Nine Paths*, in particular, the game begins when we then lift up this completed "smart" jigsaw puzzle of perennial wisdom (i.e. the deck), high above our heads, empty our minds of unnecessary distraction, and smash it hard on the floor so that all the little pieces scatter hither and thither just so, in order that they may chaotically escape their former places of comfort and natural resting.[2]

"Won't this be fun!" said The Fool, dogs nipping at his ankles and buttocks, as he steps freely off the steep cliff. The reading commences, and one is given to "expect the unexpected" at archetypal proportions in this free fall into The Intermediate Territory between the rational mind and pure consciousness. It is how tarot card readings are set in motion. They begin, that is, the moment The Traveler passes through the threshold of the Main Gates of Terminal 9, and are something akin to the Hero's quest known in the world's mythologies, of entering the forest at the darkest hour off the beaten path.

Writes Campbell:

> A hero ventures forth from the world of common day into a region of supernatural wonder: fabulous forces are there encountered and a decisive victory is won: The hero comes back from this mysterious adventure with the power to bestow boons on his fellow man.[3]

But whether conceptualized mythically, or divined through archetypal symbols, the question under discussion here is "how are such acts

---

2. For those given to less violent means, simply cutting three times from a highly shuffled deck, fanning it face down in a horseshoe configuration on the table, and then selecting intuitively one card for each position, placed, turned, and processed in order, perfectly suffices for the selection process.

3. Joseph Campbell, *Hero With A Thousand Faces.*

liminal?" Are they more "in between" than a dream, or for that matter, bungee jumping? And while we're at it, we might also be asking, "By engaging with the Tarot oracle, are we not deliberately tempting Fate? Could that be dangerous? Might our destiny be forever affected?" On all counts in this regard, the answer is yes. But as the Russian proverb goes, "He who doesn't risk never gets to drink champagne." Moreover, for people interested particularly in the nature of the mind and its many levels, it carries far greater appeal and less potential injury than the bungee.

But to the original point, divination is a liminal "altered state" of consciousness quite simply because one finds oneself, for the moment, bundled in complete mystery between two known baseline states. Like a dream, it is a relatively short-lived, temporary, transitional state, though here one may now, by contrast, wander around a bit, observe and record, digress as their mind takes them, or simply rest and absorb, as the operation itself typically eats no more than an hour of clock time. But no foreign substance has been ingested in the blood stream, and no hangover is expected. Experientially, however, from the perspectives of both reader and querent, time-wise, the procedure is virtually timeless. We can still remember who we were (or at least, who we believed ourselves to be previously) while travel is happening, we can still react, cogitate, sip our coffee, take a picture, or jot down notes while travel is happening, and even hope the operation will be successful when it is over.

Self-awareness, therefore, remains intact. Only now we must endure the process with lowered defense, openly and earnestly, though surprisingly, we might actually enjoy the experience quite a lot as most people, in fact, do; but, in any event, the experiment has begun. We are traveling imaginally, gliding through The Intermediate Territory of our minds. In the dream state, by contrast, the situation is far less "mid-stream" and liminally ambiguous, for the simple fact that when asleep we have forgotten we are dreaming, and have no familiar reference points to compare it to.

In Tarot divination we enter the Gates of the In-Between, consciously dreaming in the company of The Muses, and must surrender like The Hanged Man to this disquieting, suspended condition. It goes without saying that once past the Main Gates one is given little choice but to submit to the procedure, or go home (unless, of course, one already is at home). Though we are traveling liminally through a strange new symbol-land, we should do it fully and sincerely once aboard. No "dreamer's comfort" can be taken from the vague recollection familiar during sleeping fits that we are only dreaming, that this is not really happening, it's just a dream, and will likely be mostly be forgotten when we wake up anyway. Freud himself admitted that often he would have a dream in the night, and provide it with a perfect interpretation in his sleep, only to discover the next day upon awakening that a most interesting dream had occurred, and he had interpreted it well, but what they were about he had completely forgotten upon waking!

In a way, divination is both really happening, and not really happening simultaneously. Nevertheless, the experience won't soon be forgotten. It is why divination is more purely a liminal phenomenon than dreaming. And also, why divination is not for the faint-hearted or insecure. Nor suitable as a parlor game, or vehicle for entertainment. And why finally, in most cases, it wouldn't appeal to any man or woman already claiming complete satisfaction in their current state of health and self-knowledge. Why ever would they wish to place themselves in such a precarious, ambiguous, situation if it were not necessary? It is left, therefore, only for the rest of us, The Travelers, to atone.

Standing At The Threshold

Question: If liminal is the quality of ambiguity and disorientation that occurs in the middle stage of travel when Travelers no longer hold pre-boarding or early departure status, yet haven't arrived to their new destination or status when the transfer is complete, does it have a structure? According to van Gennep, during the liminal stage, participants must "stand at the threshold" between previous ways of structuring their identity, time, or community, and the new way which the journey will establish when it is completed.

It would seem in our present dispensation that the 21st century itself is in the throes of a liminal state.

Q: How, therefore, does one "stand at the threshold?"

As mentioned in Chapter 1, divination experiments find ideal subjects in powerful culture events as well as highly personal ones. Especially when events like the 2016 election "split" citizens down the middle, and become forcefully ambiguous, divided, and in effect, "trumped" easy solutions or conventional wisdom. Not surprisingly, "split down the middle" situations often provide a perfect station from which to enter a divinatory experiment.

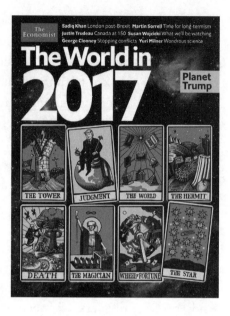

Whether by way of external rites of passage—"getting married" for example, (or "getting divorced"), or perhaps a more existentially divided concern, involving the question: "Who really am I?" or "Where am I really going?" the rule of thumb is that the more on the edge of certainty one feels in the question, the more alive the reading will be. Disturbance becomes our friend here. Crises, likewise, whether physical, transactional, emotional, political, relational, or spiritual, also provide excellent feeding grounds to partake of an oracle. While scientists of the modern age debunk anachronistic procedures like oracle work to be primitive and unverifiable, in times of great change, either calamitous or triumphant, modern science has precious little to offer by way of psychological and spiritual support, analysis, deep insight, or treatment, that is, other than opinions, consensus, conventional wisdom, and statistical probabilities. In other words, meaning is glaringly absent.

A Lighthouse

British novelist George Orwell, best known for his dystopian novel

Nineteen Eighty-Four published in 1949, eerily reminds us of the many problems we now encounter today in the American body politic:

All political thinking for years past has been vitiated in the same way. People can foresee the future only when it coincides with their own wishes, and the most grossly obvious facts can be ignored when they are unwelcome.

The same tendency of misattribution can be said, I daresay, about the bones of contention arising in personal and familial divisions, organizational competition, and at times, even scientific findings over contentious issues like abortion or climate change are, as Orwell predicted, ignored when unwelcome.[4] Orwell further prophesies what for many today is a gloomy foreshadowing of a future "doublespeak" wherein: "The very concept of objective truth is fading out of the world. Lies will pass into history." By no means a new phenomenon, this significant aberration has begun to sound the alarm bells of the 21st century as never before.

Culturally, with the rapidity and instability that characterize today's electronic and social media, where "going viral" tellingly has morphed into a desirable thing, and "fake news" calls into question the relativity of "real news" to say nothing about real "reality" itself, there is, without question, great danger afoot in the evolutionary experiment called human civilization. No guiding light is here to protect us now in the darkness beyond our established institutions of pubic welfare, education, and protection, whose own integrity and validity are themselves widely viewed to be in a state of disrepair, and therefore many sharp and dangerous rocks below the surface now obtrude, from which we must row away.

On the domestic front, important relational decisions between spouses, or in families, for example, may be helpfully sorted out with the aid of a good therapist. Help is readily attainable (if it can be afforded), as modern life is assaulted by rapid change and an anxious future, but this level of help is limited both in scope and depth. In the final analysis, it is only in the private chambers on an individual's heart and soul that true

---

4. Even though scientific evidence for warming of the climate system is unequivocal— Intergovernmental Panel on Climate Change.

light can be found and trusted. Deep wisdom is left wanting at the outer gates of institutional limitation.

There is need, therefore, for another order of guidance. Something that provides more than supportive words and rational suggestions for action and perspective. While they may be useful as physical destinations (PDs) to solve practical problems (i.e. domestic travel), their reach and depth is limited. Conventional wisdom often suffers the inherent biases and misattributions of Fates and Fortunes gone awry, to say nothing of egos, "dogs in the hunt," etc., and is susceptible to the doublespeak given us from the lieutenants and captains of sinking ships. We need guidance found and trusted only within the private quarters of the sacred interior. We need a portal to our own natural wisdom.

A lighthouse, of sorts, that provides navigation through the collective pressures and confusion in this age of institutional gridlock and ossification, heated passions, surface solutions, physical privilege, and regressive ideology. A lighthouse for inner travel crafted from the primary matter of the human soul. It is needed for the illumination of essential energies that make human beings powerful and compassionate, rather than the current technologically-seductive, lampposts that keep us busy and wanting, yet are fundamentally blind to who we really are, and where we are really going.

STRUCTURING THE LIMINAL: THE SPREAD

Were Tarot such a lighthouse, then standing naked at the threshold with tarot cards, if you will, must properly have some coherency, or systemic consistency. For this, Tarot is structured and facilitated by a seemingly "non-liminal" form—the anchoring capacity of the Tarot *spread*. With divination, we will need just enough structure to give our intuitions and deeper experience sufficient organization and context to be sufficiently grasped, interpreted, integrated, and communicated to others. Otherwise a reading can suffer for its over-generality or vagueness. In *Tarot and Psychology,* I defined these fixed, preconfigured patterns of a spread as:

a complex "field of presentation" designed to contain the constituent parts of an inquiry. It is itself neutral and static, perhaps analogous to the therapist's open engaged attention in free association, or the empty sandbox in sandtray therapy. The selected "pieces" that are placed within each container (or 'holding object') are what gives psychic life. In Tarot these pieces, of course, are the symbolic resonances of the randomly selected Tarot cards (p. 53).

Spreads have a liminal aspect as well in that structurally they live between two worlds, fixity and spontaneity. On the one hand, they have stable baselines, pre-exist to the reading proper, can be recorded and reviewed after the reading, and carry unchanging, prescribed, positions. On the other hand, what sticks to them is the gooey matter of natural randomness (via symbols), and thus they are also harbors of the unknown, the unexpected, and the nonrational. The "natural intelligence" that sticks to a spread, we remember, was selected blindly from 156 "archetypally-tinged" possibilities (if we include reversals) in a full standard deck of 78 cards, or in the abbreviated TNP deck, just 58 possibilities from a deck of 29 (including The Traveler +9 and The Four Elements card). In general, spreads provide what Giles has said about Jungian psychology in general, "a rational way to explore the non-rational." Having one foot on land, and one foot in water (like Key (14) Temperance), gives the tarot spread its unique liminality.

Examples of spread positions might include things like: "Heart," "Fears," "Foundation," "Mystery," or perhaps, "Goals." Although 156 potential possibilities, statistically-speaking, remains a relatively small number from which to boast "pure randomness," but because we are dealing with archetypal symbols here—which in each case are multidimensional, and virtually inexhaustible for their associations and correspondences as Jung and Campbell make abundantly clear, a set of 156 archetypal possibilities could literally fill a university library with related materials and references, unlike their quanta cousins, arithmetic digits.

A Tarot card carries a bevy of associations within its discrete, nonduplicated, spectrum of meaning. Number 1, The Magician, for example, can suggest change, creation, skillful speech, metaphysical knowledge, the Will, the act of intention, magical acts, "as above so below," cleverness, craftiness, stealth, application of multiple resources, visualization, unity, mental acuity, the power center, oneness—just for starters. Mythological examples of these attributes alone are found in every human culture and history from the dawn of time. Key 1, therefore, is not simply the number that precedes two and bears the properties of its mathematics; it is an entire world of possibility.

Spread positions are like coat hooks upon which random magic is hung. In theory, they could represent anything you wish to hang your hat on, providing just enough structure is given for a coherent reading. The simplest spread of one card only, might have the hook "Now_____" (pick a card). Or "Today_____" (pick a card). Even more ambivalently in true nondual fashion, simply "This!_____" (pick a card). Two card spreads like computers respond in the language of either/or, not unlike like taking a vote: "Yes_____" or No _____? " (pick a card for each), or perhaps, "This _____" or That_____?" (pick a card for each). One and two card spreads, however, are rarely used in readings because they quite simply are too non-liminal, too non-ambivalent, too cut and dry. Three steps or more seem to be where tarot cards come most alive. The more paradoxical and ambiguous the spread structure, while retaining coherency, the deeper one must drop to find its meaning(s).

Sequence and physical placement of the cards are configured so that a visual shape of the reading can be more easily apprehended, studied, and remembered; typically a preset symmetric or geometric pattern is formed, which lends visual coherency to a rich network of information and facilitates easier contemplation of the simultaneous thematic inter-relationships divined.

The choice of a question, of course, is the critical factor that remains. As a rule of thumb, one should question the edges of their experience, and move from the specific to the more general domain the question is concerned with. In the Appendix, a number of spreads that can be used with any deck but are particularly effective with TNP are offered, and seasoned readers are free to experiment with their own favorite spreads using TNP.

Preliminaries

A reading experiment is quite simple. One first chooses a spread, either an established configuration like perhaps the Eleven Card Celtic Cross Spread, or The Five Card Spread (presented in the following demonstration), though if one prefers they may craft the positions themselves, or use any other spreads they find meaningful. Before the procedure begins, one clears the mind of unnecessary distraction, and tries to locate within them some pressing need or current of change in their lives. The more ambivalent, or "at the edge" of certainty they feel about the area of investigation, the better, as there is really no point in doing a reading on something you have already made up your mind about, and it could be more confusing than helpful.

The question will likely involve several specific tributaries, perhaps financial, relational, health-related, etc., and if one starts with a very specific or local question, say "Should I go out for dinner with X?" it is better at this point to extend the question into its widest and most general domain, in this example, perhaps, "My path of relationships at this time?" or if it concerns a business contact, "My career path at this time?" This way, the cards themselves can address the specifics as you don't want to box yourself in with too narrow an inquiry. Common domains of inquiry include: relationships, career, money, health, family, love, new ideas, politics, pathways, projects, spiritual teachings, etc.

Next, the cards are exhaustively shuffled or mixed, cut three times, fanned out in a horseshoe or semi-circle, and selected face down by position, one at a time. Forming a stack of the selected cards at first until all are chosen is my own method, then placing them carefully into their configuration I find to be more efficient. If you are simply reading for yourself, and seek quick Tarot mirroring, it is perfectly fine to create a short spread for your specific purposes, prepare the cards, choose, turn, and complete the process in a matter of minutes. A businessman heading into a meeting, for instance, wanting some new inspiration for marketing his company's products, might tailor a three card spread with positions: 1) What is our current mission? 2) Where have we been most effective?

And, 3). Where do we need to grow now? If done sincerely, the procedure does not need to be elaborate.

Once the question is formulated (if there is one), a spread has been chosen, the cards properly prepared and selected face down, and placed by position into their configuration, they are turned and digested one card at time, in sequential order. At first, I recommend "feeling into" the stimulus of the card, that is, apprehending and studying it directly, before commenting, interpreting, and analyzing. Ask, "What most strikes me about this?" Typically, direct apprehension will stimulate associations, fresh ideas, and connections, as we recall "Image comes from No Image," that is, the vacant forms in the card (such as its title or number) come to life by our deep desire to find its meaning. When one "clicks" emotionally with the Image in this way, then one is ready to move on to the next card.

The process itself is timeless, and usually occurs rather quickly. Full interpretation may come at the end, when one puts their "higher order" cognitions to work, but not before a direct connection with each symbol has taken root first, within the position under consideration.

An Experiment Using The Five Card Spread

Let's try an experiment with a short spread designed for TNP, which also can be used (with the major Keys only) with any deck you prefer. The question comes after watching a news report of an explosion on New Year's Eve (2016) in a Turkish disco which killed 39 people and injured another 70. On New Year's Day morning, CNN reported:

> In Istanbul's horrific New Year terror attack the message is clear: 2017 has begun, expect more of the same to come. The echo of the black-clad gunman's bullets on such a globally festive night will reverberate long and hard.

Contextually, here was a powerful culture event "split" down the middle, forcefully ambiguous and divided, which "trumped" easy solutions or conventional wisdom. Its location in Turkey—at the very crossroads of East and West, Old World and New World, Muslim and Christian, even at this moment between the years 2016 and 2017—further exemplified its "split nature." Though despicable and tragic, it was nevertheless a perfect occasion for a reading. What could be learned?

My question, therefore, was "How Should I Relate To Terrorist Acts?" A short reading commenced. After clearing the mind of unnecessary distractions, exhaustively shuffling the cards, cutting three times, and fanning the deck face down, I turned four cards: Working For Me (16/ The Tower), Working Against Me (18/The Moon), What I Know (15/ The Devil), and What I Don't Know (8/Strength).

FIGURE 1: FIVE CARD SPREAD CONFIGURATION

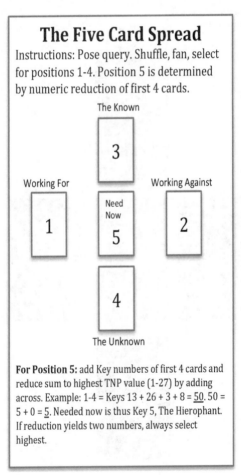

The Five Card Spread

Instructions: Pose query. Shuffle, fan, select for positions 1-4. Position 5 is determined by numeric reduction of first 4 cards.

The Known

3

Working For   Working Against

1   Need Now   2

5

4

The Unknown

For Position 5: add Key numbers of first 4 cards and reduce sum to highest TNP value (1-27) by adding across. Example: 1-4 = Keys 13 + 26 + 3 + 8 = 50. 50 = 5 + 0 = 5. Needed now is thus Key 5, The Hierophant. If reduction yields two numbers, always select highest.

The fifth card in this spread is determined by a numeric reduction of the first four, hence 16 + 18 + 15 + 8 = 57. 57 = 5 + 7 = *12*. Therefore, the fifth card would be Key 12, The Hanged Man. A simple recap of the selected cards by their archetypal principles yielded the following chart:

Q: How should I relate to terrorist acts?

POSITION	KEY	CARD	ARCHETYPAL PRINCIPLE
1 WORKING FOR	16	THE TOWER	UPHEAVAL
2 WORKING AGAINST	18	THE MOON	IMAGINATION
3 THE KNOWN	15	THE DEVIL	SEPARATION
4 THE UNKNOWN	8	STRENGTH	LIFE FORCE
5 NEEDED NOW	12	THE HANGED MAN	SURRENDER

3. The Known

1. Working For   5. Needed Now   2. Working Against

4. The Unknown

At first, as is not uncommon, the reading seems strangely counter-intuitive with The Tower/Upheaval in Position 1, Working For Me. How could that be, you wonder? On further reflection, however, The Tower card can be seen as spot on regarding the event itself, noticing the "ninja skateboarder"[5] fleeing the mayhem and destruction shown graphically in the card. One thinks, "the ivory tower of modernity, true to the card, has been attacked from the outside and is crumbling from within." But then, querulously, "how is this working *for* me?" One is now driven to drift creatively in speculation on the matter. This is precisely what an oracle wants us to do, as the 19th century French occultist Eliphas Lévi said of the Tarot itself: "It is a book that informs by making one think."

We now recall that the lightning bolt of The Tower classically points to the card's solution: namely, immediate, unequivocal action—evacuate, get out, direct your mind to safe ground outside, and strike with laser-light intensity! Radical change. Reposition yourself without deliberation. Contemplated with insight, and not simply the reactive "run for it!" the card says abandon the narrow framework of the manifest event, and view it as a symptom of a larger dynamic regarding the upheaval caused by all chaotic polarities in general splitting apart on the world stage. That operation is what is working now to your benefit.

The Moon in Position 2, "Working Against," underscores first and foremost how devoid of imagination the whole business of terrorism is. Instead, one may speculate, it is informed from a perversion of The Moon, in its shadow aspect, and signals a kind of unconscious, tribal regression out of control. As symbol of the unconscious itself, The Moon in this negative spread position "working against" reminds us of the dark and instinctive source that drives the lunacy of terrorist mayhem, and the distorted logic used to justify such actions. Positions 1 & 2, therefore, taken together illustrate the destructive dynamics taken in unison between the radical clashes of culture driven by the dark forces laden within the unconscious that from the beginning of time have accounted for the most heinous acts

---

5. This curious figure is a miniature object that was incorporated into the cards in the early 2000s.

of inhumanity, wars, genocide, and now terrorist acts. Perhaps, the one positive take-away thus far in the reading is the fierce, redirecting power of the lightning bolt, a harbinger of radical paradigm shift.

Continuing to the next spread position in this not so cheerful reading—Position 3, The Known—lo and behold, we find The Devil card, an agent of Separation. It should be reiterated that The Devil in Tarot is not identical to the Christian devil, and is more properly associated with the Jungian shadow. Here we focus on the false divisions of dualistic thinking, including the delusions and attachments that separate "self" and "alien other," that is, subject and object.

The position tells us what we are already aware of here, what we already understand (at least intellectually), that being the tragic divisiveness of shadow projection in general, and in our present question, how racial, cultural, and religious "otherness" is rife to trigger projections of "evil" onto the other, with dire and calamitous results. But knowing this intellectually, unfortunately, has not been enough to stop the bleeding. We bear witness to this flawed misattribution cycle seemingly everyday, whether in our personal relations, or societal, racial, political, national, and international divisions; The Devil, underscores the seeming incurable darkness in which still waters run deep. The terrorist act now seems simply a vicious and tragic manifestation of an otherwise archetypally-bound, pervasive collective ignorance of who we really are, and where we're really going.

What is "Not Known," however, according to the reading, speaks to the potential boon or "pay off" that could emerge IF our flawed perceptions that give rise to the abomination of terrorism were corrected; namely,the possibility of Life Force or chi), that is, the natural power and healing energy contained in Key 8, Strength. The emergence of a vast revitalization of our energy centers, and the firm, feminine mastery over "taming the beast," namely, the primitive, dualistic, tribalism that manifests in so many of the seemingly incurable human tragedies of our time, including terrorist acts. In Tarot, Strength represents gentle, regenerating power. As the reading is addressing a global phenomenon, Tarot's guidance is speaking to the world at large. At this level, the card reminds us of another Tarot Key, The World card, associated with the ancient Greek concept of the "Anima Mundi" or World Soul. The Greeks believed that there is an intrinsic connection between all living things on the planet, analogous to the relation between the soul and the human body. Plato wrote:

> This world is indeed a living being endowed with a soul and intelligence ... a single visible living entity containing all other living entities, which by their nature are all related.[6]

Finally, to complete our experiment, we move to the fifth position "Needed Now" after making the numeric reduction (summing the first four cards, adding across, and reducing), we arrive at what is Needed Now—The Hanged Man, an agent of Surrender. Surrender is not the same as succumbing to, let's be clear. The surrender needed now in Key 12 (reminiscent of The Twelve Steps) is akin to the AA slogan "Turning it over to a higher power." It means the surrender of detachment, dis-identification, and observation from a truly non-partisan perspective. The oracle upon further refection tells us to relate to terrorist attacks through the prism of wisdom teachings within our own psychological space. The reading also confirms the necessity to now embrace the lightning bolts of The Tower card, in order to activate the higher self in this matter. And also it confirms what we already know of The Devil's hand in this chronic, deadly, disturbance, yet bids us to open more deeply to an incubating regenerative potential found in the   Strength card; a taming, if you will, of "the beast within" of collective ignorance. We may invoke the vision of Anima Mundi as well, associated with the World card, where deeper resolution and integration must be accessed and actualized in response to this global sickness of our age that defiles the Earth, and symptomatically plays out in terrorist acts. Of course, deep paradigmatic change always begins with ourselves. Tarot merely confirms what we know through magical means, and thereby imprints it more deeply in our awareness.

---

6. Fideler, David (2014). *Restoring the Soul of the World: Our Living Bond With Nature's Intelligence.*

This is the way of Tarot. Invariably, it points us to a deeper level of spiritual reality where everything is interlinked by a system of correspondences and assimilations. All told, I found the experiment relevant for my own questioning concern, and would be pleased if its value was meaningful to others of equal concern. The reading was now complete.

CHAPTER 11

Time aNd TimelessNess

Time is what keeps the light from reaching us. There is no greater obstacle to God than time: and not only time but temporalities, not only temporal things but temporal affections, not only temporal affections but the very taint and smell of time.

—Meister Eckhart, 13th century German philosopher and mystic

MomeNtary Glimpses

"Time and tide wait for no man," wrote Geoffrey Chaucer in the 14th century *Canterberry Tales,* and this eternal impatience, much as our own, as first noted in the Introduction, may drive us to ponder late into the night periodically. Time measures our moments but does not share in them. It gives us things to think about, but provides no answers. The tides, by contrast, are kind enough to at least get our feet wet, and feel the soft texture of wet sand between our toes.

With Time's absence, however, comes the much coveted experience of now-ness, the freedom of abiding effortlessly in the present moment; if the great luxury or capacity for knowing this should arise, even briefly, one commonly feels its blissful sensations, and tastes the openness it provides of unlimited and clear awareness. One invariably discovers that Time's absence is a great deal less complicated than its presence. (The same thing, of course, has been said about myself on occasion), nevertheless, unlike myself, the timeless state is uniquely amorphous and immeasurable, foundationless and, indeed, ponder-less, when it is happening. It just is, clear as a starlit mountain stream. It may even be possible to activate glimpses of this experience with Tarot, at least in small denominations, on the pathways to our destination.

In Time's absence, the existential questions that might otherwise hang over us like recurring clouds of confusion, the questions we should not even have to ask pertaining to our true identity, purpose, and direction, simply dissolve, melt away, and vanish like early snowfall in a warm noonday sun. Our being is thus deeply refreshed and revitalized by it, and nothing is left wanting or missing. We just are. We may still be able to function, walk to the store, or make a cup of tea, but we do it from a different plane of awareness. The experience, we can say, is complete in itself. We have arrived, and there is nowhere else we need to go, and nothing more we need to do.

But soon enough, even from these exalted heights, the many indignities of Time (like clockwork) will mercilessly creep back in, owing perhaps to a combination of factors—the preciousness of pure consciousness itself, our inability to stabilize in duration within it, our long evolutionary march to this end (which we may be no further than midway into), and most tellingly, the deep and stubborn conditioning that keeps us bound to Time itself. Then we must ponder the when and why it has returned.

Where did the bliss go? Will it come again? How did I find the timeless state? Is there something I should do? Somewhere I need to go? An ashram, the desert, a samadhi tank? Maybe shamanic herbs from the Amazon ? Etc.

I'm reminded of the story that psychic Patricia Sun tells: "You're sitting on a rock eating an avocado and have a sudden awakening experience...word gets out, and everyone wants to know which rock you were sitting on, and what kind of avocado you were eating?" But as previously stated, this work is not meant for the permanently enlightened. The rest of us, soon again like clockwork, will sink back into those querulous sensations regarding the future that our favorite Jedi knight says is always in motion. What will it bring? Where will I be when it comes? Nobody really knows.

This fact alone, certainly, has not discouraged a confident industry of prophecy makers, forecasters of future effects, high-profile pundits, pollsters, and predictors (especially visible during the political seasons), Vegas odds-makers with impeccable track records, and of course, their alternative counterparts, the palm readers, psychics, and astrologers, to say nothing of the slightly more evidence-based professionals—psychologists, psychiatrists, and therapists, the credentialed masters of psychological determinism, and somewhere in the mix, there may even be spotted a few well-meaning tarot readers too. Predictive readers, stockbrokers, scientists, and other forecasters play with the odds, and they are easy to play with. It's a numbers game, but in the conventional sense. They deal in probabilities, not possibilities. As author/economist Nassim Nicholas Taleb observes regarding the business of economic forecasting in *The Black Swan:* "We attribute our successes to our skills, and our failures to external events outside our control"[1] One may defer, however, "Not today, thank-you," and choose to bypass the circus of future knowledge entirely simply by not bothering about where we're going at all, but the strategy still remains a far cry from abiding in the blissful timeless space.

Orwell tells us, "People can foresee the future only when it coincides with their own wishes, and the most grossly obvious facts can be ignored when they are unwelcome." We have reason for concern. Any organization or political administration bent on the normalization of untruths will, in time, devour all competing facts from sheer exhaustion, and with it, all recognition of a moral human compass. The future then becomes distinctly irrelevant, not because we have been liberated from the indignities of Time and are free to enjoy the present moment, but because we can no longer discern or verify what is actually taking place at all. We have fallen into an inescapable ditch, forgotten who we really are and where we were going; we have lost our way back.

There is a growing need, therefore, for another order of guidance, a craft or skill for accessing and navigating through the deep inner space of ourselves. It would be built by a different code and mechanism, and mandated by a very different mission than we have known, particularly when it concerns not simply the most pressing matters of our individual fates, fortunes, and destinies, but on a wider scale, our collective future as human beings on the blue planet. The need is clear as the conscious

---

1. *The Black Swan: The Impact of the Highly Improbable,* Taleb, 2007.

moon. It would require a powerful tool for soul travel and reflection within the sacred interiors of our being.

We need not quibble here over the precise meaning of the word "soul" with its many religious connotations, much as Supreme Court justice Potter Stewart declared about pornography, "I know it when I see it." We know soul, however, when we feel it. We feel it as a click in our gut, or a warmth in our heart when it is present. It touches us deeply. It is the part of *who* we are that is immaterial, and many believe immortal, and separable from the body at death; it is also, in fact, capable of moral judgment, and susceptible to happiness or misery. Author/physicist Gary Zukov describes soul like this:

> Every person has a soul, but a personality that is limited in its perception by the five senses is not aware of its soul, and, therefore, cannot recognize the influences of its soul. As a personality becomes multisensory, its intuitions—its hunches and subtle feelings—become important to it. It senses things about itself, other people, and the situations in which it finds itself that it cannot justify, on the basis of the information that its five sense can provide. It comes to recognize intentions, and to respond to them rather than to the actions and the words that it encounters. It can recognize, for example, a warm heart beneath a harsh and angry manner, and a cold heart beneath polished and pleasing words. [2]

The soul is our intrinsic nature, or essence. The craft we are developing in this book is designed to illuminate this. Some now reading I suspect may be "fortunate enough" not to feel particularly bothered by their soul, or their future development; they know it's coming, but are reasonably secure in their present, and are willing to simply "ride it out," "come what may," "live for today," as the sayings go, and will therefore, accordingly, have but passing interest in who (or *what)* they really are, or where they're really going? For the multitudes like them, no call for inner guidance seems necessary or particularly relevant. They may, nevertheless, find the Buddha's cautionary reminder on the nature of existence a

---

2. Gary Zukov, *The Seat of The Soul,* 1989, p. 34.

bit sobering, as Buddhist psychoanalyst Mark Epstein, M.D. reminds us in *Thoughts Without A Thinker:*

> The Buddha made clear that some kind of humiliation awaits us all. No matter what we do, he taught, we cannot sustain the illusion of our self-sufficiency. We are all subject to decay, old age, and death, to disappointment, loss, and disease. We are all engaged in a futile struggle to maintain ourselves in our own image. The crises in our lives inevitably reveal how impossible our attempts to control our destinies really are.[3]

Change Is Inevitable

Some mornings we wake up and look in the mirror startled by the evidence, "My god, things have changed! I look different today. Did it happen when I was sleeping?" Our intellect reminds us, change is constant, the cells in our bodies are constantly regenerating, but we just can't see it. *Dang!* We walk out of our home and start to notice, albeit subtly, things have also changed outside too. The sky looks different today, the lawn not as green, an unnoticed bush calls for our attention, the car looks older, or better, our neighbor more rushed. Change is everywhere.

But some things seem to remain the same, right? We may feel the same irritation, for instance, just at the mention of the opposing political party ... we still remain life-long fans of "da Bears" to the end of time... We always drive to work on Elm Street and go left on McDougall Court to avoid the morning crunch by the 5th Street Bridge exit... Our name has not changed that we know of... we have the same blood type, we are still African-American, still married to Shannon, still the son of Mike and Inna; we still take our coffee black, prefer the color blue, and try to play golf on weekends when we have the time and can afford it. After dinner we still help McKenzie with her arithmetic problems or current events, walk the dog, get ready for bed, watch a show and cuddle some with the Mrs., and try to get a good night's sleep. In other words, our physical footprints, destinations, and activities still seem quite the same, but we

---

3.   Mark Epstein, MD, *Thoughts Without A Thinker,* p. 44.

also quietly know the existential truth, that in Time, these things too will all change, it is inevitable.

When the question comes up—"What does the future hold?"—we tend unconsciously to apply the same reference points and time constructions to imagine how things will unfold or evolve ahead. In other words, we construct from the same thought processes we characteristically use to perceive the present, and project them out into the future, both in our personal and familial trajectories, and various other futures as well, such as business, politics, the stock market, sports, health, the environment, retirement etc.

But our perceptual focus regarding what will be is likely to remain exclusively at the level of physical destinations and ego-driven rationality, what Zukov terms the "five-sensory personality," which we privilege only because we are conditioned to do so. The same is true, by the way, when reflecting upon the past or the present. We assess the data, place it somewhere in Time, logically evaluate the pros and cons, factor in our personal preferences, past memories and emotions, etc. and hopefully arrive at an answer. This is part of the problem. We assume the familiar plodding, logical, ego-based, "objective," linear way we have been conditioned to travel and navigate by, and then project it onto the future or the unknown.

The results speak for themselves, much as does the title of a book by the late author/analyst James Hillman and Michael Ventura, *We've Had A Hundred Years of Psychotherapy and The World Is Getting Worse.*[4] The narrow way we think about Time and Change as predominantly a linear, causal, and quantifiable paradigm, is also innately dualistic, and assumes a self located in "here" and an object out "there." This ultimately is a false view that dissolves at higher levels of consciousness.

---

4. James Hillman and Michael Ventura, 1992.

This false view is notorious for producing self-fulfilling prophesies, repetition compulsions, short-lived progress, gridlock, and reinforces the limited way we think about Change. But we must remember, Time is a general concept about Change. Linear time, our dominant belief, is but one kind of Time in the face of Change. Another unfortunate side effect of linear time is that it privileges the past, as being the first, or earliest in a linear sequence, and therefore carries a certain primacy. Examples are the Big Bang, birth trauma, the "first of many," etc. Hillman further extrapolates another effect of this current cultural bias in America, namely, the tendency to overvalue youth culture and under-appreciate the dignity and beauty of aging and maturity:

> Psychology starts with an upside-down premise, that childhood is primary and determining, that development is cumulative, a kind of organic evolution, reaching a peak and declining. Not only is childhood thus overvalued, but aging is trapped in an organic, and melancholy, model. Rather than developmental psychology, we should study essential psychology, the structure of character, the innate endowment of talent, the unalterable psychopathologies.[5]

In a later work, Hillman outlines what he calls the "acorn theory" of the soul.[6] The theory states that all people innately possess the seeds to actualize specific talents and character potentials much as an acorn holds the pattern for an oak tree. The books describes how a unique, individual energy of the soul is contained within each human being, displayed throughout their lifetime and shown in their calling and life's work when it is fully actualized. Jung called this finality. A similar kind of mapping of "seed principles" from their points of Departure in the service of becoming a unique and whole spiritual individual is at the very taproots of this work as well.

From the standpoint of the linear Time bias, I believe we are left with no credible way of imagining the future at all. Any futurescape or arrival destination imagined from the narrow and suspect frame of reference of

---

5. Ibid, p. 69.
6. James Hillman, *The Soul's Code: In Search of Character and Calling*, 1997.

our current paradigm will suffer a "Jetsons Effect" (defined later in this chapter), and thereby only address surface levels of formation, will privilege physical destinations, give primacy to the past, over-value "higher-order" cognitions, and will be lacking in genuine transformational change in consciousness. In this work, we seek liberation from the constraints of linear time, but in a balanced, holistic way, where everyday functioning and compliance with the embedded structures of Time can still operate normally alongside a parallel universe of direct seeing and knowing.

Otherwise, we remain prisoners of Time as we know it, and sadly, unwitting accomplices in our own undoing. Seeking out an oracle within this dominant paradigm will seem retrogressive, pre-industrial, fanciful, strange, or frankly ridiculous, but this is only because the oracular dimension does not fit into the schematics of modern Time construction. Time, we generally believe, is external and independent of ourselves. It is tied to atomic clocks that use an electronic transition frequency in the microwave, optical, or ultraviolet region of the electromagnetic spectrum of atoms, keeping the most accurate time and frequency standards ever known, and used as the primary standard internationally to control the wave frequency of television broadcasts, and in global navigation satellite systems such as GPS. What could ever be more precise and beyond question than that?

But this proud certainty has now caught up to us in the 21st century, and the old adage "Live by the sword, die by the sword" seems apt. Linear time has certainly made the running of our lives highly efficient in terms of the holy grail of modern social attainment—"functioning"--but it has not made our lives psychologically richer, happier, or more meaningful, and we are desperately in need of another order of guidance for travel to our real destiny.

Prisoners of Time

As we become fully synchronized to the linear clocks embedded in our walls and streets, around our wrists, in our cars, phones, tvs, computers, and brains, in our new technologies, higher education, and laboratories of scientific research, Time is almost everywhere that Nature no longer reigns. But must we continue to unconsciously follow suit? Must we remain Time's prisoners? Could a different paradigm allow us to recalibrate the way in which big decisions are made vis-a-vis Time? As Jung observed: "Science comes to a stop at the frontiers of logic, but Nature does not: she thrives on ground as yet untrodden by theory."[7]

To its credit, linear time proves to be a highly efficient, logical, dependable, and indispensible basis for Change measurement, that is, for the purposes of organizing and interpreting the turnings of routine physical destinations, and the outer spaces of constant Change, up to a point. Trains run on it because linear time is not messy or emotional, and its apparent consistency and accessibility provides the perfect terminal for the empty digits and physical destinations of everyday life, where man's "higher order" cognitive functions, such as remembering, judging and problem-solving, can punch in, communicate efficiently, and get the job done.

We may recall what I've termed "The Holy Trinity of Terminality" in Chapter 4, "location, accessibility, and infrastructure." Linear time supports all three. Then again, we are not exactly freight or cargo, though we may feel like it at times. But no matter how embedded and omnipresent this Time paradigm has become, linear time remains but one particular conceptualization of Time regarding how things travel through space, move and change; there are other ways as well, some perhaps better suited for our personal and private lives. Alternative constructions found in imaginal travel, I believe, may hold the key.

Alternative Time

What we term "alternative Time" (unlike "alternative facts") was a common experience in pre-modern historic periods, and even in some sub-cultures today. Time, in fact, can be conceptualized, interpreted and lived in different ways, including: nonlinear time, cyclical time, relative time, psychological time, synchronistic time, timeless time, even esoteric time. But for the Western mind, Time and linear time have become so

---

7. C. G. Jung, *Collected Works,* XVI, para. 524.

conflated that one assumes linear time is Time itself! It is reminiscent of a joke involving two psychologists—a Rogerian (emotion based) therapist sees his very linear Behaviorist (action based) colleague go by, smiles, and casually asks: "So Miles, how are you feeling?" The Behaviorist pauses, and declares, "I don't know, I'll have to see what I do first." Old habits of thinking, whether of linear Time or behaviorist doctrine, die hard; but upon further inspection, there remains some glaring holes in the habitual assumption of linear time in particular, that come to bear frequently in human perception and relationships, the creative process, during emergencies, when traveling, witnessing rare events, watching sunsets, in optimal performance, spiritual contemplation and ritual, in understanding silly jokes, and when entering Terminal 9.

Psychological Time

When we imagine the future, we do this largely through the portals of rational cognition usually directed towards physical destinations and imagery, but with one additional and sometimes antagonistic factor: our subjectivity. Subjectivity accounts for what is termed in psychology and cognitive science—"Time perception." Let's take for example the title of this book "Tarot of the Future"...What does this suggest to you? Perhaps you imagine we are leading up a future historical stage or decade (of Tarot) still measured and assumed in linear time—say the year 2050, or sometime later in the next century—wherein the customary physical destinations and "higher order" cognitions of our thinking about the Tarot, remain structurally the same, but have incrementally evolved through the course of history, and the advances in technology and culture, to showcase at some future point in linear Time what will come... perhaps a new array of fabulous Tarot imagery, three-dimensional delivery methods, new generation virtual applications, instant accessibility everywhere, etc.? But not so fast...this would be the present paradigm projected onto the future with perhaps sexier versions of the same. Can we rightfully make such an assumption, particularly as our perception of Time is heavily tied to our subjective experience?

For those old enough to remember, we might call this fallacy "The Jetsons Effect," in reference to the animated sitcom produced by Hanna-Barbera originally airing in primetime television in 1962. The Jetsons are a regular family living in a futuristic utopia of elaborate robotic contraptions, aliens, holograms, and whimsical inventions, but they nevertheless retain a similar level of consciousness to their cartoon cousins, The Flintstones. A similar trope, as we have discussed, is carried more elegantly 50,000 years into the future in Asimov's *The Foundation*.

Change, in these examples, remains predominantly exterior and technological, manifest in shinier appearances, sleeker appliances, more sophisticated design and innovation. Apples to futuristic applesauce, if you will. As earlier mentioned, The Jetsons Effect only addresses surface levels of formation, privileges physical destinations and "higher-order" cognitions, and remains lacking in genuine transformational change in consciousness that is the hallmark of essential travel. In other words, our perception faculties remain the same, and the PDs get sleeker and perhaps better organized.

With this narrow view of Change projected onto Tarot, it is no wonder that the "practice of seeking knowledge of the future by supernatural means" seems a bit weird and suspect, far-fetched, eerie, and total "Hollywood." Better toys, speedier vehicles, craftier gadgets, some pleasant re-packaging, and a pinch of sensationalism—does not a Tarot of the future make! In truth, these alone are not enough to affect paradigmatic shift or transformation of consciousness in individuals, the Tarot, or society at large. Better think again.

On the other hand, we find the stalwart traditionalists of the Tarot, the historians and collectors, fastened to the tried and true, and the great mysteries of the old, who fiercely defend the traditional ways in the name of historical authenticity. The tradition has always served The Keepers of the Past well, and they will say, "no thanks!" "Five new cards? Too gimmicky. Too unorthodox. The Tarot belongs to its origins. We prefer it the way it was, thank-you very much! How can we trust this? By what authority could any individual have to challenge centuries of established mystery? What if this is flat-out wrong?"

And then "Always in motion is the future," we hear Yoda mumbling in our heads, and we believe him. But what our furry little Jedi friend leaves out, more critically, is that this same assessment holds just as true for the present, and for the past too! Indeed, we are always in motion, always traveling. As for the past, prior to the discovery of the Rosetta Stone in 1799, and its eventual decipherment, the Ancient Egyptian language and script had not been understood since shortly before the fall of the Roman Empire. After the discovery, voila! Our relation and understanding of ancient history completely changed. Change, in all directions, like a broken record, is constant, and it seems nothing is immune to it. Linear time, including Newton's theory of Absolute Time, not only is at its base a human construct, and its perception a psychological phenomena, but it too is subject to the infallible law of impermanence, as Sir Isaac himself may have discovered from his grave by the later disqualifying constructions of relativistic time proposed by Leibnitz and then Einstein.

Since the late 19th century, it has also been shown by the work of Gustav Theodor Fechner, one of the founders of modern experimental psychology, that every individual perceives the flow of time differently. "Time perception" refers to a person's subjective experience of the passage of time, or the perceived duration of events, which can differ significantly between different individuals and/or in different circumstances. Although physical (clock) time appears to be more or less unaffected and objective, psychological time is subjective and potentially malleable, exemplified by common phrases like "time flies when you are having fun" and "a watched pot never boils." This malleability is made particularly apparent by the various temporal illusions we experience in relation to our mood. We notice it when watching time flow variations in the second half of a basketball game, or waiting forever for the toast to pop up when we are hungry.

Any so-called "Tarot of the future" must incorporate a subjective shift in Time perception as well, affecting the very notion of what "future" even means? Things are changing all the time, including our subjective frameworks. Is the future even a thing? Or simply a construct derived from the past and applied in the present? In this work, certainly, we are not pursuing a Jetsons remix. The richness of Tarot's antiquity cannot be denied, much as the great French occultist of the 18th century, Eliphas Levi wrote of Tarot:

> It is, in truth, a monumental and extraordinary work, strong and simple as the architecture of the pyramids, and consequently enduring like those—a book which is the summary of all sciences—which can resolve all problems by its infinite combinations, which speaks by evoking thought, is the inspirer and moderator of all possible conceptions, and the masterpiece perhaps of the human mind. It is to be counted unquestionably among the very great gifts bequeathed to us by antiquity...[8]

Rather, here we call for an update and re-tuning; our charge is to maintain Tarot's foundational architecture of the past with respect for size, order, and sequence of the Major Arcana since the Tarot de Marseilles,[9] and seek both a small structural extension with the addition of five Keys, in such a way that a subjective shift in Time perception occurs, by way of The Hermit Effect. As we will discover, the re-tuning is related to contemporary philosopher of consciousness, Ken Wilber's developmental stage called vision-logic, where direct seeing overrides thinking as the order of the day. It comes with the natural flow that occurs in imaginal travel, and operates more intuitively through felt senses arising in the now.

Time Travel

As the discipline of Tarot is fundamentally a metaphysical art, and the discipline of Physics a physical science, the two would seem diametrically opposed, yet in many respects they are not antagonistic opposites, so much as complementary opposites. In certain areas they may even overlap into a single paradigm, however, time travel is not likely one of them at this stage.

---

8. Eliphas Levi, *Transcendental Magic,* (translated by A. E. Waite), 1968.
9. *A Wicked Pack of Cards: The Origins of the Occult Tarot* by Ronald Decker, Thierry Depaulis, and Michael Dummett.

Theoretical physics has long been fascinated with the outer reaches of physical possibility, and time travel surely is one of its most exotic regions to speculate and explore. From the scientific perspective, time travel refers to the possibility of changing the rate at which we travel into the future, or completely reversing it so that we travel into the past. Although a plot device in fiction since the 19th Century, time travel as such has never been practically demonstrated or verified, and may still be impossible. General relativity theory does raise the prospect (at least theoretically) of travel through time, i.e. the possibility of movement backwards and/or forwards in time, independently of the normal flow of time we observe on Earth, in much the same way as we can move between different points in space. But it is usually taken to mean that a person's mind and body remain unchanged, with their memories intact, while their location in time is changed. In other words, no rite of passage is necessary and Time perception is not properly factored in.

PHYSICS	METAPHYSICS
PHYSICAL TRAVEL	IMAGINAL TRAVEL
CAUSAL (Cause and Effect)	ACAUSAL (That which is so of itself)
LINEAR TIME	NONLINEAR TIME
"HIGHER ORDER" COGNITIONS thinking, knowing, remembering judging and problem-solving	INTUITION, IMAGINATION Visualizing, imagining, intuiting, senseing feeling, creating
OBJECTIVE	SUBJECTIVE
OCCURS EVERYWHERE	OCCURS IN THE HUMAN MIND
SEEKS GREATER UNDERSTANDING OF THE NATURAL WORLD	SEEKS GREATER ILLUMINATION AND ENLIGHTENMENT OF HUMAN CONSCIOUSNESS
USES LOGIC	USES VISION-LOGIC

At its simplest, if one were to travel from the Earth at the speed of light and then return, more time would have passed on Earth than for the traveler, so the traveler would, from his perspective, effectively have "traveled into the future." This is not to say that the traveler suddenly jumped into the Earth's future, in the way that time travel is often envisioned, but that, as judged by the Earth's external time, the traveler has experienced less passage of time than his twin who remained on Earth. This is not real time travel, though, but more in the nature of "fast-forwarding" through time: it is a one-way journey forward with no way back.

Other theoretical physicists like Kip Thorne and Paul Davies have shown how a *wormhole* in space-time could theoretically provide an instantaneous gateway to different time periods, in much the same way as general relativity allows the theoretical possibility of instantaneous spatial travel through wormholes. Time, at the quantum level, does not have a determined direction of flow from past to future.

But this too is far afield from the kind of time travel that concerns The Traveler at Terminal 9. He seeks not deeper expanses of the natural universe, but deeper entry into subtler levels of consciousness. His methodologies and presuppositions are vastly different, and their targets too are diametrically opposed, theirs being physical destinations of outer space and his being the sacred quarters of inner space.

The Tarot traveler doesn't so much care to ride on the accelerated wings of extreme Time, than to obliterate Time entirely in immediate experience. Then the wisdom agents may do their work. In the timeless state, much as entering the Main Gates of Terminal 9, we leave our baggage behind (including our theoretical baggage). We travel lightly so as to freshly see without preconceptions, personal investments, and loyalties. That is the proper way to engage an oracle. We may return later to the place we were before, though likely with a new and expanded sense of who we really are (a function of The Hermit Effect), and after many previously unimagined places we have gone. We will be free then to reclaim all the baggage as we like, but here in the liminal realm of divination, things are quite different.

Interestingly, regarding state of the art "time travel," though mind-bending streams of new ideas continue to surface at the edges of theoretical physics, one scientific observer notes, "with all of these schemes and ideas, it does not look to be possible to travel any further back in time than the time at which the travel technology was devised."[10]

---

10. "Exactly What Is Time?" http://www.exactlywhatistime.com/physics-of-time/time-travel/.

From Terminal 9, of course, our technology is timeless, and time travel is really about the subjective shift away from ordinary time perception by way of the oracle, and, in particular, the direct apprehension of living symbols found in Tarot, the deck of possibility. We turn now to an experiment in esoteric time I originally launched in cyberspace in May of 2008 at Tarotpsych, a Yahoo discussion group which I own and moderate.[11]

An Experiment with Tarot Time

A famous metaphysical study of the first half of the last century and relevant to our discussion was undertaken by J.W. Dunne in 1927, and published in a book called *An Experiment with Time*.[12] Dunne, a physicist, was inspired by his vivid dreams that somehow seemed to precipitate an odd slew of waking events, including volcanoes and fishing adventures. He decided, therefore, to conduct an experiment where he (and eventually others) logged their dreams for a period of time, and tracked their content. Subjects would then reread their logs within a week or so and note whether the events that occurred in their dreams were either in the past, had happened in the short time since the dream, or had never happened. Often, subjects would find a mixture of past, present, and future events in a single scene. The connection of waking events to dream-state events was the heart of his experiment with time.

Dunne considered himself an "abnormal" subject, as his dreams equally consisted of past and future events. He believed that the time humans understand and live in during waking consciousness (Time 1, Waking Time) follows a linear path, while the state of dreams existed in a separate, non-linear consciousness (Time 2, Dream Time). This dream-state of consciousness (Time 2) was composed of a mixture of past, present, and future events. Dunne also believed that humans were capable of a fourth-dimension (Time 3), a time/space state that does not correlate to a directional or observable scale. This dimension held that "neither

---

11. See Tarotpsych at https://groups.yahoo.com/neo/groups/tarotpsych/info.
12. J.W. Dunne, *An Experiment with Time,* London: Faber and Faber, Ltd., 1927, 3rd Ed. 1958.

past nor the future was observable" and that "all observable phenomena lay in a field situated at a unique 'instant' in the time length," or, as we know it, the momentary present.

I wanted to see what would happen if we added what might be called "esoteric time" into the mix by adding Tarot divination. Accordingly, I designed an exercise or "cyber-experiment" on Tarotpsych that utilized what I called *The Three Windows of Time:* The Window of Reality, The Window of Dreams, and The Window of Now. Tarot would be used as the independent variable for all three windows. Twelve people participated for a period of three weeks. They were instructed to divine (i.e. randomly select) a card for each of the three windows twice a week. The windows were meant to correspond with Dunne's Time 1, Time 2, and Time 3. Subjects were asked to reflect upon personally meaningful synchronicities after divining the tarot card for each window in question, and post their answers online. As participants were scattered all around North America, Europe, and India, the cyber experiment attempted to exploit the easy sharing, unedited recordings through posting, and the instantaneous delivery opportunities afforded by the internet from great distances and diverse time zones. All subjects were students and practitioners of the Tarot.[13]

For Time 1 (Reality), to control for confounding interpretations of so-called "reality," participants were instructed to read the top story appearing on Google News at any moment as their reality measure[14], then blindly select a card, reflect upon the meanings found concurrently between their "card/outer event" synchronicity, and post it on the site. For Time 2, participants were likewise asked to randomly select a card immediately upon awakening from a dream they remembered, reflect upon the "card/inner event" synchronicity (i.e. the dream), and post it on the site. Posts on the website, of course, could be made anytime, night or

---

13. Author's comment: Using the power of the internet for experiments in divination and synchronicity is what I have called "the global method."

14. Google News is a free news aggregator provided and operated by Google, selecting news from thousands of news websites, and gets auto-refreshed throughout the day.

day, from any time zone and would remain on the site for all to read. For Time 3, following a similar protocol, participants were instructed to pull a card either during meditation, or anytime they felt glimpses of timeless momentary awareness, reflect upon the "card/moment" synchronicity, and likewise post this onto the site. Subjects were asked to do this twice a week at their own pace, keep a log of their results, and post the entire log onto the site at the end of the three weeks.

The results were fascinating in many cases, but problems with inconsistent compliance, the relative looseness of the design, access issues to the internet, and the exploratory nature of the experiment in general, did not lend themselves to careful statistical analysis. What resulted, however, was a fruitful discussion about this exploratory area of inquiry itself, speculations for future experimental possibilities through cyberspace, but most significantly, the personal insights themselves gained from the various synchronicities that were touched. One subject posted, for example:

> Regarding the news article, ...picking up the pieces after an embarrassing "gaffe"—likely has to do with my initial feeling after submitting that very personal post. In essence, however, my Self is rescued by this exercise (The Knight of Swords), I'm continuing to learn through my dreams (King of Swords – the teacher) and am experiencing more of a sense of mind over matter more fully developed (the Emperor).

I believe the difficulties with this experiment are not atypical of any pilot study that attempts to measure the highly subjective and nearly invisible variables and effects of the liminal world, but I highly encourage future attempts with respect to tighter design and the proper scientific attitude be undertaken. The metaphysical dimension remains like uncharted terrain at the bottom of the ocean, and I believe a treasure of riches can be found there in deep explorations in the future. Beyond lending greater reach and legitimacy to these methods, as stated in Chapter 1, great value can be gained through clever experimentation, as the unseen and invisible forces that operate beneath the oracular process are brought into clearer focus, awareness, understanding, and vision. The final frontier, as it were, of inner space!

A Liminal Spread

One of Dunne's key terms is the notion of *association,* where one links events in their mind to other events or images because of possible similarities or connections in the mind of the subject. Dunne believed that, "the Time dimension, for any given observer, is simply the dimension in which his own world-line happens to extend through the four-dimensional continuum." Imperative to Dunne's thesis is the notion of a series, which "is a collection of individually distinguishable items arranged, or considered as arranged, in a sequence determined by some sort of ascertainable law." Time 2 (Dream Time) connects events from different series' and rearranges them in a revised order that does not correlate with any ascertainable law that we, as humans, have created in Time 1 (Reality Time). But what is learned of the oracular (Time 3) in this respect?

The answer again must be uniquely liminal, that is, in between. At first, the cards appear dreamlike and lawless in their surreal imagery when they meet the eye; the coherency of their assigned meaningful numbers places them, but not so much in Time, as Space, that is, inner space. The Matrix further gauges their precise spatial location aided by The Hermit Effect, and the magical properties of 9; but not in physical space so much as metaphysical space. Space, in fact, will be the topic of the next chapter.

Divination then scatters their innate meaningful sequence into seemingly chaotic, lawless patterns like a dream, but also like a dream, a story is being told. It is not a vacant, or frivolous tale; Nature is speaking to us through the wisdom of the oracle. And as we discussed with the *I Ching* in Chapter 3, the images arise, ironically, through the process of our interpreting the abstract forms originally given, for the purpose of obtaining relevant meaning. We ourselves co-create the stories out of our undying passion to awaken. Meaning, therefore, is generated in Time 3 as we sincerely search through our deepest interior to find connection.

Timeless Seeing

We come to the close of this "middle phase" Section called Transfer, marked by its liminal state of consciousness, its shadowy contents with

Death, The Devil, and The Tower cards, as well as The Moon, and equally its magical invitations from The Wheel of Fortune, Justice, The Hanged Man, Temperance, and The Star. Let's revisit the transpersonal bandwidth of "vision-logic" as it pertains to Time. In this model, vision-logic is considered the highest structure of the personal realm, a narrow region of consciousness, "higher" than our rational ego-driven consciousness (Piaget's "formal operations"), commonly understood as normal rational thought. In this respect, it is not that far away from everyday adult thinking, and is accessible in principle to anyone reading this book.

As discussed earlier in Chapter 3, vision-logic is characterized by a dialectical, integrative, and synthetic thinking style. It is naturally geared for working intuitively with imagery. And as we noted, vision-logic marks the subtle shift of awareness that comes with intuitive seeing, that is, the direct apprehension of images without interpretation. A natural outgrowth of frequent Tarot use, this transition to "seeing" most notably entails a freeing from the limitations of dualistic thinking, wherein a subject stands apart and separate from all the objects of awareness, including the constraints of linear time which is "out there."

While more advanced research into "esoteric time" will include deep meditative concentration and visualization, shamanic, occult, and magical relationships to time perception to invoke deeper levels of awareness (i.e psychic, subtle, or causal),[15] the perceptual shifts most germane to oracle work operate rather narrowly within this level of vision-logic, as described by Wilber.[16]

Trump Experiment

At the very beginning of this section, recall Figure 1, in which a random display of 5 TNP cards was given. At the time of my writing, it was meant to introduce the unprocessed, twilight quality or rainbow realm of the in-between region of mind we have described as Transfer. As we have discussed its key features, including The Liminal, Meaningful Numbers, The

---

15. Carlo Dorofatti, *Soul and Reality,* 2011.
16. Ken Wilber, *A Brief History of Everything,* 1996.

Hermit Effect, Divination, and in this chapter, Time and Timelessness, let's revisit Figure 1 (of Section 2), and further it along by way of a short reading experiment.

As we have on occasion utilized current public events and figures in previous discussions, including the early candidacy of "DJ" in Chapter 1, but also the passing of Mohammed Ali in Chapter 2, and the Turkish Terror Attack in Chapter 10, on January 17, 2017, a full year after the original Trump reading before the first Presidential primaries began, a kind of synthesis might provide an interesting conclusion to Section 2.

Accordingly, the five random cards previously shown in Figure 1, were shuffled exhaustively, and fanned face down, etc. asking the question:

What will be the fate of the Donald Trump Administration?

The result was impressive (see spread on the following page), if only from the numeric requirement. On the very first attempt at the fine witching hour of 5 AM, a pattern was divined that met the numeric requirement perfectly, and reduced quite appropriately to the magical number 9!

But the significance of the reading itself in lieu of the question is all the more compelling and relevant, certainly from my own subjective vantage point, and perhaps yours as well. What we know, for instance, judging from Position 3, The Traveler reversed, is that the Administration itself has no idea of who it really is and where it is really going! And working against it, certainly, with The Magician also reversed, to me suggests loss of power, thwarted intentions, and a dark struggle to identify its objectives, and ressurect its mojo. The Magician when reversed often feels impotent, and directionless.

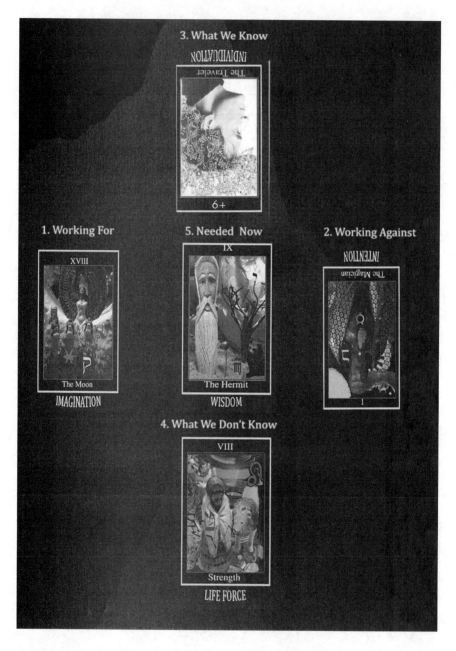

Q: What will be the fate of the Donald Trump Administration?

But I leave it to the reader to ascertain the rest, and make their own experiments with the question. Reversals, it should be noted, can work on several levels, but the first to consider is the shadow side of the card, suggesting either blockage in this area, a distortion, or perversion of the lesson called for. What, for example, should we make of The Moon, bastion of the unconscious, to serve in the position of "Working For?" Should more information about card meanings be needed, the reader may consult the Lexicon in the Appendix to learn more about the many spectrums of meaning contained in each card. And should they have a deck of TNP, they might try laying these same cards in the spread configuration, and let them marinate for a while.

A tarot reading's value is not assessed in its so-called "accuracy" so much as its relevancy. "Accurate" I ask, "compared to what?" The rational schemata of your beliefs, opinions, and interpretations? Well, maybe. Subjective reality offers little in the way of accuracy "fact-checking." The "prime directive" that I teach readers is to remember the one rule of thumb: "The card is always right!" It remains for us hard-working interpreters to discover just where and how its import and relevancy (true to its established spectrum of meanings) should be directed to gather most coherency and click. No doubt, this particular question for Americans, if not citizens all around the world, is juicy, and will be revisited many times again in the coming years. A tracking of a series of readings over time is often the most telling approach to a seminal subject matter of this order, and rest assured I myself will be experimenting with great curiosity.

SECTION 3

ARRIVAL (Z)

CHAPTER 12

INNER SPACE

SPACE CRAFT

A spacecraft is a vehicle, or machine designed to fly in outer space. Spacecrafts today are used for a multiple purposes, including communications, earth observation, meteorology, navigation, space colonization, planetary exploration, and transportation of humans and cargo. Like conventional aircraft, they are geared to physical destinations and travel, and they too require terminals— 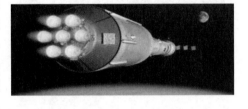 both for physical locations from which passengers or cargo may depart, transfer, or arrive at destinations, such as the International Space Station or perhaps one day Mars—but also they require terminals in terms of points of connection for closing electric circuits, including *ground* terminals, for example, which encode digital data and transmit information via laser light from specially equipped ground stations to a commercial communications satellite, as well as *flight* terminals necessary to transmit and receive optical signals, which may include telescopes, lasers, mirrors, detectors, a pointing and tracking system, control electronics, and modems.

The passenger terminal shown on the next page in Figure 1 may conjure uplifting fantasies of future space travel with its sparkling, fanned geometric canopy, airy, spiraling swirls of pleasing, softly-lit openness, and the bubbly white spaces in the interior. Amazing terminals of the

Figure 1

future where passengers will board spacecraft to starships and travel to other worlds, someday... when space travel becomes widely commercially available! But, in fact, Figure 1 is a picture of the Chhatrapati Shivaji International Airport, reconstructed in 2014, a conventional modern airport now serving the greater Mumbai metropolitan area in India largely for business travel to Delhi.

So hypnotic these Jetsons Effects can appear! Especially when imaginations are given license to envision both the future and outer space! Like kids in the proverbial candy store, the possibilities are exotic and unending, but imaginations will surely take a nosedive back down to earth, and must recalibrate to a very different territory when the focus shifts to the future and *inner* space.

At that point, we no longer travel in "spacecraft" but rather *by* space "craft" in a metaphysical sense, that is, by the skill (or craft) in making something (such as a journey to self-realization), from the old English word "craft"—meaning *strength and skill.* Ironically, *space craft* as such resembles more a thing of the past than the future.

To be *crafty* means to show ability, capability, competence, art, talent, flair, artistry, craftsmanship, expertise, proficiency, adroitness, adeptness, deftness, and virtuosity. These are the skills of direct apprehension, reflection, and interpretation we hope to develop in our oracular craft. In the pip cards of the 8 of Pentacles (or Coins), images of the craftsman engaged in spiritual development are symbolized. The apprentice is focused, humble, well-practiced and hard at work in his space craft.

The Old Craft

Rider Waite Tarot (1909)   Golden Tarot (2004)

Uniquely, the visual compositions of TNP were themselves crafted humbly in a small sandbox in the author's home office, via the medium of Sandplay Therapy, a Jungian technique of active imagination, by his own hands, sweat, and toil. Each Key was contemplated meditatively for its Hermit Effect (ie. in the service of spiritual individuation), and then intuitively "sculpted" in the sand from a menagerie of miniature objects collected from the author's travels. Later they were digitally photographed, layered with established Hermetic correspondences, and crafted in Photoshop. Note that, to begin this process, the designer (or client) first engages with his blank canvas by confronting the open space of an empty box. He is instructed to empty his mind, and "make a scene in the box," spontaneously allowing any number of objects from the adjacent shelves to, in effect, "pick him," and place them in the box just so. This is much in keeping with the so-called "random" selection of cards in a divination. The objects and sand may then be moved rather like finger-painting, to form a scene until the designer *feels* complete. Then he stops.

Crafting space

Sandplay miniatures

ARTIST'S TECHNIQUE

The Sandtray

TNP's "blank canvas"

In my case, the task was not quite as pure and agenda-less as is normal for this technique; I trusted that if my theory of the incomplete Major Arcana would stand up to inspection, the missing five Keys would arise organically, and synchronistically in the sandbox, of their own accord, and the puzzle of The Matrix would be solved. My theory had been presented at several conferences before the deck was even launched, but I knew that because Tarot is primarily a visual art, a new deck that could both assist in channeling the missing pieces, and house them properly and aesthetically in one coherent whole, would be necessary. From the very start this was the impetus behind making the *Tarot of the Nine Paths*. To assemble a completed Major Arcana, with the addition of five emerging archetypal principles, invoked by The Hermit Effect, and the magical properties of 9 which I was convinced carried the inner code of the canon, even in its incomplete form.

As Travelers from Terminal 9, I suspect, we are not really artists so much as craftsmen apprentices of cartomantic skill and strength, namely, in order to travel imaginally into the sacred realms of interior space. As craftsmen, we travel without frills, oxygen tanks, or hard-shelled space suits, and we attune to the present moment, and follow the click. But to do so, we must first understand what space is.

Space Defined

Simply defined, space is a continuous area or expanse that is free, available, or unoccupied. Much as we saw in the last chapter, we are conditioned to think of space like we think about time—as something outside ourselves, independent of our perception, measurable, and objective. In everyday language, space is something we all know. It is measured in the three dimensions of distance: length, width, and height. If we are a closet *trekkie* like me, then etched into our minds are surely the most sanguine command orders of all time: "Space, the final frontier. These are the voyages of the starship Enterprise. Its 5-year mission: to explore strange new worlds, to seek out new life and new civilizations, to boldly go where no man has gone before." In modern physics, space is understood as a "boundless four-dimensional continuum" known as *spacetime*. There is disagreement, however, much like with time travel, about whether this is an entity that actually exists, or is rather just part of a conceptual framework.

Psychological Space

Psychologically, space is quite a different story. As the poet Rilke wrote: "The essence of mind is like space; therefore there is nothing that it does not encompass." Western psychology, with the exception of William James, has generally ignored any relationship between space and mind, owing we may suspect to the lingering influence of Descartes, who separated the world into the thinking substance of mind as over against the spatially-extended substance of matter.

Transpersonal psychology is the exception, which has taken a keen interest in the psychology of space and consciousness. Author/psychologist John Welwood, for instance, has distinguished five distinct types of psychological space operating in inner travel we may consider: perceptual space, conceptual space, oriented space, feeling space, and open space, noting:

> Although the notion of psychological space has been avoided and neglected by Western psychology for the most part, it has a potentially important descriptive and heuristic value for understanding the nature of consciousness and the way we create our world.[1]

---

1. John Welwood, *The Journal of Transpersonal Psychology*, 1977, vol. 9, no. 2 .

In summary, *perceptual* and *conceptual* space are the two most common notions of psychological space in Western culture. *Perceptual space* is "out there," we can see it, and to a lesser extent, feel it in a tactile way with our bodies. In Tarot it is the physical touch, shape, and direction of the cards and spreads themselves. Perceptual space is characterized by three-dimensionality, juxtapositions, form and distances, and directionality (forward, back, up, down, left, right, under, around, and so on). *Conceptual space,* on the other hand, is a postulated abstract continuum, defined primarily by mathematics and physics, and accounts for the locations and relations of physical objects. The sequential template of The TNP Matrix is an example of conceptual space. In both cases, Welwood observes, the eye has been the chief organ for developing our sense of space and spatial relations, giving rise to the development of geometrical space, which served as the basis for classical physics. As mathematics and physics have established the basic conceptual model for the world that modern Western man accepts as real, their definition of space has become dominant. Since perceptual and conceptual space can be objectively defined and measured, they are generally thought to comprise all that space "really is."

Space-As-Experienced

But the notion of space may be approached in another way, in terms of *lived space,* that is, space-as-experienced. It is here we find relevance to the spatial craft of Tarot. Lived space is not readily measurable by any of the sense data or yardsticks that are used to define perceptual or conceptual space. Nevertheless, it clearly can be experienced in the human psyche, and it is this order of space that pertains to our study. It refers to our living, pre-articulate feeling-sense of space, just as "lived time" is the felt sense we have of becoming and change, different from any mathematical or diurnal measurements of "objective" time as we saw with perceptual time.

With respect to the oracular experience, it becomes obvious to an initiate that anyone who has not experienced this firsthand, who has yet to enter the lived space and time of this process, can only comment on it from the sidelines through an conceptual framework subject to one's embedded biases. That is where the skeptics and naysayers set up their tents and pontificate smartly on its quackery and sleight-of-hand, but with absolutely no first-hand experience of what they are talking about. To them, I would simply say, why not come by for a reading yourself? You might be surprised by what you will discover really happens. Oracular space is real enough from within its own side and workings, but just like kissing, it cannot be correctly understood from the outside looking in.

Welwood distinguishes three interrelated kinds of lived space within psychological space: 1) *oriented space* that is experienced *bodily*; 2) *feeling space,* the spatial quality of the felt environment we create around ourselves, and I would add, within ourselves too; and 3) *open space,* a totally unconditioned, formless dimension underlying all our activity, which can be understood and realized as the essential quality of awareness itself. Any true Tarot of the future, I believe, must evolve specifically in the areas of feeling and open space, or fall prey to a Jetsons Effect, and be no more than a derivative of the Tarot, past and present. As space travelers, our explorations must take a vertical, interior descent into the depths of human consciousness.[2]

Feeling Space

A major dimension of feeling space is that of expansion and contraction. When feeling good, naturally, we are generally more expansive, moving outward, action-oriented, and able to take on more of the world without hesitation. When stressed, our movements tend to tighten and contract, we become less patient, and more reactive. Let's examine feeling space through the direct apprehension of a Tarot card, in this case, Key 2, The High Priestess of TNP.

Simply gaze into this image without interpretation, and ask: "What

---

2. Whether we speak of consciousness as being "higher" or "deeper" is an arbitrary distinction based on the perceptual and conceptual space models of the observer.

II

The High Priestess

INTUITION

strikes me first on a feeling level?" Do I find it pleasant or unpleasant? Calming or thought-provoking? Warm or cool, comfortable, edgy, friendly, mysterious etc.? What are the feeling words I would choose to describe my first experience here? Let these impressions sink into your feeling space and expand naturally as you approach the card. Include in your direct gazing all words, glyphs, and numbers, as well as colors, and even suggestions that are not shown overtly, and do this non-analytically, that is, without interpretation.

In this exercise, unlike your usual rush to determine its meaning and significance, simply continue to follow your felt senses that arise in direct apprehension of this stimulus, until something inside of you clicks. In a recent class when I tried this exercise I was surprised to hear a great divergence of impressions, from delightful to bordering on terrifying. Recall that by "click," we mean a sense of resonating with your natural being as clear and true to your experience, and stands out as your strongest impression. Is this click one of expansion or contraction for you? Are there other related words, memories, mental images, or associations that come to you without thinking? Just note these impressions without feeling pressed to interpret their significance.

A Tibetan Buddhist slogan of Chogyam Trungpa I've found useful for this kind of approach is called "First thought/Best thought." It addresses the best way to think creatively and also as I've found to conduct divination experiments. "First Thought, Best Thought," however, refers not chronologically to the first shred of content that pops into your mind, but rather, qualitatively, to the first clear impression, idea, expression, or "felt sense" which arises effortlessly in consciousness, in other words, the first click. It is often preceded by a momentary "gap" (or pause) in the mindstream, and has the resonant quality of simply "feeling right" whether or not it is logical. This is the best way to first perceive a Tarot card as well, with no pressure to take it any further than this. Now take a breath.

A second dimension of feeling space is that of surface and depth. Feeling spaces may be flat, shallow, and two-dimensional, or they may be charged with depth, volume, and vivid texture. Affective space, as such, has depth when it is textured with many levels of meaning. Looking again at The High Priestess, one may see a highly textured affective space with many levels of meaning. Too often readers unwittingly interfere with a richly textured feeling space by way of premature intellectual analysis, over-talking it, and quick reduction into known quantities, thus cutting-off any natural arising of the click. To symbolists, this is what is known as the "degradation of the symbol."

The classic example is seen in traditional Freudian dream analysis where spontaneous, naturally arising images are quickly named, associated, and reduced into psychoanalytic constructs such as "penis envy" or "castration anxiety," and interpreted. The Jungian approach, in contrast, seeks not to reduce the image but rather to amplify its symbolic content in the widest possible way, including correspondences to cross-cultural, historic, scientific, metaphysical, or mythological associations while still honoring its living uniqueness in itself. An important aspect of Tarot craft, therefore, is pre-interpretive, as the greater resonance with the momentary stimulus of the card deepens its impact on the soul and leads to more meaningful discoveries. This perhaps is why reading applications on the internet typically fail to generate sufficient lived space for a reading to really take hold.

Intuitive Space

Another dimension of space not covered by Welwood, but especially relevant to Tarot and its bandwidth of vision-logic, is intuitive space. Jung defined intuition as "the psychic function that perceives possibilities in the present," and Frances Vaughn, a pioneer in intuition research, notes: "Receptivity to imagery is the vehicle to intuitive insight as imagery is the language of intuition."[3] The deeper one travels, as a general rule, the wider and more enduring will be experiences of intuitive space. Tarot, of course, is primarily an image net, and as well, a "synchronicity generator" and many are drawn to it simply to develop their intuitive faculty.

Intuitions naturally gather when we first gaze upon the stimulus of a tarot card without interpretation, or apprehend it (fearlessly), and then bring our awareness to the feeling space, and wait for the click. This usually occurs in very little time if one focuses properly, no more than a matter of moments, as intuitions bubble up freely from the mindstream in the post-rational level of vision-logic, where "light-touch" seeing gradually replaces discursive thinking as the dominant perception. The High Priestess, incidentally, is an agent of Intuition. She is the guardian of deep memory and subtle knowledge, "the keeper of the Akashic records" some would say, and represents the part of us that retains access to subtle metaphysical experiences normally filtered out by the so-called "higher-order cognitions." Another aspect of Her insight is the penetration of opposites, as depicted in the two pillars of the Temple of Solomon, Boaz and Jachin, the first temple of Jerusalem, suggesting nonduality beneath the veil.

Intuitions may be reported as felt-senses, hunches, "feelings," spontaneous thoughts, ideas or "flashes," images popping up in the mind without prompting, psychic impressions, and so forth. Often they are pre-articulate, and assigning words to them fails to capture perfectly their nuance or suchness, until one begins to develops a vocabulary suited for these momentary inklings. Giving them sounds or guttural expressions ("Ahhhhh"), movement, artistic engagement, automatic writing or journaling, doodling, humming, tapping, or poetic metaphor is helpful to better capture and forward these intuitively perceived, present possibilities, and should generally precede the more rational-analytical function of interpretation.

Meditators may give breath to their intuitive and feeling spaces, or simply sit with these manifestations for a while, relax, and contemplate. Amplification through correspondences, whether mythological,

---

3. Frances E. Vaughn, *Awakening Intuition,* 1979.

philosophical, literary, scientific, or cultural, can at times broaden an unassembled intuition, though other times, and this happens quite frequently, an intuition's meaning simply jumps out, clicking immediately and resoundingly, we can feel its essential rightness throughout our being, and we may, therefore, choose to place absolute trust in its appearance and relevance, even should it seem at the moment, well, *counter*-intuitive! "Live by the sword, die by the sword," said Agamemnon. As with all arts and crafts, of course, knowing the best treatment comes with experience.

Open Space

A third kind of lived space goes beyond the purely psychological dimensions to the ontological level of our basic being. Open space refers to the groundless, insubstantial, omnipotential awareness that underlies our more conditioned mind-spaces. From a Buddhist perspective, our basic nature in essence is open space, which allows for the possibility of

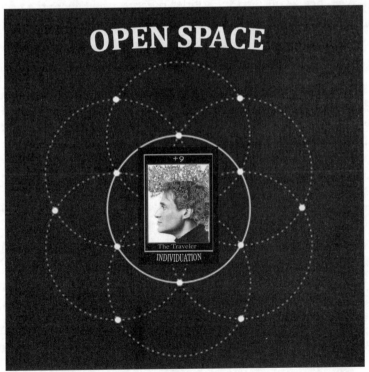

liberation from ego-based positions, attitudes, and perceptions that seem fixed or imprisoning. In open space, Time becomes timeless, foundations foundationless, and the boundaries between self and other dissolve into a state of nonduality, that is, one undivided without a second.

For our purposes, open space is understood as the surrounding context and container that informs the narrow band of higher consciousness we are now traveling, the oracular dimension of post-rational, vision-logic, the initial phase of "The Intermediate Territory." As Wilber notes, the shift to vision-logic brings to awareness the limitations of dualistic thinking that posits separation between a subject "inside" in relation to a world "out there." Mindfulness meditation encounters this same artificial dichotomy which is part and parcel of formal operations, that is, the normal way we think and perceive.

A deepening of these higher states of awareness naturally bleeds into the next level organically, with practice. For example, from vision-logic one's awareness evolves to the subtler psychic level, where the power of inner sight has become more direct than the power of thought, marking the beginning of transpersonal insights and subtler levels of self-reflection, and so forth, through the subtler bands as shown earlier. Tarot work in its deepest applications can extend into the most subtle regions of The Intermediate Territory (causal level), but we limit our discussion here to vision-logic, which I believe is more accessible, and the next likely step of conscious development for most individuals, and even collectively on a societal level as well, which Tarot and related tools can greatly facilitate.

As we grow collectively at this level, intuitive seeing increases powerfully, and our faculty for perceiving new orders of possibility in the present expands, opening uncharted territory for the emerging human civilization. The world about now is critically wanting in most every quarter for new possibilities in the present, guided by natural wisdom-light, and this is clear as stars in frosty night. But at every stage and level of awareness, including the formal operations of our ordinary, ego-based awareness, it is important to recognize that open space surrounds and contains our thought processes, both inside and out, mostly without our even realizing it.

KEY ZERO

The Tarot card that most corresponds to open space is Key 0, The Fool, an agent of pure Possibility. Tarot, therefore, with The Fool as its alpha and omega, begins and ends paradoxically in a never-ending cycle of beginningless time and open space. In its distinctly Eastern flavor, this paradoxical condition marks the context of all our travels, and rather curiously, we confront this implicit absurdity that surrounds us of already having arrived before we depart, and accept it. This is the trickster nature of The Fool that dances wistfully in what to us is a paradox. Our journey is simultaneously both meaningful and devoid of meaning entirely. The Fool reminds us that it is well to maintain our sense of humor with what is occurring here. Too often this "crazy wisdom," as the late Tibetan meditation master Trungpa Rinpoche called it, gets buried under the heavy weight of spiritual practice. In Tarot in general, much like The Hermit

0 The Fool (Possibility)

The Trickster; spirit in search of experience/total potentiality; open space; the unconditioned mind; undifferentiated spirit; freedom to make mistakes, without situational karma; beginner's mind; crazy wisdom; divine child archetype; freedom; inventiveness and eccentricity; (reversed) foolishness, menace.

Spectrum: Possibility, Openness, Discovery, Play. [Note: as in classic tarot, The Fool retains his placeless/numberless position at both "end and beginning" of The Matrix, bearing the dual, paradoxical number analogues 27 and zero. This echoes the Buddhist cosmology of beginningless time]. (Air)

0

The Fool

POSSIBILITY

Effect in TNP, The Fool is always present in the proceedings. In the Lexicon (see Appendix), The Fool is given above.

Open space itself is the ultimate matrix through which, on a relative basis, The Traveler takes his rites of passage to go places, to travel, in the service of spiritual individuation. The Oracle teaches there is no other way, as essential lessons must be learned, stages passed through, and pathways traveled down before one can fully and consciously arrive to completion, whereupon the journey itself either spirals for another round, or dissolves into open space and one finds oneself, in TNP parlance, "off-grid." In either case, from the Tarot perspective, we will have arrived.

WHERE SPACE, TIME, AND NUMBER FULLY CONVERGE

Here is a riddle for the Tarot savvy: Where is it that Space, Time, and Number fully converge? Hint: you can find it in the Past, feel it in the Present, and plan for it in the Future; it defies linear Time and thrives in lived Space, and you can now set your datebook by it?

Answer: Hermitized Constellations on The Matrix! See the following chart.

1	2	3	4	5	6	7	8	9
10	11	12	13	14	15	16	17	18
19	20	21	22	23	24	25	26	27

Let me explain. First I must concede that Time, Space, and Number have already converged, and done so nicely, in the modern Tarot (overlooking, for the moment, the ghastly Overbite). In what have been called Tarot Constellations, first introduced by Arrien in San Francisco in the 1970s, a method of using numeric reduction to calculate calendric patterns, thereby ascertaining what are called "Soul and Personality cards," has been a commonly applied Tarot forecast procedure derived from the numbers in one's birthdate. Other numbers including addresses, numerically-converted names, goals, ideas, etc. can likewise be calculated for their Tarot equivalency. Mary Greer has written a concise workbook, entitled *Tarot Constellations* (1987), which clearly lays out this fascinating forecasting approach sometimes offered before a formal divination is undertaken.

For example, suppose you, (or more likely your child), were born on the very day of Donald Trump's Inauguration: 1/20/2017. Adding across via mystic addition yields $1 + 2 + 0 + 2017 = 2020 = 4$. The Emperor. Interesting, no? Referring back to The Matrix, you see that The Emperor, is an agent of Dominion, and rests in the fourth column of the first row, or in TNP terms, in Departure X on Path 4, Transformation. Directly below and one row down we

JANUARY 20, 2017

$1 + 2 + 0 + 2 + 0 + 1 + 7 = 13 = 4$

4	13	22
THE EMPEROR.	DEATH.	THE FOOL.
SOUL	PERSONALITY	HIDDEN FACTOR

see Key (13) Death, and below that (Key 22) The Fool (that is, on the old map that only admitted 22 Keys in total, not 27 as found in TNP). In Constellations, your Soul card is therefore (4) The Emperor, because it has primacy as the root number and earliest in the series, and your Personality card is (13) Death. What do these designations mean? One's Soul card, in theory, represents what I think of as the archetypal "individuation mandate" of your core self or, from an Eastern perspective, the core karmic pattern you've incarnated in countless previous lifetimes, that is, your old soul.

Your Personality card is considered more contemporaneous, and thought to be that archetypal core pattern most significant for this particular lifetime you now inhabit. Personality cards always correspond to two-digit numbers between 10-22 (in the old model). Sometimes Soul and Personality cards can result in the same card, owing simply to the way the numbers kick out. I, for instance, am what's called a "double 5," i.e. Hierophant soul, Hierophant personality $(1/7/1950 = 1 + 7 + 1950 = 1958. 1958 = 1 + 9 + 5 + 8 = 23 = 5)$. Notice that because there is no card 23 in the old system, one must continue to add across to arrive at 5. Carl Jung, born on July 26, 1875, by this method most fittingly is a Moon/Personality and Hermit/Soul, born $7 + 26 + 1875 = 1908$; $1908 = 1 + 9 + 0 + 8 = 18$ (Personality); $18 = 1 + 8 = 9$ (Soul).

Greer notes a surprising number of "imaginative realist" writers with (18/9) Hermit/Moon constellations, including as Nabokov, Vonnegut, and Anais Nin, and as well many deeply intuitive thinkers and highly creative artists, including among my favorites: Nostradamus, Bach, Tesla, Gandhi, Kahlil Gibran, Roberto Assagioli, Carlos Casteneda, Ray Charles, Yoko Ono, Allen Ginsberg, Robin Williams, and of course, my own two children (though they are double 9s).

But as the final number only goes up to 22 in the standard system, for matrix numbers higher than 22, one must continue to add across. In the Greer method, the four-digit number (e.g. 1958) yielded from adding the day and month to one's birth year is termed your "Destiny Year." I think of this as the year, whether in the past or the future depending upon how the numbers kick out (in my case, it occurred when I was 8), one's Destiny Year exemplifies, or sets in motion, the core life lessons and themes throughout one's entire lifetime. But another function of our re-tuning of the map requires some slight changes and reconsideration of the Constellation model currently in play. With the TNP system there are some fascinating adjustments to be found. Though one's Soul card and Destiny Year remain unchanged, in about 20 percent of cases the cards assigned to their Personality now change; in fact, the underlying constructs of Soul and Personality cards have been "hermitized" by the additions and re-tuning of The Major Arcana according to the magical properties of number 9 in TNP!

A third card, configured in traditional constellations, one that Greer calls "The Hidden Factor," now becomes more problematic in the new system. In the Emperor/Death example of Trump's Inauguration, for instance, The Fool (22) would be designated The Hidden Factor. This is determined by ascertaining a second card in the Matrix that also reduces to your root or soul number (i.e. 4), but is not your Personality card. And, regrettably, not everyone gets one! If it sounds unnecessarily complicated, that's because it is. In theory, The Hidden Factor represents a more private, interior dimension of your personality, equivalent, perhaps, to your alter ego or Ascendant in Astrology. The full constellation here of Trump's Inauguration would now be Soul: Emperor (4); Personality: Death (13); Destiny Year: 2020; Hidden Factor/Fool (22).

But here again we push against the "missing pieces" problem on the third row. To date, there simply are no cards corresponding with 23-27 (and The Fool's placement at 22 to my mind remains suspect!). Equally awkwardly, it has been explained away that Keys 5-9 simply don't possess "hidden factors" in The Oracle's counsel, and that is that. But for a celebrated metaphysical system that otherwise appears perfectly integrated and whole, I have never been able to fully swallow this glaring inadequacy, no matter how ingeniously it is justified. The "constellation problem," as such, was instrumental in my motivation to update and re-tune the map in order to eliminate "special cases" and bring final symmetry and completion to its sacred structure.

Constellating 9

What is implied, but has not clearly been accounted for in Tarot Constellations theory, is that the entire operation rests squarely on The Hermit Effect, and the magical properties of Number 9. Take for example The Emperor/Death/Fool constellation which we just viewed, or numerically simply the 4/13/22 constellation; what connects these numbers both symbolically and arithmetically (as with all constellations) is +9! If one's birthdate happened to numerically reduce to say 6 (i.e. Soul/6, Personality/15), as one easily can determine, the Hidden Factor should be 24, which also reduces to 6, but no luck! There is no Key 24, thus we must continue to add across. Perhaps it is not that certain "factors" are *not* hidden, but that the grid itself is undone!

The problem has been solved in TNP with the addition of five cards on the third row of The Matrix, and with this expansion I propose a different way of approaching constellations in general. It is simply to view all cards by their respective stage (X Y or Z) and Path (1-9), ascertain the corresponding rite of passage, and dispense with the construction of "Soul, Personality, and Hidden Factors" altogether. The triad will be the thing, and all stages of it will carry relevance on The Nine Paths. Thinking in terms of "stage" in the growth process, such as TNP's "Departure/Transfer/Arrival," or if you prefer, simply "Beginning/Middle/End," opens a more universal portal of oracle work, where dates, time, and even space now become more consciously and transparently interwoven with number archetypes, and most conspicuously, by virtue of Number 9 and The Hermit Effect. The result, therefore, will be clear and cohesive, and gives this work a distinct objective, namely, to become a whole spiritual individual. Isn't that what it was meant to do?

Going With The Flow

Tarotists, when left to their own devices, take every opportunity to connect with what might be described as the "arcanic flow," that dynamic underground stream of number-wisdom and archetypal imagery that circulates eternally throughout The Matrix, whether they do so for healing benefits, spiritual re-tuning, or just for the fun of it. As Dion Fortune writes:

> A man's soul is like a lagoon connected with the sea by a submerged channel; although to all outward seeming it is land-locked, nevertheless its water-level rises and falls with the tides of the sea because of the hidden connection. So it is with human consciousness, there is a subconscious connection between each individual soul and the

World-soul hidden in the most primitive depths of subconsciousness, and in consequence we share in the rise and fall of the cosmic tides.[4]

A Tarot practice in this regard for the calculation of Growth Cycles and Year Cards from dates, by locating the corresponding Key on the map, I think best captures the spirit of Constellations. It can stimulate a fascinating reappraisal of historical patterns, offer a parallel universe to linear time, and orient oneself esoterically to the passing of years and the stages of their lives. The year 2017, in this light, numerically reduces $(2 + 0 + 1 + 7 = 10)$, and is thus viewed as a Wheel of Fortune year. One may contemplate the events of any chosen year through this lens, and make choices and decisions with an awareness of the arcanic backdrop. Arrien,[5] (with the help of Twainhart Hill), has produced a Year Card Chart from 1880-2095 with this method shown here on the next page, based on the standard matrix.

A careful inspection of the chart and one notices the curious ways in which number cycles flow through Time, and occasionally take an unexpected leap, observed just in the calendric years. But when the vast symbolism of Tarot Keys are tied to the numbers, a year is given a far deeper and more interesting dimension of meaning with respct to Time, Change, and lived space.

With the expansion and re-tuning given in TNP, something quite fascinating occurs: some years now correspond to the emerging agencies that didn't consciously exist before. Their arrival casts some interesting reconsideration of what was, and what will be. Cycles of Time, you will discover, are affected slightly in the TNP model, but much as we saw just with Waite's re-ordering of Strength and Justice, the ramifications in metaphysical space can reach cosmic proportions.

---

4. Dion Fortune, *The Mystical Qabalah*, 1935, p. 17.
5. Angeles Arrien, *The Tarot Handbook*, 1987.

(Trad.) YEAR CARD CHART (1880-2095)

Left-hand columns = Base Numbers; Right-hand columns = Year Cards

Year	Card	Year	Card	Year	Card	Year	Card	Year	Card	Year	Card
1880	17	1916	17	1952	17	1988	8	2024	8	2060	8
1881	18	1917	18	1953	18	1989	9	2025	9	2061	9
1882	19	1918	19	1954	19	1990	19	2026	10	2062	10
1883	20	1919	20	1955	20	1991	20	2027	11	2063	11
1884	21	1920	12	1956	21	1992	21	2028	12	2064	12
1885	22	1921	13	1957	22	1993	22	2029	13	2065	13
1886	5	1922	14	1958	5	1994	5	2030	5	2066	14
1887	6	1923	15	1959	6	1995	6	2031	6	2067	15
1888	7	1924	16	1960	16	1996	7	2032	7	2068	16
1889	8	1925	17	1961	17	1997	8	2033	8	2069	17
1890	18	1926	18	1962	18	1998	9	2034	9	2070	9
1891	19	1927	19	1963	19	1999	10	2035	10	2071	10
1892	20	1928	20	1964	20	2000	2	2036	11	2072	11
1893	21	1929	21	1965	21	2001	3	2037	12	2073	12
1894	22	1930	13	1966	22	2002	4	2038	13	2074	13
1895	5	1931	14	1967	5	2003	5	2039	14	2075	14
1896	6	1932	15	1968	6	2004	6	2040	6	2076	15
1897	7	1933	16	1969	7	2005	7	2041	7	2077	16
1898	8	1934	17	1970	17	2006	8	2042	8	2078	17
1899	9	1935	18	1971	18	2007	9	2043	9	2079	18
1900	10	1936	19	1972	19	2008	10	2044	10	2080	10
1901	11	1937	20	1973	20	2009	11	2045	11	2081	11
1902	12	1938	21	1974	21	2010	3	2046	12	2082	12
1903	13	1939	22	1975	22	2011	4	2047	13	2083	13
1904	14	1940	14	1976	5	2012	5	2048	14	2084	14
1905	15	1941	15	1977	6	2013	6	2049	15	2085	15
1906	16	1942	16	1978	7	2014	7	2050	7	2086	16
1907	17	1943	17	1979	8	2015	8	2051	8	2087	17
1908	18	1944	18	1980	18	2016	9	2052	9	2088	18
1909	19	1945	19	1981	19	2017	10	2053	10	2089	19
1910	11	1946	20	1982	20	2018	11	2054	11	2090	11
1911	12	1947	21	1983	21	2019	12	2055	12	2091	12
1912	13	1948	22	1984	22	2020	4	2056	13	2092	13
1913	14	1949	5	1985	5	2021	5	2057	14	2093	14
1914	15	1950	15	1986	6	2022	6	2058	15	2094	15
1915	16	1951	16	1987	7	2023	7	2059	16	2095	16

Based on the work of Angeles Arrien

To close this chapter, I have made a small sample of both systems side by side, where the variance is most remarkable. For a comprehensive study of Year Cycles in TNP, I have included more extensive charting in the Appendix. Remember, that (Key) 22, formerly held by The Fool, is now (Key 22), The Well, an agent of Renewal, as we will discuss in the next chapter.

YEAR CHART 1970-1999

STANDARD WAITE-BASED							ADJUSTED TNP-BASED				
1970	17	1980	18	1990	19	1970	17	1980	18	1990	19
1971	18	1981	19	1991	20	1971	18	1981	19	1991	20
1972	19	1982	20	1992	21	1972	19	1982	20	1992	21
1973	20	1983	21	1993	22	1973	20	1983	21	1993	**22**
1974	21	1984	22	1994	5	1974	21	1984	**22**	1994	**23**
1975	22	1985	5	1995	6	1975	**22**	1985	**23**	1995	**24**
1976	5	1986	6	1996	7	1976	**23**	1986	**24**	1996	**25**
1977	6	1987	7	1997	8	1977	**24**	1987	**25**	1997	**26**
1978	7	1988	8	1998	9	1978	**25**	1988	**26**	1998	**27**
1979	8	1989	9	1999	10	1979	**26**	1989	**27**	1999	10

Note: Shifts in TNP are in bold

CHAPTER 13

The Re-Tuning

Let's recap the main ideas discussed thus far to properly reset a return to Terminal 9. For instance, early on I made mention of my previous description of Tarot as "one finely-tuned, intricately engineered, new class of psychological vehicle."[1] In Chapter 1, we suggested that a true scientific attitude with respect to experimentation ("try it, and see what can be learned") benefits Tarot practice by bringing clearer focus and understanding to the mysterious mechanism (synchronicity) and deep template (The Matrix) behind Tarot's operation. We also described the uniqueness of Tarot readings to be like snowflakes of psychical proportions, and suggested Tarot begins in the realm of imagination, "where it is possible to travel instantaneously into the past or future, to other lands, beyond the earth, and even to realms that don't exist in the material dimension" (Giles, 1994).

We have spoken of travel as "the act of going places," and suggested vigorously that we are always traveling somewhere, knowingly or unconsciously, and importantly, there are many levels of travel, including physical destinations in outer space like to your car on the street or Alpha Centauri, and also various regions of mental travel in inner space, including East and West, either with, or apart from, our so-called "higher order cognitions" operating, i.e. the ego-driven rationality (the formal operations of Piaget) that we normally think of as adult thinking. More provocatively, I suggested that we don't really know where we are going, nor who or *what* is doing this going, beyond the physical level. Our ignorance here is dramatically limiting to Man's exploration of human possibility, though rarely recognized as such.

---

1. Arthur Rosengarten, *Tarot and Psychology: Spectrums of Possibility.*

In this paradoxical condition, going but not knowing, we have introduced The Traveler as our protagonist and everyman, whose mind is routinely confused and over-run with random thoughts and images, who has grappled with change and impermanence mostly through addiction, avoidance, and denial, but who now seeks to enter a spiritual path, by way of Tarot and the oracular dimension, in the hope of discovering who he really is, and where he's really going. His attitude becomes far more humble and open-minded when he leaves his baggage behind and steps into the liminal "in between" dimension of divination. Navigation, we noted, is essential for effective travel in all areas, as are terminals, from and to which traveling regularly occurs, becoming his indispensible aids. We observed the general consensus of transportation experts that long-term success of all travel terminals will depend upon the "Holy Trinity of Terminality" of location, accessibility, and infrastructure. These factors were recognized to be true equally for inner travel.

We observed that all levels of travel, like all levels of human narrative (given fundamentally, that Man is a storyteller), will structurally carry a beginning, middle, and ending phase; further borrowing from the metaphor of transportation, we designated the three phases as the XYZ stages on The TNP Matrix: Departure (X), Transfer (Y), and Arrival (Z). In Section 2, we delved into Tarot's liminal phase of Transfer, and saw how the act of divination was itself an "in-between" liminal undertaking, quoting Jung's famous observation in the Terry Lectures at Yale University: "The shortcoming of Western religious rituals is the emphasis that is placed on highly structured, as opposed to spontaneous, religious experience." I noted that a kind of spontaneous, natural divination process with minimal structure would allow the freedom for things to arise of their own accord in their natural wholeness and simplicity.

We have also explored another dimension of Time, Space, and Number to include psychological and experiential dimensions outside the conventional scientific paradigms, and regularly overlooked in the general discussion, which may otherwise contribute significantly to what is discovered in our travels. The only thing faster than the speed of light, we should remember, is the human mind. In this context, the constructs of "future" and "past" take on new meaning, recalling Alan Watts' pronouncement in the Introduction: "...when the world is inspected directly, and clearly, past and future times are nowhere to be found." Yet it remains to be seen in this last section how "the future" as such fleshes out, in the oracular world of ideas and perceptions.

Finally, we have introduced the idea of Terminal 9, an imaginary portal or gateway into subtler levels of awareness via the Tarot oracle, that facilitates exploration of "The Intermediate Territory," a mental realm of progressively higher (or subtler) levels of consciousness, beginning with the philosopher of consciousness Ken Wilber's post-rational band of awareness called "vision-logic" where Tarot work makes its first home (and evolves progressively to the psychic, subtle, and causal bandwidths), all "situated" in awareness between the formal operations of ordinary thinking and final enlightenment (shunyata, nonduality, nirvana, open space etc.) that are themselves "off-grid" and exist beyond Tarot. Tarot is seen as a journey of preparation that facilitates the becoming of a whole spiritual individual, who may then take his journey in the direction he likes.

With The Tarot Matrix, we have examined discrete, universal, developmental stages for socio-cultural and psychological maturation, that normally adhere to a triadic pattern, which we call "rites of passage," and we further distinguished a metaphysical formula along these lines embedded in Tarot's Major Arcana, that I have termed The Hermit Effect (or +9), related to the magical mathematic and symbolic properties of the Number 9. Hopefully, this is now clear as as a cube of solid sunshine and diaphanous gems. We may thus proceed to stage Z, including what are termed "the emerging archetypes of finality" in the following chapter to complete our arrival.

Thαt Which Is So of Itself

The great American modernist poet of first half of the 20th century, William Carlos Williams, in his most anthologized short poem, *The Red Wheel Barrow*, writes:

so much depends
upon

a red wheel
barrow

glazed with rain
water

beside the white
chickens.

The poem holds relevance to our discussion with respect for the necessity of *things arising of their own accord*...just so. It speaks of an unfiltered, natural intelligence. The ancient Taoist sage, Chuang Tzu, called this "that which is so of itself." And for the proper expansion of Tarot, so very much depends upon that which is so of itself! The natural world in its fullness is inherently whole and complete in one-ness, unblemished, for better or worse, by the intrusions of "higher order cognitions" from Man, that is, until Man insinuates himself into it, and tinkers. Things then are no longer simply as they were, pure and unfiltered, in harmony with their natural order, and neither in opposition to, nor domination over, unless such constraints occur in their native condition. In many respects, this perspective is in keeping with Hermeticism, the Perennial Philosophy, Taoist and Eastern sensibility, Native American and Shamanic teachings, American Transcendentalism, Environmentalism, modern Humanistic, Jungian, Transpersonal, and Integral philosophy, and, as well, the way of Tarot.

It would seem, therefore, that tampering with the Higher Arcana as I have proposed would be a rather crude violation of a natural law handed down through the ages, and indeed, the Tarot authorities and The Keepers of the Past should be notified at once! By what legitimate power could any individual, a psychologist no less, deem to make so metaphysically weighty an intervention? Specifically, I refer to the author's call for a revision of the third row of 9, the Arrivals (Z) stage of our Matrix, whereby (Key 0) The Fool card has been absconded from its traditional 22nd "terminal" resting spot, and slid over to the 27th position. Moreover, five new Keys would by necessity be added, bearing emergent archetypal agencies of our time, to follow in procession *beyond* the triumphal conclusion of Key 21, The World card. No matter the merits of this enlargement, the intent alone must surely seem an effrontery to the sacred order of this Renaissance oracle map! But herein, Tarot colleagues, lies the first rub.

Disclaimer

It is not the author who moves like a thief in the night to steal away the sacred relic from its original store... but The Oracle Himself, through his own encoded assurances, that transparently dictates The Call for an update, and indeed, a "re-tuning." By re-tuning is meant a small but critical adjustment or fine-tuning, as one does with a musical instrument like a guitar or violin to gain the correct or uniform pitch. In this work, it is to attune the Tarot, presumably, a Tarot of the future, to a new frequency by applying the so-named Hermit Effect (+9) to its erstwhile crocodilian overbite! It is time. But an orthodontist I am not, merely a faithful scribe of the sacred canon who can see the writing on It's walls. Symmetry and completion are the primary intent. As I anticipate the procedure will not be undertaken without resistance, the fine-tuning will be further demonstrated in the present chapter. While the adjustment may seem minor, I echo William Carlos Williams—so very much depends upon it!

Moreover, the author makes no claim as a tarot historian himself, as one finds in the brilliant and thorough study of Tarot and Renaissance mysticism by Robert V. O'Neill[2] and others, but rather an average translator sitting off to the side, a loyal student to be sure, though one who pays special homage to The Oracle's hidden teachings in concert, of course, with his own intuitions and feeling space. His chosen task is to re-tune the Tarot map accordingly, but with unswerving respect for what has gone before. With great assistance from the occult author and scholar, my colleague and friend Lon Milo DuQuette, I have incorporated, and

2. Robert V. O'Neill, *Tarot Symbolism*, 1986.

successfully extended, all firmly established Hermetic correspondences to each card, including the additional five, and embedded them into the composition of each illustration, without interruption, redundancy, or contradiction (see Correspondences in Appendix). In effect, *Tarot of the Nine Paths* is meant to add a final wing to the "edifice" without disturbing the foundation and sacred architecture, by addressing the nasty overbite with respect to nine-ness, the number of spiritual Man. No doubt, somewhere on Mount Helicon in Boeotia, The Nine Muses are now dancing!

Questions may arise from concerned readers to which I will for the time being remain silent: Is this what is meant to be The Tarot of the Future? Are the proposed adjustments meant to be incorporated in new decks other than TNP? Is there a way to scientifically or metaphysically validate this hypothesis? What if I agree with your hypothesis but I don't relate to the imagery? These questions and more will be answered in time, but first let's quickly review the historical precedents of the Major Arcana's composition and order, which brings me to the second rub, if you will, with respect to the potential heresy of tampering.

KEY ZERO REMAINS SUPREME

It is a curious fact, as O'Neil and other scholars have shown, that in the earliest Italian decks significant variance with respect to card membership, number assignment, sequencing and attribution, size, and naming of the Major Keys abounded; like most modern practitioners today, we have therefore accepted The Marseilles convention stemming from the mid-seventeenth century in France (with the slight early 20th century adjustment by Waite of Keys 8 and 11) to serve as standard-bearer. We may recall from Chapter 9 our first adjustment of this modern matrix was "Step 1" shown here again:

Note that Key Zero is taken out of the 22nd position, and placed into the 27th; this effect signals that The Journey of The Nine Paths remains well within the auspices of pure Possibility, The Fool and His Journey.

Step 1: Key 0 The Fool is moved to the final position as the 27th card, thereby retaining its termainal status of ending and beginning anew. As such, Key 0 now completes the 9th Path, The Path of the Sage.

We further identified the supreme importance of this archetype as Tarot's alpha and omega, the place wherein the story begins, ends, and begins anew, providing a never-ending spiral of Beginningless Time and open space, within which The Journey only deepens, in keeping with the wisdom doctrines of East and West. What remains of our re-tuning efforts, therefore, is a further investigation of the five missing pieces of the third row (Keys 22-26) as well as some discussion of the new implications of The Fool in the 27th position, now the final card of the 9th triad, more elegantly as the denouement of The Hermit and The Moon, on The Path of The Sage.

A Grand Central Station of the Mind

Welcome Arriving Travelers

TERMINAL 9

	THE FOUR ELEMENTS	↓ X	Gate 1-9 Departures		+9		
D O M E S T I C		↓ Y	Gate 10-18 Transfer				E N T E R
USE GTE 28 →		↓ Z	Gate 19-0 Arrivals		The Traveler		←
	Quaternity	⊘ Ego	NO ENTRY Baggage		INDIVIDUATION		

The 9 PATHWAYS: TNP MATRIX

X	1	2	3	4	5	6	7	8	9
Y	10	11	12	13	14	15	16	17	18
Z	19	20	21	22	23	24	25	26	0

DEPARTURES X
1 The Magician/Intention
2 The Priestess/Intuition
3 The Empress/Passion
4 The Emperor/Dominion
5 The Hierophant/Spirit
6 The Lovers/Union
7 The Chariot/Challenge
8 Strength/Life Force
9 The Hermit/Wisdom

TRANSFERS Y
10 Wheel of Fortune/Synchronicity
11 Justice/Balance
12 The Hanged Man/Surrender
13 Death/Dissolution
14 Temperance/Synergy
15 The Devil/Separation
16 The Tower/Upheaval
17 The Star/Essence
18 The Moon/Imagination

ARRIVALS Z
19 The Sun/Consciousness
20 Judgement/Awakening
21 The World/Integration
22 The Well/Renewal
23 The River/Flow
24 The Ring/Wholeness
25 The Dragon/Initiation
26 The Great Web/Interbeing
0 The Fool/Possibility

NOTE: NEW Z GATES 22-26

22	23	24	25	26
THE WELL Renewal	**THE RIVER** Flow	**THE RING** Wholeness	**THE DRAGON** Initiation	**THE GREAT WEB** Renewal

By returning to Terminal 9, we may row re-examine why and wherefore these emerging five principles, as the author contends, arise by their own accord at the bidding of The Oracle himself, through his embedded magical code termed The Hermit Effect (+9).

TRIADS 1-3

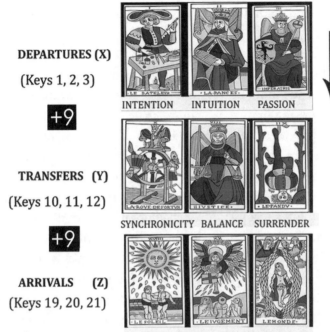

DEPARTURES (X)

(Keys 1, 2, 3)

+9

INTENTION   INTUITION   PASSION

TRANSFERS (Y)

(Keys 10, 11, 12)

+9

SYNCHRONICITY BALANCE SURRENDER

ARRIVALS   (Z)

(Keys 19, 20, 21)

CONSCIOUSNESS AWAKENING INTEGRATION

Using the classic Tarot De Marseille of Jean Dodal (c. 1701)
superimposed over the corresponding TNP Keys, the same
archetypal pattern is revealed in the metalogic of The Oracle
with respect to The Hermit Effect (+9). Note, in this
pre-20th century deck, Justice retains the number 8, that is,
before it was re-tuned with (Key 11) Strength, by A.E. Waite
(1909).

The first three unaffected triads (above) present a clear model of
The Oracle's original thinking process, so let's engage this more closely
with respect to The Hermit Effect. I have chosen for illustration purposes a Marseilles deck (the Dodal, c. 1701) for this demonstration to
reinforce Campbell's insight regarding multiplicity, "the hero with a
thousand faces" effect—that is, though archetypal images of The Hero,
or any Tarot archetype, will appear differently in different decks due to

artistic execution, interpretation, and personal conceptualization of the designer, the fundamental principles they represent are the same, eternal, singular, and unknowable, as Jung distinguished as the *archetype per say*.

In the diagram we can see plainly The Oracle's metalogic at play; from each Departure Gate shown (Intention, Intuition, or Passion), The Traveler descends more deeply into what is directly below him, from Departure into the liminal Y Transfer stage, then on to the Arrival Z where the journey resolves. The significance of +9 means, of course, The Traveler moves *in the service of spiritual individuation*. This is his modus operandi throughout the nine pathways of The Matrix, however, until now the third stage was left wanting on five of The Nine Paths. I suspect this is because human consciousness had not evolved to the point where they were ready to be seen and addressed, that is, until now.

Recall that the notion of "Individuation" is arguably Jung's major contribution. He defines it "as becoming a whole psychological individual." As a metaphysical map for spiritual travelers, we have extended Jung's definition to the becoming of a whole spiritual individual. Not unlike in Patanjali's classic Eight-Limbed Yoga System, we find in Tarot many roads and practices one may take in the pursuit of spiritual wholeness, which we call "Paths." The specific practices and techniques are left to the individual to find from the vast offerings now accessible in the psychospiritual universe. Tarot Paths merely point to the thematic emphasis and purpose for which skills should be applied. In this respect it is like a terminal, a Grand Central Station of the Mind.

Returning to Path One—MASTERY, as first introduced in Chapter 6, yields (by way of agency alone) the following formula:

Intention (+9) → **Synchronicity** (+9) → Consciousness

Before we now step any further down these pathways, I think it will be less cumbersome if we abbreviated the phrase "in the service of spiritual individuation (or +9)" as "ITSOSI" (in the service of spiritual individuation). It helps me tor remember this visually as "IT-SOS-I" (a kind of cryptic warning not to regress into a thing). The formula above, therefore, in longhand will be called "Intension ITSOSI leads to Synchronicity. Synchronicity ITSOSI resolves in Consciousness. By card, we denote it simply as Magician (+9) →Wheel (+9) →*Sun*. At first gaze, the teaching appears almost counter-intuitive, seeming at odds with The Magician's focused deliberation, defined and will-directed Intention, leading now to the rather mellow, liminal condition where The Wheel of Fortune's magical release manifests in a kind of blissful timelessness, with luck, magic, and spontaneity gathering together as Synchronicity—meaningful coincidence—but again we remember: this connection only occurs through +9, that is, when actions are taken in the service of spiritual individuation! In effect, the TNP archetypes have all been alchemically "hermitized" in The Oracle's Matrix.

As one becomes familiar with these agencies and dynamics, the Keys alone become sufficient to describe specific rites of passage, and soon just the images will tell the story because the spectrum of teachings within each card have been fully absorbed with continued use, and will speak in the prescribed manner without need for words. That is when the "light seeing" perception of vision-logic truly takes over and the elevation of consciousness is fully underway when actions are taken is service of spiritual individuation (ITSOSI).

We see in the same basic pattern and

PATH 2: INSIGHT

The High Priestess

INTUITION

↓ +9

Justice

BALANCE

↓ +9

Judgement

AWAKENING

metalogic in the remaining eight paths. Path Two—INSIGHT, therefore, yields by way of agency:

Intuition (+9) →Balance (+9) → Awakening

Longhand, the teaching is Intuition ITSOSI leads to Balance; Balance ITSOSI resolves in Awakening. By card, simply as: Priestess (+9)→Justice (+9)→Judgment. Simpler still, by number alone we find the following equation: 2 (+9)→11 (+9)→*20*. The Traveler is here commissioned to learn what occurs when the agency of Intuition is "hermitized" by +9 on The Matrix: Intuition, he finds, leads to Balance, equanimity, and poetic justice (Key 11), which in turn, resolves in final Awakening (Key 20).

As with most tarots, in TNP a variety of nuances and textures are depicted in the illustration itself to give further clues with symbolic intent; a story on many levels is being told in a single card as one examines each illustration more closely, though it may be left to the reader to tell it. One also discovers in TNP intentional linkages to other cards, and correspondences parallel to the hermetically-sealed systems of astrology, numerology, and Kabbalah. It is not necessary, however, to ascertain all meanings of the full display, and with continued practice, new details will come into focus for reflection. For skilled readers, the devil is in the detail; for psychic readers using tarot cards, a single detail often provides ample spring-boarding stimulus for expansive psychic association.

In divination, of course, as the Keys have been smashed up and scattered about, likewise our own personal world views too, in effect, are being smashed up and scattered about similarly. This occurs particularly when baggage has been left behind. At such times The Matrix offers a secondary function of portable roadmap and navigation tool, to help remind us of where we've been and where we're going, and better contextualize our incoming tarot lessons in metaphysical spacetime. Are we spending more time in "departures" for example, or perhaps "arrivals" or "transfer stations?" Guidance from the map can help us navigate preferred avenues, as it were, or in the least, present a glimpse at the road ahead. Let's take a practical example. Suppose an important goal has come into mind—the direction of a relationship is unclear, or perhaps, you've decided to run for Prime Minister of the Canary Islands, but you don't even know where the Canary Islands are? Could be a problem...

Naturally, your first rational step would be to find a map of the world you are traveling to, assess your present location to better navigate, and get some idea of the lay of the land. "Aha!" you exclaim, "There it is! Right near Morocco, who knew?" You then do your due diligence, in this case, you research everything you possibly can find about the Canary Islands, its governing bodies, air fares and so forth, consulting conventional resources available, having conversations with people who have been there, books, etc. until it occurs to you before going any farther that a Tarot reading would be useful to check in with yourself on a deeper level, so you choose to enter Terminal 9, leaving all your baggage behind as required.

You draw (Key 7) The Chariot, an agent of Challenge, in the first position (Working For You) and say (Key 16) The Tower, an agent of Upheaval, in the second position (Working against you). Hmmmm. After directly apprehending these first two cards, passing through the various stages of interpretation,[3] you notice that your original question pertaining to running for political office in a foreign country has now shifted somewhat, as often occurs. It has been de-colorized, stripped of the particulars, and plays now more on the order of "seeking a position of power and governance in an exotic distant land." No problem, you go with it. You may then choose to visit The Matrix and locate where Keys 7 and 16 fall on the map, and to your surprise, you discover they are linked by The Hermit Effect, and form the first and second stages of Path 7: The Universe. Now this is getting interesting, you think. What is this pattern telling me? It may not be clear at first, so you listen through your feeling and intuitive spaces. You might ask yourself: Is there a discernable regularity (that is, a pattern) with my other random selections? What can be learned from this? You decide to sit back and let it marinate.

---

3.   Interpretative styles: analytical, therapeutic, psychic, magical, [and global]; see Mary K. Greer's *Tarot For Your Self* (1987); detailed further in *Tarot and Psychology, Spectrums of Possibility*, Rosengarten, 2000.

You may contemplate a little longer, asking "What does becoming a whole spiritual individual mean to me?" You wonder: "How do these archetypes I've chosen find resolution on the map? It might be good to know where I'm really going?" A novel idea, you think. You notice the associations that now arise in your mind, and the subtler felt sensations, images, fantasies, memories, etc. In other words, you sit, reflect, and work with it. This is when a reading comes alive.

At every position and stage, of course, The Oracle counsels like a broken record with one over-riding reminder: "Approach _____ in the service of your spiritual individuation." Do so, that is, to advance your self-awareness and consciousness. Become more of a unique and whole spiritual individual. This is what the wisdom of Tarot always wants from us. It is not unlike the final words given by the Buddha often translated as "Seek your own salvation with diligence!"

> Then the Buddha addressed all the monks once more, and these were the very last words he spoke:

> "Behold, O monks, this is my last advice to you. All component things in the world are changeable. They are not lasting. Work hard to gain your own salvation." (Pali Canon)

But though The Oracle may be an alien intelligence, "He" is not monolithic or single-minded as far as the means are concerned. He recognizes there are many ways, as the saying goes, "to dive into a pool." Perhaps the Canary Island idea, in retrospect, was only what got you to The Terminal in the first place, and for that you are grateful. But it changed! Surprise, surprise... Everything changes. Take what you get, and use it in the service of your spiritual individuation.

You undertook all the conventional initial steps first as one should, and your initial query morphed into another, before (or during) your brave decision to enter Terminal 9. Now, as is often the case, the question's import has became infused with a distinctly spiritually-directed layer, and your choices and actions that result will be laced with higher purpose—becoming a whole spiritual individual (and not regressing into a thing!). It may not at all be why you came initially, you may not quite know what this even means, but the seeds have been planted in any case, and you will leave, (consciously or otherwise) so affected. The roadmap has opened new territory perhaps, a world of potentially unlimited mind travel, which, quite naturally, carries its own set of rules and new terrain to be sure, and even if you suspected there might be some deeper process underlying your initial fantasy, well, yes, it is now definitely confirmed! You have slipped through the doorway and opened your mind to inner spiritual travel.

This is the predictable result of consulting an oracle—one is always directed to consider what is most advantageous for one's wholeness in becoming more spiritual, that is, relating to or affecting the human spirit or soul as opposed to material or physical things. Suppose after your baggage was left behind, your question morphed as in the above example, and at the conclusion the reading did not seem to produce the original insight you had initially sought? Take what you get! You will still gain a deeper, and relevant sense of self and purpose in the undertaking, regardless. Tarot, in this respect, is infallible. We learn firsthand what seasoned Travelers know: life is an ongoing journey at many levels, new possibilities appear no matter where we currently are, and the process gets easier and more satisfying with continued practice. And more often than not, as a bonus, your life will be rewarded serendipitously, an effect of the good karma from which your actions have sprung in undergoing this procedure with sincerity.

The Oracle's Counsel

"Paths" in TNP can be thought of as fully "vetted," differentiated, and non-duplicated, triadic structures connected meaningfully and quantifiably by The Hermit Effect (+9) on The Matrix, and bearing unique rites of passage to higher levels of awareness. The "vetting process" has been determined in the wisdom-mind of The Oracle, and we take this on faith, and, of course, by way of direct experimentation and the proper scientific attitude. But The Tarot Oracle, we must remember, is not some lovely fellow; "He" is not a person, not a prophet, not invested in you or me, and never preaches or proselytizes; He is a true, non-ego-mediated source. This in itself makes cartomancy a strange and alien practice, but also, a great rarity and opportunity. Without negative connotations, He may be considered an alien intelligence, that is, from *inner* space. He serves us as a mirror of our sacred interiors through curious pictures, and is consistently a shrewd, knowing guide and beacon. One enters His auspices in Terminal 9 by personal choice only. There is no other way.

As we now understand, by the mysterious guidance of The Oracle's Counsel, Nine Paths have been fully crystalized in the re-tuning, repre-senting nine, three step, rites of passage for the transformation of con-sciousness extending the original Tarot map to a state of completion, per-fection, and symmetry. The author has given The Nine Paths descriptive titles for easy identification:

Rosengarten's

TAROT OF THE NINE PATHS

THE TNP MATRIX

	1st	2nd	3rd	4th	5th	6th	7th	8th	9th
X	1	2	3	4	5	6	7	8	9
Y	10	11	12	13	14	15	16	17	18
Z	19	20	21	22	23	24	25	26	27

The Nine Paths

PATH ONE: MASTERY
PATH TWO: INSIGHT
PATH THREE: JOY
PATH FOUR: TRANSFORMATION
PATH FIVE: PEACE
PATH SIX: RELATIONSHIP
PATH SEVEN: THE SEEKER
PATH EIGHT: THE UNIVERSE
PATH NINE: THE SAGE

X = DEPARTURES   Y = TRANSITIONS   Z = ARRIVALS

  (P1) The Path of Mastery
  (P2) The Path of Insight
  (P3) The Path of Joy
  (P4) The Path of Transformation
  (P5) The Path of Peace
  (P6) The Path of Relationship
  (P7) The Path of The Seeker
  (P8) Path of The Universe
  (P9) Path of The Sage

Working with *Tarot of the Nine Paths,* it is well to remember the deck's subtitle: *Advanced Tarot for the Spiritual Traveler.* The mandate is clear. TNP is no parlor game, and unlike say the beautiful and quite popular *Lenormand,* a (non-tarot) deck created in France during the Napoleonic era, whose divinatory focus is the outer world and its happenings, TNP, by contrast, is decidedly inner world-oriented, spiritual in nature and purpose, and designed for the transformation and expansion of consciousness. Without meaning offense, we might say in the words of Michelle Obama, "When they go low, we go high!"

In Arrival (Z), where van Gennep's final stage "re-aggregation or incorporation" is consummated, the Path is, in principle, "completed." This is analogous to Campbell's "Return" phase in the hero's quest, whereupon The Traveler assumes a "new" station, and re-enters society "with a certain new status," as for example, "Today I am a Marine!" (or perhaps, a "grandmother!"). But less we forget, the territory of Tarot, of course, is a metaphysical and intermediate realm in the vast suprastratum of the realized human mind, and thus not primarily geared to the kind of physical destinations that van Gennep and Campbell speak of, or for that matter, the kind of penultimate liberation sought by yogis and monks; consequently, Arrivals serve not so much as "incorporations to a new social status," but rather completions of discrete pathways to higher consciousness.

In practical terms, Arrivals often help Travelers primarily as destination pointers on our journey. I think of Arrivals in the vain of Werner Erhard's observation: "the future that one *lives into* shapes one's being and action in the present [italics mine]." As we *live into* a Path's Arrival, such as we have discussed with The Sun's Consciousness, or Judgement's Awakening, our being and actions are shaped accordingly. We have established, in effect, "fully-vetted" targets of awareness, and now truly will know where precisely the deepest part of ourselves is really going!

Completion

We draw an important distinction in this work between being "complete" and being "finished," as in "the party's over, let's go home and get some sleep." In Buddhist terms, when we are complete, our travel continues to unfold as a product of karma, but we're no longer creating new karma. This is an important distinction. As wisely taught by the Australian creator of the Radiant Mind training, Dr. Peter Fenner, "karma is only created when we're holding onto or rejecting what's happening now," in our travels Our actions are incomplete, therefore, because we are projecting a time in the future when the results of our actions will come to fruition. When we truly are clear and complete, our transient moods such as excitement, enthusiasm, doubt, embarrassment, resignation, and boredom will slowly disappear from our experience and be replaced by serenity, sensitivity, natural patience, vulnerability, invincibility, unconditional forgiveness, openness, supernal bliss, joy, and love.[4]

The only reason we have felt incomplete all this time is that we have not really known who (or what) we are, or where we are going. As conditioned, "higher order" rational, ego-driven human beings, sadly, our minds reflexively are self-placed into the past or future, wanting things to be different than they are, feeling something is missing, and wishing to be somewhere else. A Buddhist teaching to this point claims only four things make us unhappy: Not having what we want. Having what we don't want. Not being with who we want to be with. And being with who we don't want to be with. This about sums it up, no?

Erhard observes:

> The reason that it appears that the past shapes one's being and action in the present is that for most people the past lives in (shapes) their view of the future... it's only by being complete with the past such that it no longer shape's one's being and action in the present that there is room to create a new future.[5]

The Last of the Completed Paths

Let's take another look at The Oracle's Counsel as it presently stands in Path Three: Joy. Here we find established in the Marseilles-Waite

---

4. See Peter Fenner, *The Radiant Mind*, (2007).

5. Werner Erhard, "A Breakthrough in Individual and Social Transformation," Presentation at the Eranos Conference, Asconia, Switzerland, June 18, 2006.

PATH 3: JOY

The Empress

PASSION

⤛ +9

The Hanged Man

SURRENDER

↓ +9

The World

INTEGRATION

convention, Passion (+9) → Surrender (+9) → Integration (see diagram). In longhand, we say Passion ITSOSI leads to Surrender; Surrender ITSOSI resolves in Integration; or simply by card: Empress (+9) → Hanged Man (+9) → World.

In this rite of passage, we track the evolution of The Dancer, a metaphor for The Empress, associated with anima, or the feminine principle, fertility, universal love, nature/nurture, the divine mother and so forth which have been wrapped in TNP under the agency of Passion (See Lexicon).

By The Oracle's Counsel, we observe The Hermit Effect deepens The Empress's effusiveness of emotion and passion into what may appear at first to be a rather dampening Transfer, namely, to (Key 12) The Hanged Man, an agent of Surrender. The Hanged Man's brand of Surrender, however, is highly conscious and self-aware, and includes dis-identification, mindfulness, and detachment, much in the vein of the 12 Step slogan: "Turning it over to a higher power" for Step 3: "Made a decision to turn our will and our lives over to the care of God *as we understood Him.*" One may hesitate, however, and protest: "But she is The Dancer! Why not just let her dance?" Such is a matter to be taken up with The Oracle himself, who, as we know, always has the bigger picture in mind, always thinks in three steps, with an unapologetic agenda for the transformation of consciousness.

One may only surmise His thinking regarding pathways, and as merely a humble emissary, I will make such an attempt. The liminal mandate to now surrender her otherwise sparkling, effervescent nature, by the magic of +9, is ordered to serve perhaps an even larger aspiration, namely, to become a whole individual. It entails a certain standing back from herself, a mindful re-gathering of her potent instinctive feminine energies, in order to complete Her higher destiny of Integration, that is, at the very center of the Wheel of Life, (Key 21) The World card, Anima Mundi, World Soul, and Dance of Life.

In Arrival, we see The Empress now turned around, face-to-face with us, within the healing aura of her diety consort, the Hindu God Shiva Nataraja, the cosmic ecstatic dancer; The Empress has transformed to Lila, the dancer of all reality in the cosmos, a universal consciousness that is the outcome of creative play with the divine absolute. In (21) The World card, therefore, The Empress becomes complete, an Integration of spirit in the material world, whereby no separation exists between realization and the mundane life of everyday reality.

The four angelic animals positioned around her outer mandalic wreath, represent Quaternity, (The Four Elements) showing the worldly square of mundane existence now contains and supports Her integration of spiritual fulfillment in Earthly existence. It is quite possible, you know. The Oracle's Counsel reveals on the current map, the penultimate finality and completion distinguished for the higher learning of material Man. (21) The World card, that is, up to now, marks the highest attainment possible for man and woman, and the vastness of this achievement cannot be denied. But TNP opens still another gate, as we shall see.

AS FAR AS HE CAN GO?

Now comes the erstwhile roadblock. The next five triads by virtue of The Overbite have no third stage, no Arrival Z, no finality, and no completion. They are left hanging dualistically in the liminal phase, without further passage. Their precursors: Death, Temperance, The Devil, The Tower, and The Star are given nowhere to advance to a final stage of completion. It is so sad. Although true, in 9th Path, The Path of The Sage, The Moon has indeed found a place to go, namely, reset with Key Zero who now completes Her in the 27th place, and happily, this speaks volumes for the future of Her agency, Imagination. The tinkering of TNP has indeed affected The Fool's course and purpose as Tarot's first and final representative, and The Moon now promises to inspire it from the lunar depths of the human soul. Will this, however, critically alter the entire fabric and trajectory of The Fool's Journey, which is, of course, Tarot's journey? The answer is yes. Beyond our Imagination, if you will. The so-called "Emperor-Fool" will be replaced by the "Hermit-Fool," unquestionably a more mystical combination. This means, metaphysically-speaking, the pathway of Possibility will no longer be rooted in The Emperor's Dominion, but rather, in The Hermit's Wisdom. This transposition cannot be overstated.

Many questions arise. Let's now take a pause and allow the new cartography to marinate a bit in our thoughts, and try to imagine how our map will find its completion. What lessons and rites of passage remain? Will the re-tuning for this Tarot of the future be true to the perennial wisdom-teachings that have consistently marked the way of Tarot? Moreover, what now must we make of the notion of the "future" itself? Will we again come to discover, in the words of the celebrated 19th century French occult scholar, Eliphas Lèvi that:

> The Tarot informs by making one think... An imprisoned person, with no other book than the Tarot, if he knew how to use it, could in a few years acquire universal knowledge and would be able to speak on all subjects with unequaled learning and inexhaustible eloquence.[6]

---

6. Eliphas Lèvi in *Dictionary of Symbols,* Je Cirlot, p. 329.

CHAPTER 14

ACORNS TO OAK

"As above, so below, as within, so without, as the universe, so the soul..."

—Hermes Trismegistus

A Tarot of the future, if so titled, must not be a Tarot of the past. It should not, therefore, be "re-descripted" in the vein of neuroscience, or jettisoned by The Jetsons Effect. This is clear as spring water in the high rocks. We've seen far too many shiny new additions to the archives, and the temping frontiers of brain-oriented correspondence will do little to lessen the problem, or further the cause, if Tarot truly be a transformational and paradigm shifting tool in lived experience. Despite monumental advances that science has gifted our world, as Asimov lamented, "The saddest aspect of life right now is that science gathers knowledge faster than society gathers wisdom."

Wisdom by all measures has shown paltry gain in the long and storied history of Humankind. Its highest achievements remain ancient in origin and ageless in practice. Its opposite, human ignorance, continues its furtive run for planetary dominance, and seems lately to be gaining steam. Psychology has largely passed over wisdom in favor of "functionality," as it is far easier to measure, define, and control, and organized religion has handily neutered wisdom's place in their priorities and supplied too few tools to broaden it. In the time-worn streets and squares of 21st century Western civilization, wisdom is rarely to be spotted, or championed in its arts, crafts, and popular culture which shows far more interest in fighting, fashion, and football. There are no wisdom factories in Taiwan or Mexico, and in the gargantuan fast lanes of the world-wide-net, it lays mostly inert or hidden below the blast of information, promotion, and pornography.

In the divided, contentious, and thorny global political climate of our time, ageless wisdom is staunchly eclipsed and undone by the timeless "three poisons" at the center of the Buddhist Wheel of Samsara, namely, hatred, greed, and delusion. I think it is no overstatement to say that human civilization is now showing serious signs of global decay and even mortal danger, and without a resurgence of wisdom, planetary survival may be at stake. Time and tides wait for no man, and for those with eyes, by all outward appearances, the prospects for the future would seem rather dim at the present moment.

But all is not lost. The "good news about the future," originally laid out in the Introduction, as framed by the predictions of research-psychologist Evans for the American Psychological Association's Millennial Edition (December, 1999), namely, that in reaction to the escalating trend towards social isolation and addiction wrought by rabid information technology, as well as the increasing biomedical dominance in the treatment of mental disturbance throughout the century, a small but strong *spiritual and mental counter-movement* will arise, dedicated to coping in a world without chemical or mechanical aids. These movements, predicted Evans, will develop radical therapies and group cultures, rejecting all but the most primary and personally human relationships. But should they stand a chance, I daresay, their funnel must reach deeply down into the earthly soil of the human soul, from which wisdom springs. We will first need to know, accordingly, who and *what* we really are, which we will finally address before this study's close.

If the Wisdom, in symbolic form, we have ascribed to (Key 9) The Hermit card and The Hermit Effect (+9) of Tarot can finally, and one hopes, ebulliently, spring to life and be disseminated in an updated, re-tuned, and completed map of consciousness, there remains but two minor matters still to be settled in this study. First, what, on God's green Earth, *is* the future? What does it even mean? Should we be attempting to predict it, or writing a book about it? Secondly, will this much talked-about "re-tuning procedure," once and for all, lead us to answer our study's central (and occasionally annoying) leitmotif, namely, *"Where are we really going?"*

Future's Naysayers

Could it be, as respected Western teachers of Eastern wisdom, like authors Eckhart Tolle, Alan Watts, Peter Fenner, John Welwood, and others tell us unequivocally: the future is an illusion and errant concept. Things can only occur in the Now, and, therefore, sadly, the future is rather moot, not unlike the past. Says Tolle:

> Your life is always null, never, not, Now; what we call past and future—their only reality is that they are thought forms in the human mind. In your immediate experience, they cannot exist, they do not exist. There is no past and future; all you can know is what time does to things.[7]

Certainly, all notions of "future" imply Change of some sort, though rarely can we witness its operation in action per say, only its effect ("what it does to things"). Take the future of January 7, 2050 (my 100th birthday!) for example. Assuming the merit of Werner Erhard's insight that "the future that one *lives into* shapes one's being and action in the present," a normal thinking type, for instance, will likely see his future as an idea, ascribe to it the conclusion of a linear sequence, and then shape his present being and actions accordingly. A feeling type may value it most for its newness in light of the past, and delight in the difference and comparison. The sensate type will want to get his mitts on it in the present, and make it do something functional or interesting. And the intuitive type, in his less common, mysterious ways, will want to feel into its movement and depths, sense where it's going, and jump ahead in imagination. After all, it is only human to reify, that is, to want to make a "thing" out of it.

But our study, quite succinctly, has not privileged physical destinations or thingness whatsoever, in fact, quite to the contrary. What then

---

7. Eckhart Tolle, *Doorway Into Now*, 2014.

to make of a metaphysical future? Can it be found if it doesn't exist as a thing or a "potential thing" measured in time, space, and quantity?

MEANINGfUL NON-THINGS

I suggest, within the landscape of The Intermediate Territory, things are quite a bit different (no pun intended). For a Tarotist, life becomes an adventure inside an illusion (i.e. a story), and we make no bones about it. Before us, all manner of "things" are quickly transformed into "non-things" by way of an image-language like that of dreams, called Tarot. Future things are thereby "de-thingified" if you will, and no longer subject to the rules and conditions that things are innately charged with, including the conventional laws of physics, Time, Space, and Number. The "future" thus becomes a hazy and textured world as we reconstruct it accordingly, the very stuff that dreams are made of: imaginally malleable, liminal, and layered with meaning. But "meaning," we must keep in mind, is something primarily that one sees, lives and feels, whether or not it is understood perfectly by the "higher order" cognitions we have come to cherish so. The intellectually-inclined will likely suffer it like a color-blind bridge partner who finds numbers qualitatively meaningful and doesn't know how to count.

With thanks to their modern luminaries like Freud, Jung, Calvin Hall, Campbell, Hillman, and others, we know that dreams much as symbols, myths, and indeed, tarot cards, are not merely vacant forms we project upon, or the epiphenomena of the brain that some cognitive scientists would have us believe; they directly inspire and carry meaning from their own side, and are tied to an inner intelligence native to our deep psyches, as anyone can attest to who has had one. Meaning, which in some cases is "terminally" relevant to who and what we really are, and where we are really going. We may further distinguish dreams, therefore, and all non-rational narratives in general, as meaningful non-things!

Previously, we described dreaming as a kind of unconscious realm of divination, pointing to an advantage that true divination has over these sleepy nocturnal outpourings for the simple fact that we are awake when they happen. In both cases, dream and Tarot, they are liminal, "in-between," dimensions of mental travel and are not party to the same rules as solid states. Moreover, from the eye of the metaphysician, we may further accord these liminal, meaningful, non-things their most defining trademark, namely, to show Travelers that "nothing is isolated inside its own existence and everything is linked by a system of correspondences and assimilations."

Key 26, The Great Web/ Interbeing, or "dependent origination" (in Buddhism)

This extraordinary realization, namely, the inter-connected linkage of all manifestation, we may assume extends to things and non-things alike, physical and mental destinations, throughout the Universe(s) of spiritual Man. As a cross-cultural vision constructed in myriad of narratives, found in the earliest creation myths of primitive and ancient Man to the furtherest edges of modern contemporary science, the very notion of "an interconnected Universe" is an archetypal reality, and therefore, timeless and eternal, and as Jung wrote, "born anew in the brain stem of every individual."

The beloved Vietnamese Zen master of our day, Thich Nhat Hanh, has coined a word for this arhetypal reality: "interbeing." It is akin to the Buddhist doctrine of dependent origination. The Japanese term is *engi* which means "arising in relation." Nothing can exist in absolute independence of other things, it is believed, or arise purely of its own accord, everything is inter-related.

This is true within The TNP Matrix as well, and the principle of arising in relation (above), has been incorporated into the final Key of the five "Emerging Archetypes of Finality" in TNP: this is (Key 26) The Great Web, an agent of Interbeing. We will come back to this crowning final Key in the next and final chapter of this book.

Emerging Archetypes

In philosophy, systems theory, science, and art, *emergence* is seen as a phenomenon whereby larger entities arise through interactions among smaller or simpler entities such that the larger entities exhibit properties the smaller/ simpler entities do not. In the political sphere, we can think of federal governments exhibiting properties of governance over smaller entities like cities and states, for example. Cities, in our current dispensation, do not have standing armies.

Symmetrical fractal patterns emerging in snowflakes

The formation of complex symmetrical and fractal patterns in snowflakes also exemplifies *emergence* in a physical system (see illustration). Emergence is believed to be central in theories of integrative levels and complex systems. By integrative levels (or levels of organization such as TNP's XYZ) is meant a set of phenomena emerging on the backs of pre-existing phenomena of lower levels. Other examples include life emerging from non-living substances, and consciousness emerging from nervous systems.[8] This too can be applied to the emergence of cards in Tarot.

In our study, emergence refers to the larger archetypal entities (such

---

8.   See Joseph Needham, "Integrative levels: a revaluation of the idea of progress", in *Time: The Refreshing River,* Allen and Unwin, London 1943, p. 233-272.

as Interbeing) arising through smaller and simpler archetypal principles on the TNP Matrix (Life Force and Essence in Path 8). We have earlier spoken of the intricacies of snowflakes for their exquisite six-sided symmetry, comparing them to the uniqueness of reading patterns in tarot divination, though here we compare the emergence of snowflakes from fractal patterns to the emergence of 5 new Tarot Keys from established matrix patterns based on the properties of 9. We will include, naturally, their relevance for human consciousness, and suggest some of their socio-cultural implications for our time.

Could larger archetypal entities, therefore, be emerging in the collective consciousness of our time, which may simply be accounted for naturally, that is, in effect, "their time has come," because they have not heretofore had the necessary evolutionary span of development to appear consciously, and be recognized collectively as such? The hypothesis is in keeping with Dion Fortune's observation mentioned with respect to Qabalistic symbols blossoming now in the modern age: "more is to be got out of them today than in the time of the old dispensation because our mental content is richer in ideas." We might add as well, that we are living today with more global consciousness than at anytime previously in human history.

The answer to this thinly-veiled rhetorical question, I believe, is yes! And within the historic canon of Tarot, accordingly, we contend that five larger archetypal entities are now "emerging on pre-existing phenomena" of the lower level archetypes (in stages X and Y). Four of the Arrivals Z, as we discussed in the last chapter, have already been well known and accounted for in Tarot's 600 year history, namely: (19-22) Sun, Judgment, World, and Fool. The remaining five, I believe, have been breaking into collective consciousness perhaps over the past 60 or so years, and are akin to Joseph Campbell's famous "Earth As Seen From Space" conjecture with regard to the emerging myths of our age.

Within Tarot, as inferred by this author via The Counsel of The Oracle, we might say, five original "archetypes of finality" are emerging collectively in our time: by agency, they are Renewal, Flow, Wholeness, Initiation, and Interbeing. I suspect they have been swirling in the planet's *noosphere*[9] for at least the past fifty years, and will not appear unfamiliar or especially exotic when first apprehended today. By their given titles, they are respectively, (22) The Well, (23) The River, (24) The Ring, (25) The Dragon, and (26) The Great Web.[10] But before we say much more about them, let's lay some further groundwork before exploring in detail these extraordinary emergent wisdom teachings.

EARTH AS SEEN FROM INNER SPACE

In the remarkable series of interviews on PBS between Bill Moyers and the distinguished mythologist Joseph Campbell entitled *The Power of Myth,* shown in America in 1988 (a year before Campbell died), and considered among the most popular TV series ever aired on public television,[11] at the close of the long series  of interviews Moyers asks about the emergence of new myths in our time, to which Campbell responds:

> (Campbell): You can't predict what a myth is going to be, any more than you can predict what you're going to dream tonight. Myths and dreams come from the same place; they come from realizations of some kind that have then to find expression in symbolic form. And the myth, the only myth that's going to be worth thinking about in

---

9.   The *noosphere* (/ˈnoʊ.əsfɪər/; sometimes *noösphere*) is the sphere of human thought. The word derives from the Greek νοῦς (nous "mind") and σφαῖρα (sphaira "sphere"), in lexical analogy to "atmosphere" and "biosphere". It was introduced by Pierre Teilhard de Chardin in 1922 in his Cosmogenesis.

10.   It may be noted that titles (e.g. The Well) were chosen for their universal recognition, their timeless, cross-cultural, and multi-layered wealth of mythic antecedents, their non-redundancy with other established arcanum, and their obvious correspondence to the archetypal agencies they were assigned to represent. A full-bodied list of associations and phrases are given for each card in The Lexicon in the Appendix of this book, and *The Travel Guide* that comes with each TNP deck.

11.   Joseph Campbell, *The Power of Myth,* with Bill Moyer, 25th Anniversary Edition, 2013.

the immediate future is one that's talking about the planet, not this city, not these people, but the planet and everybody on it.

(Moyers says): There's that wonderful photograph you have of the Earth seen from space, and it's very small and at the same time, it's very grand.

(Campbell closes with) You don't see any divisions there of nations or states or anything of the kind. This might be the symbol, really, for the new mythology to come. That is the country that we are going to be celebrating, and those are the people that we are one with.

Campbell's vision remains truly inspiring today. But what of Earth as seen from *inner* space? Is there a corresponding internal emergence? An "as without, so within" in the spirit of correspondence? What larger archetypal entities may now be emerging in our time through interactions with smaller or simpler entities, such that they exhibit properties the smaller/simpler entities do not? The answer, if one can be determined, would certainly be highly consequential! It might reasonably serve to guide a conscious course of development advocated by teachers, leaders, theorists, writers, scientists, and consciousness researchers, energize popular "counter-movements" in its wisdom light, and conceivably bestow significant impact on the psychospiritual direction of an entire global culture, whether consciously or unconsciously.

Does it matter? One need look no farther than the ways "Earth as seen from space" has outwardly impacted our collective view. In the Age of Space, according the NASA's Chief Historian, Steven J. Dick, the search for microbial life has been a main driver of space exploration, in particular with regard to Mars, but also now extended to more exotic environments like the Jovian moon Europa. With the search for life on new worlds, planetary protection protocols have been put in place, both for our own planet and others. Contact with intelligent extraterrestrials beyond the solar system remains a more remote possibility, but when and if it happens, well, everything, no doubt, changes dramatically in the history of human evolution.

But the immediate impact of the Space Age is far more diverse than the ultimate discovery of life in space. In *Rocket Dreams: How the Space Age Shaped Our Vision of a World Beyond*, Marina Benjamin argues that space exploration has shaped our worldviews in more ways than one:

> The impact of seeing the Earth from space focused our energies on the home planet in unprecedented ways, dramatically affecting our relationship to the natural world and our appreciation of the greater community of mankind, and prompting a revolution in our understanding of the Earth as a living system.[12]

The Politics of Paradigm Shift

The question, therefore, "Earth as seen from *inner* space?" should equally raise the hands of many serious and dedicated practitioners of guidance and wisdom persuasions, and it would seem an absurd and fruitless task to attempt to ferret out the best candidates from the bunch. Mainstream political, technological, economic, theological, psychological, and medical avenues, in today's climate, would seem to be dead-on-arrival resources for advocacy, funding, and support. They have far too much invested in their own doctrines and beliefs. Asimov's long view of evolutionary change in *The Foundation* reminds us that transformational growth requires many cycles of Time, centuries of it, though, again I am heartened by researcher Evans' speculation that though "such movements will be looked on with disdain by the biomedical Establishment [they] *will gain strength* as the 21st century ends."

But for spiritual individuals, free of the shackles of conventional norms that privilege physical destinations and the "higher order cognitions," the entities that, as Orwell prophesized, are the bearer of "Who controls the past [and thereby] controls the future. [And] Who controls the present controls the past," notwithstanding, still nothing really stands between The Traveler and his cards in becoming a true spiritual individual NOW. For all intents and purposes, individuals in this country at least remain free and unshackled to practice the craft, for now. But by

---

12. Marina Benjamin, *Rocket Dreams: How the Space Age Shaped Our Vision of a World Beyond*, 2004.

what measure then, from a consciousness perspective, free of all sectarian bias that invariably attaches to organizations and governing bodies, could this thankless task of mapping this emergent inner space possibly be determined?

Here again we see something of an advantage with Tarot. For one thing, we can limit our search to an already existent body and map, namely, the 22 Major Arcanum of the Tarot, which provides a centuries-old heritage of transformational wisdom within the universal psyches of the human mind; it rests perfectly (though incompletely) in a magic square upon which new interactions may germinate and multiply. Though, of course, politically, we probably must be content to limit our conclusions within the outer reaches of the canon and its esoteric teachings, and resist generalizations and proclamations beyond it to the larger world, less the source of our realizations itself comes into question, albeit wrongly, and once more Travelers become marginalized by the internecine battles of the controlling establishment, as metaphysical teachings invariably have known before. One must try to be realistic about the world, such that it is, unfortunately, when we hunger for full societal change.

The Tarot remains at the fringes of conventional wisdom, perhaps as it should be, and it is not likely any time soon that it will rise to a more widely-held status. It exists essentially for Travelers, ordinary human beings like you and me, unclear about their true identity and purpose, who suffer impermanence, and the indignities of Time and culture, and are wanting more of their time on Earth than satisfaction of surface needs, who, therefore, elect to undertake a spiritual journey to discover themselves, who they truly are as whole and unique individuals, though in principle, we are all Travelers, are we not? Therefore, we do best to speak of our findings at the "present dispensation" only insofar as The Oracle's Counsel is concerned; the revelations we may wish to trumpet to the world exist only in terms of Tarot's thinking on the matter, we bite our tongues, that is, until conditions are favorable, and leave it at that. This is not to say any limitation should be put upon the revelations and deep development that will come from our efforts. There can be, nevertheless, astonishing power that emanates from humble ponds, and I am reminded of Giles' timely observation:

> Magical philosophy blossoms when old structures of cultural clarity
> start to crumble—much the way flowering vines will insinuate them-
> selves to the cracking walls of an abandoned building.[13]

In recent political matters, it was often said that Barack Obama's international strategy was to "lead from behind," which personally always struck me as a very shrewd way to lead, despite objections from the body politic. Regardless, in matters that concern us here, I believe our task will likely be to lead from below and above. That is, from the wisdom teachings that flow at the depths of our sacred interiors, and soar above to our highest levels of awareness.

Entelechy

From the Late Latin *entelechia,* the Greek *entelecheia,* or *enteles* (complete), and *telos* (end, completion) + *echein* (to have)] comes the word "entelechy," the ancient Greek belief behind what we have previously called the "acorn to oak" principle. I was first exposed to this Aristotelian idea in a brilliant lecture by Dr. Jean Houston at The Parliament of World Religions (Centennial), in Chicago, 1997. It was referenced with respect to theories of the early 20th century French visionary-philosopher and Jesuit priest, Pierre Teilhard de Chardin. This resonated deeply with my own core intuition that the Major Arcana of Tarot was really a cosmographic map that revealed the entelechy of higher consciousness. I went on to develop TNP with this principle in mind, coupled with the related philosophic construct of "finality" as postulated by C.G. Jung.

For Aristotle, entelechy meant the "end within"—the potential of living things to become themselves, e.g., what a seed has that makes it become a plant, that is, its actuality, or realization of its destiny. In Aristotle's use, entelechy is "realization or complete expression of some function; the condition in which a potentiality has become an actuality."[14] It addresses a particular type of motivation, a need for self-determination,

---

13. Cynthia Giles, Tarot: History, Mystery, and Lore; NY: Simon and Shuster, p. 121.
14. *The Oxford English Dictionary,* Oxford University Press, London, 1933.

and an inner strength and vital force directing life and growth to become all one is capable of being.

In TNP, entelechy is perhaps best represented in (Key 8) Strength, an agent of Life Force, or chi energy in the Oriental system. The card's classic motif of the woman taming the lion suggests by subduing his powerful jaws in her hands a firm but decidedly feminine mastery over the instinctive libido, this is true strength. In TNP, a shamanic process is implied in the medicine woman, to channel this vital chi in the service of becoming a healthy and actualized being, energetically similar to kundalini yoga.

Dodal, 1703   **TNP, 2009**

Developmental psychologist Deidre Lovecky who researches gifted individuals, writes:

> Gifted people with entelechy are often attractive to others who feel drawn to their openness and to their dreams and visions. Being near someone with this trait gives others hope and determination to achieve their own self-actualization.[15]

---

15. Deirdre Lovecky, "Warts and Rainbows: Issues in the Psychotherapy of the Gifted," *Advanced Development*, Jan., 1990.

Years after her childhood time with Teilhard de Chardin, psychologist Jean Houston in *The Hero and the Goddess,* wrote:

[We need] to attempt to tap into a symbolic or archetypal expression of the entelechy principle operating in our lives. Entelechy is all about the possibilities encoded in each of us. For example it is the entelechy of an acorn to be an oak tree, of a baby to be a grown-up, of a popcorn kernel to be a fully popped entity, and of you and me to be God only knows what. It is possible to call upon the entelechy principle within us in such a way that it becomes personal, friendly, and even helpful. This entelechy principle can be expressed symbolically as a god or a guide. We feel its presence as the inspiration or motivation that helps us get life moving again after times of stress or stagnation. There are many ways to engage the symbolic forms of the entelechy principle...[16]

In TNP, we have seen The Hermit Effect (+9) account for the entelechy of all Keys on The Matrix. For instance, on Path One, the entelechy within Intention (The Magician) accounts for its fruition in Consciousness (The Sun), as in Path Two, the entelechy within Intuition (The High Priestess) accounts for its fruition in Awakening (Judgement), and so forth. But what of Path Eight that departs with (8) Strength (Life Force) or entelechy itself? The final result in this case is Key 26, The Great Web, Interbeing! (Life Force→Essence→Interbeing). How do we know this? By the meaningful numbers tied to The Hermit Effect (+9). 8/Life Force +9 ≅ 17/Essence +9 ≅ 26 Interbeing. It's right there on the map, just go to Path 8, The Universe. One begins to truly appreciate the treasure trove of wisdom teachings within the amazing deck of possibility.

It might be noted that the liminal phase of each triadic rite of passage (Transfer Y), in the above examples, respectively, Synchronicity, Balance, and Essence, addresses the unconscious developmental agencies at work and necessary for each of the nine "acorns" or seed principles to self-actualize, and "arrive." The Matrix reveals this by "hermitizing" each

16. Jean Houston, *The Hero and the Goddess: The Odyssey as Mystery and Initiation,* 1992, p. 62.

seed principle (X) through the addition of 9, and a second time to the middle phase (Y), before finally "arriving" at its targeted completion. Psychologically, as we have discussed, +9 means embracing a card "in the service of spiritual individuation." Writes Jung:

> I am persuaded that the true end of analysis is attained when the patient has arrived at an adequate knowledge of the methods by which he can maintain contact with his unconscious, and at a psychological understanding broad enough for him to discern, as far as possible and whenever necessary, the direction of his life-line, for without this his conscious mind will not be able to follow the flow of the libido and consciously sustain the individuality he has achieved.[17]

17. From *Philosophical Issues in the Psychology of C.G. Jung*, Marilyn Nagy, p. 212.

CHAPTER 15

Completion

What to the causal view is fact, to the final view is symbol.

—C. G. Jung

In the Jungian perspective, the final view is an expression of the purposive course that psychic energy follows that leads the individual to higher understanding. Finality, we can now see, is interwoven in the related concepts of emergence and entelechy that we have discussed. All are concerned with the prospective function, that is, the future and where we are going. We have narrowed our application to spotlight The Immediate Territory of higher consciousness, as these principles are often met with some resistance in the modern natural and psychological sciences, and we need not go far afield from our study's limits: the imaginal bandwidth of the human psyche that begins in vision-logic. In TNP, finality is related to the principle that guides The Hermit Effect within The Matrix, that is, the purposive course that leads The Traveler to higher understanding, activated by the magical properties of 9.

We have spoken of emergence in terms of larger archetypal entities arising on the backs of smaller and simpler principles, whereby entelechy is the vital force that turns tarot acorns into oaks. The groundwork has been set, therefore, and we are now ready to properly introduce the five missing pieces to our puzzle, that being, the Completed Matrix of the Major Arcana. Let's begin with the first new addition, Key 22, The Well, an agent of Renewal. One now sees it at the Arrival (Z) stage of Path Four, Transformation. The Well sits where formerly The Fool was given residence (at the termnal ending/new beginning spot), but who has now been slid over to the final position of the final path, namely, Path Nine, The Sage. The Well is described in The Lexicon as follows:

> (22) The Well—Replenishment, healing waters of salvation; sublime aspirations; the "silver cord" attaching man to the center; rebirth, nourishment, refueling. "When the well's dry, we know the worth of water" (Ben Franklin). Medicinal rites, baptism, purification, resurrection; related to "the lake" as with fishing—symbolic of drawing out and upwards the numinous contents of the deep; divination, mystic contemplation; (reversed) sterility, the barren, resistance, addiction, disease, ghostly realms, wasteland, death by drowning, purgatory, or else (subjectively) catharsis, "wishing well," meditative cleansing of the mind, resting in healing bliss awareness.

As the archetype of rebirth, (Key 22) The Well signals an emerging future Renaissance, or cultural reawakening, not only in the storied evolution of Tarot itself, but one may imagine, the planet at large. The World card (Key 21) previously carried top honors as the deck's final integration—Spirit in Matter—now with the advent of TNP, The Well fills us with a larger view, and significantly, quite another turn to a possible future. The journey, it presages, continues on in sublime aspirations... for complete fulfillment in spiritual transformation. This again reminds me why I call Tarot "the deck of possibility." It pushes us to imagine beyond our wildest dreams, or as Lévi said, "it informs by making one think."

PATH 4: TRANSFORMATION

IV
The Emperor
DOMINION
⬇ +9

XIII
Death
DISSOLUTION
⬇ +9

XXII
The Well
RENEWAL

Here in Path Four, The Oracle has taken the departure of The Emperor and his Dominion (i.e. dominance, command, structure, and control) in Form and construction, then by the liminal waters of (Key 13) Death, deconstructed and dissolved Form into its opposite, Formlessness or Emptiness, and now beckons us further: we must ready ourselves for a baptismal rebirth ritual into the supernal regions of higher consciousness, all, of course, to the central purpose and master plan of becoming a whole and complete spiritual individual. It's as if The Oracle is saying, "Wait, there's more. The party's not done yet." Refuel yourself in the deepest purifying waters before proceeding on the final stretch of the complete journey. The formula for Path Four/Transformation, simply put, is control→dissolve→renew, or in the Buddhist sense, Form→Emptiness→Rebirth.

What then, one may ask, is waiting when the extended wing of the sacred edifice is now opened? The Answer is revealed next in Path Five, The Path of Peace. Here the emerging Key is called (23) The River, an agent of Flow. In this larger archetypal entity, Earth as seen from *inner* space is like the Tao, or Great Way, continuous, melodic, bliss-filled, flowing, and transcendent. In *The Lexicon* (see Appendix C), The River card is associated with:

(23) The River, an Agent of Flow: The mindstream, "the watercourse way" (Watts), the Tao; journey, passage through change, river of time, the eternal, Michael Jordan's number, impermanence; floating, fluidity, natural flow, going with the flow, downstream, free flow, "being in the zone" when time vanishes; non-attachment, groundlessness; evolution, "Never the same river twice" (Heraclitus), time-travel; all channels, currents, streams (metaphysical); navigation, the riverboat and raft; life, blood, the cradle of civilization, sacred river (Nile, Ganges, Mississippi, Styx etc.); fertility, floods, Oedipus, Buddha, Huck Finn; (Reversed) blockage, flooding, stagnation; or else (subjectively) flow, effortlessness, not making problems out of problems.

In Path Five, the sublime aspirations renewed by The Well evolve into the pellucid sensations of pure peacefulness, the natural flow of being ("in the zone") where time utterly vanishes. We have arrived, therefore, via our Departure in Spirit of (Key 5) The Hierophant and his agent of Spirit, by the province of +9, then transported to the blending synergistic waters of (Key 14) Temperance, and arrived, finally and gracefully, to the sweet intoxicating melodies of Dixieland jazz on the Riverboat of Life. Not bad work if you can get it!

As we navigate these higher realms of imaginal travel it is well to remember that the *Tarot of the Nine Paths* is "foundationless" (void or empty) in terms of religious, philosophical, or theoretical doctrine. And unlike the psychologist's Rorschach inkblots, or animal faces projected by day-dreamers onto random cloud formations, tarot archetypes are not hollow and meaningless from their own sides, but rather universal denizens of the imaginary world, numinous, and irreducible.

The River reminds us that divinations with Tarot are never replicable in their specifics because as you recall, "You cannot step into the same river twice," the pre-Socratic Greek mystic-philosopher Heraclitus of Ephesus observed, adding "for fresh waters are ever flowing in upon you." The rite of passage for The Path of Peace, therefore, is Spirit→Synergy→Flow, where The Hierophant's spiritual "bridge-making" talents have been brought to the subliminal artist's pallet of (Key 14) Temperance, The Middle Path, at the exact midpoint of the New Matrix, where Temperance's blending of water and earth synergizes one's canvas in the service

PATH 5: PEACE

The Hierophant

SPIRIT

⬇ +9

Temperance

SYNERGY

⬇ +9

The River

FLOW

of spiritual individuation, resolving in The River the eternal, harmonic, archetypal riverboat ride of the mind.

One may notice the winding river's tail eventually lifts off the Earthly plane itself and continues into limitless space. This marks the beginning of TNP's "trans-terrestrial" span, where "Earth as seen from inner space" no longer demands gravitational fealty to the home planet. The River extends us freely without end out to the galaxies, as it must, and by The Oracle's Counsel, I suspect, in time we must as well.

We have now but three emerging pathways to consider, and, of course, as promised, a discussion of The Fool's new home as the terminal final in the deck, on Path Nine, The Sage. But first we must revisit Path Six, The Path of Relationships. Tarot readers and therapists alike know well it is upon this path that the majority of inquiries are formulated and set. *"Relationships*—can't live with them, can't live without them..." etc. among the common grumblings they inspire. You may recall earlier in Chapter 9 we discussed why the sixth path brought the most obvious proof of Tarot's current incomplete state, and urgent need for re-tunement. We highlighted the "overbite problem," which I believe most detrimentally affects the unresolved face-off between (6) The Lovers (Union) and (15) The Devil (Separation). The two cards being nearly identical in composition in both Waite and Marseilles versions, show respectively, a naked couple connected by an angel, or a devil, reflecting the bright and dark sides of the relationship archetype. But they are split dualistically, showing only "thesis" (Lover/Union) and "antithesis" (Devil/Separation), with no final synthesis. Accordingly, the relationship archetype is left hanging in The Devil's grip of bondage, addiction, anger, black humor, deception, attachment, and separation, with no resolution in sight.

The Lovers/Devil Dichotomy

We speculated further that this dichotomy was surely evident in the global uptick in divorce, (and probably porn and drug addiction as well), which in present-day America is nearing, by some estimates, a divorce rate of 60 percent, and the future survival of the traditional institution of marriage itself has begun fraying at the seams. A deeper resolution, if it resided somewhere in the sacred canon, would be greatly welcomed. In Key 24, The Ring, an agent of Wholeness, I believe the call has been answered. In the Lexicon, The Ring is associated with:

> Wholeness, conjunction, cosmic union, the round, *coincidentia oppositorum;* the "I/Thou," inclusion, fidelity, eternality; the *ouroburos* (snake biting its own tail) i.e. the Self in totality, the mandala. Also tied to "the remaining link" of the chain; the relationship of the future; light radiated from the ring symbolizes eternal wisdom and transcendental illumination. In Tolkien trilogy, "The One Ring" (aka The Ruling Ring, The Ring of Power) is made of simple gold, but virtually impervious to damage, destroyed only by throwing it into the pit of the volcano; the wearer is partly "shifted" into the spiritual realm. (Reversed) power lust, incompletion, infidelity, or else (subjectively) Circle of Seers, withdrawing projections, nonduality.

Viewing the established progression from Union to Separation, it seemed obvious and perfect that the third of this triadic constellation would be Wholeness. I think the idea of wholeness is a good example of an emerging archetype that has been "swirling around in the noosphere" probably since the 1960s; it is spoken of all the time, particularly in the world of holistic health and psychology, but what does it mean for relationship?

To begin with, Wholeness provides a larger archetypal entity to contain the separating antagonism of (Key 15) The Devil, without invalidating its often necessary, though difficult, role in the service of achieving mature harmony in relationships. In separation, said Otto Rank, we rediscover our aloneness, in union our sense of belonging. Both are essential for becoming a whole individual, and this card represents a higher level of understanding in partnership. Relationships large and spacious enough to contain the natural ebb and flow of these competing human

PATH 6: RELATIONSHIP

The Lovers
UNION
⬇ +9

The Devil
SEPARATION
⬇ +9

The Ring
WHOLENESS

needs are contained in The Ring, a symbol of eternal love, commitment, trust, and wholeness. The principle of Wholeness makes it possible for relationships to achieve a higher level of union without ego-attachment based on fear, insecurity, and possessiveness.

In all three cards of this path, the same male and female imagos are shown, but in different relational postures. In The Lovers card, they sit facing each other in the shared gaze of mutual belonging, though in the crystal ball above the male's shoulder is a more lurid fantasy version of his physical desire. It is of this "intrusion" that The Lovers card is often associated with Choice, whether of spiritual or carnal union. In The Devil card, we see the severed heads (i.e. egos) of The Lovers, symbolizing a stage wherein their shared departure has been cut off and compromised, and transferred liminally into the lap of the Devil's shadow. Outwardly, this phase may manifest in estrangement and discord of many varieties, including infidelity, addiction, depression, acting out, deception, etc. I believe the prevalence of devilish phenomenon is a symptom of the dualistic pressures created in the union/separation polarity. It is suffocated by an "either-or" choice.

But in The Ring, we can see how The Lovers have resolved again in harmony, but at a higher level of connection, the shadow issues have been worked through, and the partnership resolves in a circle of transcendent light. The Edenic symbolism of apple and serpent is meant to underscore a return to the purity and natural intelligence of true Wholeness. But here, The Lovers have successfully weathered the fall of taking of the fruit, worked through this evolutionary stage, and grown organically and more wisely to include a higher synthesis of light and dark. They find their power through the light radiating from the ring, a symbol of eternal wisdom and transcendental illumination.

We may now move on to the seventh path, The Path of The Seeker. It is the path of the hero within us, and true to form, by his own birthdate numerology, *The Hero With A Thousand Faces* author, Campbell himself, was, as you might expect, born onto The Path of The Seeker.[18] There are no accidents, are there? Path 7 is perhaps the rockiest and bravest path one must travel on The TNP Matrix, as would only befit The Seeker. (Note that by countless testimonies of truly brave heroes, we know that though they may seem to act fearlessly, heroes too suffer fear like anyone else, it just doesn't impede their quest).

The hero-seeker, by way of his Chariot, is deigned to pursue that which demands the hardest challenge, and is practiced by the fewest, for this is why, after all, he is a hero. Among my favorite secrets revealed by occult author Lon Milo DuQuette, concerns the real mission bequeathed The Chariot card. According to DuQuette, it is not to be found in the person of the charioteer, nor uncovered in the clever mechanics of his golden carriage, nor even in his furious team of stallions running afront— it is actually the secret cargo the hero is carrying within The Chariot: the sacred Holy Grail cup! The hero-seeker's mission, therefore, is in the deliverance and dissemination to the world of the sacred teachings it contains.

On his great journey, as begets a quest, the hero is first transported to the liminal realms where he finds himself in the throes of war, and under attack, in the Lightning Struck Tower; chaos and upheaval abound, as the old order is now crumbling from within and torn asunder from without. The Ivory Tower is finally collapsing, as Humpty Dumpty

---

18. Joseph Campbell born March 26, 1904 = 3 + 26 +1904 = 1933 (Destiny Year). 1933 = 1 + 9 + 3 + 3 = *16.* 16 = 1 + 6 = *7.* Path 7 (Chariot →Tower→*Dragon*).

PATH 7: THE SEEKER

VII

The Chariot

CHALLENGE

⬇ +9

XVI

The Tower

UPHEAVAL

⬇ +9

XXV

The Dragon

INITIATION

watches passively from the wall where he sits, and therefore, the hero-seeker must be evacuated at once, radically, skillfully, and without equivocation.

At his disposal, as we saw in the Tower's push-plunge of Chapter 7, is only the lightning bolt, a messenger from the gods known well to churn up a slew of internal reactions of heightened necessity. In essence, bolts of lightning ignite the deeper self, as we have discussed, tapping our most primal, basic emotions, and are often used as power symbols in many of the great spiritual traditions.

This is fortuitous, considering the Challenge that remains in store for him, namely, (Key 25) The Dragon, an emerging agent of Initiation! Of all five emergent finals, this one is probably the hardest to explain. And it is here, rather late into the arcanic flow, where I believe the next great initiation must occur. It symbolizes the final gates through which the journey must pass before liberation into The Great Web. An allusion to the three witches of Macbeth stand in the background, there to set an ominous tone that an initiation is immanent, because like all true initiations, it will be exceedingly difficult, if not outright terrifying even for the hero.

I was heartened to hear recently from a student that Campbell himself picked "the dragon" when asked what animal, if he could choose, would he most like to come back as! The Dragon is certainly among the most universal, numinous, magical, and ancient symbols in human history *not* to be found in the Tarot, until now. In The Lexicon, (Key 25) The Dragon is associated with:

XXV THE DRAGON, an Agent of INTIATION (Key 25)

The primordial enemy with whom combat is the supreme test. Things animal, adversarial, instinctive, terrorism, perhaps evil; something terrible to overcome; confronting the collective shadow; the way through all things—He who conquers the dragon is a hero; initiatory tests; slaying the monster; assoc. with plagues, sickness, giants, ogres. Passage through the gates, beyond terrestrial identification and limitation; is strong and vigilant with keen eyesight, used to guard temples and treasures, as emblems of imperial power. "Come not between the dragon and his wrath" (Shakespeare). (Reversed) inner demons, wrathful deities, bullies, disease, or else (subjectively) direct encounter with Man's deepest shadow fears, tantric initiations, secret societies of the future.

The hero's mission, therefore, at this final stage, after liberating himself from the war and chaos on the ground of The Tower, is nothing short of passing through the terminal gates of archetypal evil, that is, the non-personal darkness we must all encounter at the highest levels, and bravely push through before attaining final liberation. This, indeed, is the primordial enemy with whom combat is the supreme test. Found in children's fairytales around the world, The Dragon in TNP represents the final and most fierce obstacle that stands in the way of The Fool's Journey. It is the collective shadow of humanity in multitudinous forms, and ultimately must be encountered directly and vanquished, before liberation is attained.

In science fiction, The Dragon corresponds to the alien force who challenges our terrestrial identifications with the home planet we have only known, and pits us in the frightening mirror of who, ultimately, and *what*, we really are? In this alien and uprooted context of Path 7, The Traveler's koan carries a kind of gravitation-less gravity, if you will, I imagine it to be not unlike spacewalking high above the Earth and gazing far out, into the cold, unfathomable, endless galaxies while moored semi-securely to your space capsule. It is perhaps the shadow side of open space. But as we are speaking primarily of inner space, the parallel is accompanied not with myriads of stars sparkling in the firmament, but rather a myriad of fantastic beasts, sirens of the night, ancestral beings from the past, goetic demons, idle sorceries, and the like, laden in the collective shadow of humanity, that would otherwise drive us back from the iron will of our quest. The hero, therefore, must summon profound courage at this stage, and untested, bravery sufficient to pass through The Dragon's doors, and arrive triumphantly to the other side. If you thought Tarot was all fun and games to this point, well, here you may be roundly disabused of any such fancy.

The final emergence, which we have previously alluded to, is The Great Web on Path Eight, The Path of The Universe. In *The Lexicon,* (Appendix C, Key 26) is associated with:

XXVI THE GREAT WEB, an Agent of INTERBEING (Key 26)

Interwoven nature of all existence, the law of resonance, "an inescapable network of mutuality" (Martin Luther King), deep ecology, the world-wide-web, the veil, the Gateless Gate, superstrings, interdependency, "interbeing" (Thich Nhat Hanh); Buddhist doctrine of "mutual co-arising" (dependent origination)—"all things co-arise"; "engi" (Japanese) arising in relation; linkage, correspondence, "nothing is isolated inside its own existence and everything is linked by a system of correspondences and assimilations" (Eliade). Related to Hindu 'maya', the weaver of appearances and the cosmic web of illusion (of separate existences); fabric of space-time, the drum, spiders, also "Indra's Net "the vast net extending throughout space where at each crossing point a radiant jewel reflects all others ad infinitum." (Reversed) disconnect, enmeshment, a snare, isolation, or else (subjectively) compassion for all beings, cosmic sympathy, citizenship of worlds.

In *Acorns to Oak* we referenced The Great Web to be the final destination of Life Force or chi, the entelechy of the biggest picture of all, that is, the universe itself! We noted that Path Eight departs with (8) Strength (Life Force), and resolves gloriously in the final (Z) emergence,

PATH 8: THE UNIVERSE

The Great Web, Interbeing! But we have yet to fully examine the intervening liminal Transfer (Y) that makes this all possible, namely (Key 17) The Star, an agent of Essence.

In TNP, Strength's vital life force, when hermitized by the addition of 9, is transported to a liminal transmission process underway, an exchange between The Traveler and the Tibetan Buddhist Goddess deity, Tara, though any goddess of infinite love and wisdom will do. In Sanskrit, Tara means star. Tara (the Liberator) is a Buddha who represents all enlightened beings' skillful activities, or the means by which they communicate with and guide us according to our ability. The ordained Tibetan Buddhist nun Kathleen McDonald tells us "contemplating Tara brings quick results in whatever we want and need. Known as the Mother of all Buddhas, she is our mother too, because she awakens and helps fulfill the potential to attain enlightenment."[19]

In The Star's transmission with this goddess deity, The Traveler visualizes rays of light with nectar running down them like raindrops running down a wire; the rays and nectar flow continuously, reaching you, and all the beings surrounding you, purifying your hindrances on the spiritual path and the obscurations to liberation and enlightenment. This is the essential level of starlight, where the formula "As above, so below" is most active. In its realization, we fully experience our own existence interlinked with everything in the universe through correspondences

---

19. Kathleen McDonald, *How to Meditate: A Practical Guide*, p. 118.

and assimilations. The formula, therefore, presents a direct passage through the fabric of spacetime to compassion for all beings, cosmic sympathy, and at the imaginal level, at least, an experiential elevation or promotion, we might say, from our solely terrestrial identifications, to a sense of holding citizenship of all worlds. This is the Tarot's cosmic destiny realized in the actualization of The Great Web.

Final Travel Concerns

As we approach the completion of the re-tuning, and as well, our study as a whole, there remain several last matters to attend. We have given no conclusive answers to our questions of "Who are we really?" and "Where are we really going?" Additionally, we have not clearly arrived at an answer with respect to the so-called "future," from a Tarot perspective, which in the short remaining time I intend to address. But first, let's examine what on Earth has become of The Fool, Key Zero, and His alpha and omega status of the Tarot itself. Because of what I have playfully termed "the overbite problem," *Tarot of the Nine Paths* was conceived and developed in such a way that a careful re-tuning of the Major Arcana could take place, without damage to the well-established architecture of the sacred edifice. In the process, The Fool has been moved to the very final position of the third row in the expanded matrix, in what has been called Path Nine: The Path of The Sage. Let's examine the metaphysical implications of this not insignificant move.

In *The Lexicon that follows*, it says this about Key 0:

0 THE FOOL, an Agent of POSSIBILITY (Key 0)

"Spirit in search of experience," total potentiality, possibility, open field, open space; undifferentiated spirit; everything that can be, Journey of The Keys, freedom to make mistakes (without karmic consequence); beginner's mind; crazy wisdom; the divine child, the puer aeternus. Without guile, innocence, wonder, the bumpkin, Parsifal; distinguished from the others because it's unnumbered (the zero); outside movement, becoming, or change; eccentric, a clown, the master/fool, unconscious/supraconscious, alpha and omega; (reversed) foolishness, menace, imbecile, imposter, humiliation, stupidity, or else (subjectively) emptiness (shunyata), No-mind (Zen), final liberation, crazy wisdom, the unconditioned mind.

Most telling about The Fool's new dispensation are the smaller archetypal entities from which it now emerges, namely (Key 9) The Hermit, an agent of Wisdom, and (Key 18) The Moon, an agent of Imagination. No longer the aftermath of The Emperor and Death, The Fool now is set in motion by the much discussed initial Wisdom of The Hermit himself, which now, quite interestingly, is transported by the addition of 9, to The Moon! The Mother of the Unconscious, and matrix of the human mind, Luna, has become the new liminal transfer station that hereby brings Wisdom to Possibility, Hermit to Fool. As Campbell believed, all the mythologies of the world since time immemorial can be reduced to but two, over-riding cardinal symbols, namely, The Sun and The Moon. Is there not, therefore, a kind of unblemished elegance to discover at the base of The Fool now resides the agencies of Wisdom and Imagination!

For me, the beauty of this transposition is that Imagination and, in effect, the imaginal realm itself, become the archetypal entities that now nourish and animate The Fool's Journey of Possibility. The re-tuning allows and indeed encourages far greater spaciousness and creativity in our travels. The Traveler is thereby given full permission to develop his imaginal faculties

PATH 9: THE SAGE

from the deepest depths of The Moon, which as we have discussed, is the mother of intuition, imagination, visualization, felt-senses, psychic impressions, music and artistic productions, romantic relationships, and more, all in the service of becoming a whole spiritual individual. I believe the re-tuning has now achieved its original mandate throughout, and The Matrix is complete.

The Future Is A Paradox

The nature of the future is a central question of our study. From The Oracle's perspective it seems the future is Now, open, and unlimited, albeit, metaphysically-speaking. This means it is a story within an illusion, a kind of timeless seeing process directed to the imaginal future. As an example, let's revisit "time travel" into the future, for years a great fascination for many at the vanguard of theoretical physics and, of course, science fiction. In the thought experiment of traveling at the speed of light, if one were to actually do this, it is generally understood today that one would not really be traveling into "the future" per say, but rather accelerating time as judged by the Earth's external time, such that the traveler would have experienced less passage of time than his twin who remained on Earth. But, as was pointed out, this is not real time travel, but more in the nature of "fast-forwarding" through time, a one-way journey forwards with no way back.

But The Traveler at Terminal 9 is not concerned with the future of outer time travel, or particularly, outer space travel. He seeks not deeper expanses of the natural universe, but deeper entry into subtler levels of consciousness in inner space. And as we have also seen, unlike conventional time and space travel that privileges causality, linearity, physical destinations, and "higher-cognitive faculties," the future to the Tarot Traveler is acausal, synchronistic, nonlinear, nonrational, and momentary; it is like a rainbow, at once exquisite, serene, colorful, seen by multiple observers, magical, and supra-mundane, but also delicate, short-lived, and mysterious. We should remember too that it is always shifting, changing, and impermanent, as fresh waters are ever flowing in upon him. Impermanence, as taught The Buddha, is inevitable even for The Traveler.

But with respect to the much coveted "Now" experience, Tarot seems to run against what the wise "future naysayers" of Eastern awareness would tell us, namely, that the future is a moot point, irrelevant, and nothing more than a thought-construction, for this key reason: Tarot is metaphysical, and carries special freedoms and assimilations that conventional reality does not, not unlike its more random, elusive, and unconscious counterpart, dreams.

The Tarot of the Future is, in fact, an imaginary destination, and therefore, it both fundamentally exists and, paradoxically, does not exist, like all non-things. Typically, nondual inquiries in Eastern teachings like Zen, Dzogchen, and the Madhyamika schools of Buddhism, which ply their methodology in the attempt to deconstruct words by "thinning out" or dissolving thought-constructions embedded in language (i.e. higher order cognitions) in order to enable clear (direct) seeing, or insight. What was conventionally called "meaning" based on logic, physics, common sense, and reason, thereby dissolves into nothingness, openness (or emptiness). That is their purported goal.

But here in the metaphysical ethers of non-things and the very question of meaning, including that of "the future," becomes uniquely paradoxical. Much as it says in the ancient Mahayana text, The Lankavatara Sutra: "Reality is not as it seems. Nor is it different." In Tarot, imagery and the eye are the primary mediums of the cartomantic art, yet light-touch seeing through vision-logic replaces formal thinking in rational logic. Conventional meanings, immediately, are deconstructed by translation into an image-language like that of dreams, a kind of visual mythopoesis occurs, and no longer is one given to think hard about meanings with his cognitive faculties, so much as seeing, living, and feeling them directly, through the imagery, synchronicity, and intuitions that are activated. The gradual shift of emphasis from "thinking" to "seeing" in higher levels of consciousness development becomes its modus operandi. Non-things become that which is so of itself at first apprehension, and pictures become worth a thousand words. As Watts observes: "The ear cannot detect as many variables at the same time as the eye, for sound is a slower vibration than light."

On one level, therefore, a reading is totally meaningless, no more than random projections onto vacant forms like an inkblot test; on another it is richly meaningful and relevant in deep, life-affirming, and self-affirming ways, with the kind of meaning one can directly see, live, and feel, that resonates within the soul, warms the heart, and brings with it an inaudible vibratory click (even if we cannot fully understand it by our rational thinking). Therefore, the future is a paradox in The Immediate Territory, both meaningful and meaningless simultaneously, something that does and does not exist at the same time. Travelers awake!

All the World's a Journey

We have been tripping over two existential questions throughout, neither of which have I answered clearly. The first one, as to who or *what*, we really are? My guess is no better than yours. That is why I am a traveler. The best answer for me at the moment that brings satisfaction in view of our study is that, in essence, we are storytellers, and the tales we tell are about our travels. We construct reality by way of narratives, and this includes what in science is called "objective reality," in religion "God," in philosophy "Truth," in business "Success," in the arts "Beauty," in psychology "Sanity," and so forth.

Purveyors who claim expertise are those who attempt to find proofs of their beliefs and perceptions through their own set of narratives, i.e. stories. And this is the world we outwardly inhabit. But there is one fact that everyone has in common, we are all travelers, and where we choose to go will be a function of the stories we tell ourselves and listen to the most. The great problem we encounter regularly is that we have forgotten we are but storytellers and, much as Shakespeare famously wrote in *As You Like It*, "All the world's a stage, and all the men and women merely players..." I would paraphrase: "All the world's a journey, and all the men and women merely travelers!" It remains so, even at the sharpest edges of the worlds we inhabit, war, climate change, disease, politics, loneliness, loss etc., these too are stories, nothing more, nothing less.

This realization, for The Traveler, is a great comfort. It gives encouragement and motivation to enter places where the stories he encounters will provide the most benefit and growth for himself, and the characters who populate his world. Experience has shown him that the stories about the future he lives *into* by his conditioning and habit have not satisfied, elevated his consciousness, or advanced his personhood as a whole individual. Those outcomes too often have become predictable, superficial, cynical, and limiting, and inevitably, they too will be ravished by the forces of impermanence.

Some travelers who have read this book will take the risk, suspend disbelief, and choose to enter Terminal 9, periodically! There can be no harm in trying it. You will at times have no idea where you're going but, beyond your physical destinations and rational thinking, you can be no worse off than where you are. At Terminal 9, not knowing is never a problem. To the contrary, it is the proper way to begin your journey. All that is required is your sincerity, curiosity, and open-mindedness, and that you leave your baggage behind. It will be waiting for you when you return.

The Terminal is open, and you are welcome to enter.

Appendices

Appendix A

TERMINAL 9

THE FOUR ELEMENTS

Quaternity

I – Intuition   S – Sensation
T – Thinking   F – Feeling

DOMESTIC USE GTE 28 →

↓ X	Gate 1-9 Departures
↓ Y	Gate 10-18 Transfer
↓ Z	Gate 19-0 Arrivals
⊘ Ego	NO ENTRY Baggage

+9

The Traveler

INDIVIDUATION

E N T E R

←

The 9 PATHWAYS: **TNP MATRIX**

X	1	2	3	4	5	6	7	8	9
Y	10	11	12	13	14	15	16	17	18
Z	19	20	21	22	23	24	25	26	0

DEPARTURES X
1 The Magician/Intention
2 The Priestess/Intuition
3 The Empress/Passion
4 The Emperor/Dominion
5 The Hierophant/Spirit
6 The Lovers/Union
7 The Chariot/Challenge
8 Strength/Life Force
9 The Hermit/Wisdom

TRANSFERS Y
10 Wheel of Fortune/Synchronicity
11 Justice/Balance
12 The Hanged Man/Surrender
13 Death/Dissolution
14 Temperance/Synergy
15 The Devil/Separation
16 The Tower/Upheaval
17 The Star/Essence
18 The Moon/Imagination

ARRIVALS Z
19 The Sun/Consciousness
20 Judgement/Awakening
21 The World/Integration
22 The Well/Renewal
23 The River/Flow
24 The Ring/Wholeness
25 The Dragon/Initiation
26 The Great Web/Interbeing
0 The Fool/Possibility

Appendix B

TNP'S HIGHER LOGIC

"We study the self to forget the self in order to know all things," taught the Buddhist monk Dogen, 12th century founder of Zen. A similar mandate and paradox is at the heart of *The Nine Paths.*

Correspondences are never accidental in The Higher Keys but interwoven into the universal fabric by its original designers. From timeless laws, critical *rites of passage* are revealed for travelers of mind and spirit concerning humanity's higher destiny, challenges, and the completion of consciousness, according to this sacred corpus.

Oracle wisdom captures *snapshots of experience* by translating problems into "image-narratives" like in dreams; fresh possibilities arise and unconscious forces shaping each moment and circumstance are made transparent to the observer.

Read or contemplate these symbols **without pressure to obtain** something beyond the experience itself. Synchronicities and paradoxes will naturally occur in this heightened mind-state but should not be misconstrued as "ways around" difficulty so much as windows opening to a deeper reality.

TNP QUICKSHEET

DEPARTURES
1. THE MAGICIAN/Intention
2. THE HIGH PRIESTESS/Intuition
3. THE EMPRESS/Passion
4. THE EMPEROR/Dominion
5. THE HIEROPHANT/Spirit
6. THE LOVERS/Union
7. THE CHARIOT/Challenge
8. STRENGTH/Life Force
9. THE HERMIT/Wisdom

TRANSFERS
10. WHEEL OF FORTUNE/Synchronicity
11. JUSTICE/Balance
12. THE HANGED MAN/Surrender
13. DEATH/Dissolution
14. TEMPERANCE/Synergy
15. THE DEVIL/Separation
16.. THE TOWER/Upheaval
17. THE STAR/Essence
18. THE MOON/Imagination

ARRIVALS
19 THE SUN/Consciousness
20. JUDGEMENT/Awakening
21. THE WORLD/Integration
22 THE WELL/Renewal
23. THE RIVER/Flow
24. THE RING/Wholeness
25. THE DRAGON/Initiation
26. THE GREAT WEB/Interbeing
27. THE FOOL/Possibility

OFF GRID
28. THE FOUR ELEMENTS/Quaterni
+9 THE TRAVELER/Individuation

Appendix C

The TNP LEXICON

From Rosengarten's *Tarot of the Nine Paths: Advanced Tarot for the Spiritual Traveler,* 2009.

DEPARTURES (X)

I THE MAGICIAN, an Agent of INTENTION (Key 1)

Magician in the lab of life, the transformer (darkness to light, difficulty to ease, chaos to form, the ideal to the real, etc.); skillful means, ingenuity, "focused intent," aim, mastery, the will; associated with Thoth, Hermes, Mercury; quickness of mind, stealth, changeability; clever and resourceful mind, artistic, creative and pragmatic; **(Reversed)** manipulation, cunning, black magic, "mantic warfare," sleight of hand; magical (infantile) thinking, powerlessness, impotence, or else (subjectively) inner magic, mantras, spells, active meditation, psychic abilities, creative vision, remote viewing, etc.[1]

II THE HIGH PRIESTESS, an Agent of INTUITION (Key 2)

Goddess of the psyche; knower of the subtle and the hidden; occult knowledge, hidden reality, the "records"; perceives through psychic impressions and hunches, a trusted keeper of secrets, feline, a witch and wise woman; deep intuition and memory; "female intuition"; non-rational thought, innate wisdom, natural intelligence; she equalizes the opposites; **(Reversed)** blocked psychic channels, espionage, betrayal, revealed secrets,false memory, or else (subjectively) clairvoyance, subtle bodies, inner truths.

---

1. By "subjectively," the reversal's meaning is not negative so much as it privileges the inner or interior dimension of the card, like "inner tennis."

III THE EMPRESS, an Agent of PASSION (Key 3)

Nature and nurture, the feminine spiritual principle (the anima); natural beauty, affection, exuberance, sweetness, sex appeal; passion, compelling enthusiasm, love, and dersire; creativity; healing and sympathy, supporting life, the Earth Goddess; mother, mater, matter, the material; fertility, the body, the womb, sensuality; basic trust, universal love and compassion; associated with Venus (Aphrodite), Demeter; (Reversed) smothering, infertility, lifelessness, the pampered damsel, the "animus ridden" woman (Jung); or else (subjectively) sensory awareness, pregnancy, incubation, self-nurturance, self-healing.

IV THE EMPEROR, an Agent of DOMINION (Key 4)

The leader, captain, father, master and commander, the CEO; leadership, power, responsibility, and authority; the animus figure or "golden man within"; "Individuals have dominion over the property that is their bodies," wrote John Locke (1690), "and by extension, they own what their minds and hands produce and have the liberty to do with it as they please." Authority, law, power, severity; Freud; Captain Kirk, magnificence, a benign king; the masculine principle: logos, structure, order, organization, quaternary; the temporal, status quo, establishment, four-square reality; associated with Aries, ruled by Mars; (Reversed) imperious, controlling, "mind control," disorganization, ineffectiveness, shadow government, or else (subjectively) inner law, infrastructure, the dharma.

V THE HIEROPHANT, an Agent of SPIRIT (Key 5)

The teacher and the teachings, spirit in worldly realms, community, human complexity, ethics, values, spiritual needs; bridge-maker, peace-maker, guru, psychologist, spiritual authority; the capacity "to walk the mystical path with practical feet" (Arrien); Dumbledore to Dalai Lama; somewhat cloistered, institutional, dependent upon flock or following; (Reversed) pontifical, dogmatic, overbearing, self-righteous, predatory, corrupt, critical superego, or else (subjectively) inner guide, conscience, personal code of ethics.

VI THE LOVERS, an Agent of UNION (Key 6)

The art of relationship; harmony, chemistry, romance, desire, attraction of opposites; two as one, communication, union, partnership; intimacy and otherness, the heart-to heart, the anima/animus (Jungian); soulmates, Tristan and Iseult, Romeo and Juliet, Tony and Maria, hormones and fantasies; choice between passion v. compassion, cherishing v. self-cherishing, virtue v. vice, integrity v. temptation; "love is a choice, not a feeling" (The Road Less Traveled); **(Reversed)** love-sickness, uncertainty, betrayal, hate, narcissism, apathy, secret attraction, affairs, merging, fusion, sex-and-love addiction, self-pleasuring; or else (subjectively) the *soror mystica* (mystic union), Platonic love, yin and yang.

VII THE CHARIOT, an Agent of CHALLENGE (Key 7)

Taking charge, action, challenge; the quest; the hero; enlistment, victory over obstacles; Hercules, Joan of Arc, Gilgamesh, Batman, Florence Nightingale, Jesus, Achiles, Mickey Mantle, Gandhi, John Lennon, Patton etc.; master of Language and communication; the grail; political power; speaks to masses, great expanse; triumphal nature; **(Reversed)** Ruthlessness and aggression; stalled at the gate, cowardice; or else (subjectively) inner quest.

VIII STRENGTH, an Agent of LIFE FORCE (Key 8)

Strength of character, natural confidence, basic trust; vitality, libido, chi, shakti (creative power), the life force; the regenerative power of the feminine, taming the beast, beauty and the beast; the triumph of intelligence over brutality, Leo vanquished by Virgo. Kindness, the "charm offensive," soft muscle, aggression subdued by diplomacy ("We confide in our strength without boasting of it; we respect that of others, without fearing it," Thomas Jefferson); incorporation of one's "instinctive" side, sympathetic magic, homeopathy, akaido, fortitude, endurance, regeneration, courage to take risks; overcoming obstacles; **(Reversed)** psychic weakness, fear of the unknown, machismo, illness, bullying, cowardice, or else (subjectively) inner strength, natural intelligence, yogic bliss.

IX THE HERMIT, an Agent of WISDOM (Key 9)

The Wise Guide, wisdom and tenacity in pursuit of true self, "individuation"—the process by which a person becomes a psychological "individual" (Jung), or "self realization." Fiercely independent and self-directed; Dylanesque, a master of the invisible; cares little for outside approval, Holden Caufield, values aloneness, ndependence; He seeks his own salvation with diligence' (as the Buddha advised for us all). His motto: To Become One Of Clarity and Light Within the Fabric of Universal Spirit As Revealed in Immediate Experience (i.e. the symbolism of Lamp, Mantle, Staff); life purpose; introspection, the maverick; (**Reversed**) isolation, cold, paranoia, antisocial, or else (subjectively) ascetic monk, arhat, creative artist, mystic.

TRANSFERS (Y)

X THE WHEEL OF FORTUNE, an Agent of SYNCHRONICITY (Key 10)

The secret of timing, the master of change; knowing correctly when to move, when to stand pat; "synchronicity" or "acausal connection through meaning" (Jung); life's roulette wheel; coincidence, simultaneity, nonlinear time; associated with destiny, serendipity; karma (the law of cause and effect) and the (Buddhist) Wheel of Life; the laws of change, cycles, seasons, rotation, and all circular patterns; occult powers (siddhis), the unexpected, the educated guess, the gamble; opportunities; (**Reversed**) stagnation, grasping, "spin," going in circles, repetition compulsion, addictive disorders, or else (subjectively) inner certainty, rhythm, prescience.

XI JUSTICE, an Agent of Balance (Key 11)

"Poetic justice, just deserts"; balance, fairness, alignment, adjustment; harmony, equilibrium, equanimity, equality; discriminating mind, restoration, truth, clear seeing; karmic fruition, "what goes around, comes around," (divine) retribution, sin and punishment; the object of law, the sword of discrimination (Prajna), the scales and seeds of Justice, the dream and foundation of democracy; courts of law, accountability, proportionality; **(Reversed)** one-sidedness, imbalance, corruption, criminality, bias, prejudice; or else (subjectively) inner balance, grace, compensation, flexibility.

XII THE HANGED MAN, an Agent of SURRENDER (Key 12)

"Turning it over to a higher power," Letting go, non-attachment, surrendering (the struggle); related to Buddhist mindfulness, dis-identification, detachment, awareness; to be "in the world but not of it (Jesus)"; "witness consciousness," immunity from ordinary influences; levitation, magical powers; self-sacrifice, Odin (Norse), descent, central pillar on the Tree of Life (Qabalah); reversal, turning the world on its head, "stop the world I want to get off"; thinking out of the box; **(Reversed)** aloofness, self-obsession, dissociation, holding on, compulsivity, or else (subjectively) self-observation, mystical vision, creative ambiguity.

XIII DEATH, an Agent of DISSOLUTION (Key 13)

Loss, dissolution, death, and ego death; the end of an epoch; loss of control, fear of finality; like Shiva, Death transforms beings by destroying their form without annihilating their essence; dematerialization, the inevitability of decay, dissolution, and release; "melancholy decomposition" (Cirlot), Thanatos, "the daughter of night and the sister of sleep"(Greek mythology). Transformation, death/rebirth; reincarnation, the void, extinction, end of the line; **(Reversed)** lethargy, fear of extinction, petrifaction, sleep, or else (subjectively) grief, sorrow, liberation; dissolving into nothing, doing nothing until it is obvious.

XIV TEMPERANCE, an Agent of SYNERGY (Key 14)

The Middle Path: tempering the fires, reconciliation, the blending of opposites; patience ("the highest enlightenment" Ven. Rina Sircar), straddling, Obama, one foot on land, one foot on water; bridging, centering, synergy, synthesis; the wisdom of water, the Lady of the Lake (Arthurian), water colors, water falls, etc.; "the ceaseless circulation through formation, regeneration, and purification"(Cirlot); pacing, matching energy, the "both/and," not this, not that ("neti neti") paradox central; **(Reversed)** intemperance, impatience, impulsivity, or else (subjectively) incubation, the inner craft, alchemy, Madhyamaka (Nagarjuna).

XV THE DEVIL, an Agent of SEPARATION (Key 15)

Falsity, illusion, bondage, duality, deception; the Jungian shadow (projection), The Three Poisons—hatred-greed-delusion; the devil's advocate, the scapegoat; black humor, sensuality, mirth, "creative energy in its most material form...the masculine of masculine" (Crowley); associated with Pan (naturally repugnant, hypersexual, transcends all limitations), basic forces, raw instinct, Baphomet, Satan, Voldemort; **(Reversed)** shadow projection, repressed rage, evil, anti-Christ, or else (subjectively) recovery from addiction, shadow awareness, withdrawal of projection, black humor, courting the senses (Tantra).

XVI THE TOWER, an Agent of UPHEAVAL (Key 16)

Radical immediate change; instability, turmoil, shock, destruction/ deconstruction; sudden awakening (satori), danger, upheaval; attack from outside, 9/11, or decay from within. Unequivocal need to shift position, "abandon ship," react, evacuate, run for cover, reorganize; the "ivory tower," one's positionality, territory (ego-sphere) no longer tenable; corruption, cancer, terrorism etc., necessitating a "forced" restructuring of laser intensity; lightening rod; **(Reversed)** shake-up of core values, hitting bottom, shell shock, nervous breakdown, self-imprisonment, or else (subjectively) radical transformative breakthrough, deconstructing fixations, intentional re-direction.

XVII THE STAR, an Agent of ESSENCE (Key 17)

Essential, elemental being; energy, transmitted light, sparkle, radiance, vibration; the cosmos, Nuit (Egyptian), cosmic consciousness, the extraterrestrial; "the soul uniting spirit with matter"(Oswald Wirth); hope for higher, brighter things, 'as above so below', higher intelligence above reflecting off the waters below (human emotion); enlightenment, invoking the compassion of Green Tara (Mother of All The Buddhas), Her mantra [pronounced om-ta-ray-too-ta-ray-too-ray so-hah] opens hearts to this transmission. Guru yoga; emergence, rising star, stardom, celebrity; beacon, guiding light; (Reversed) dullness, stage fright, hubris, darkness, exhibitionism, abduction, or else (subjectively) Guardian Angel, inner light, higher Self, divinity.

XVIII THE MOON, an Agent of IMAGINATION (Key 18)

The non-rational, psyche or soul; the unconscious (personal and collective); instinctive and magnetic, id, night-time and moonlight, the dream world, goblins and witches, fantasy, romance, "by the light of the silvery moon," menstrual cycles, fluctuation, emotional lability; shows "the strengths and the dangers of the world of appearances and imagination"(Cirlot); the imaginal world, magic, howling at the moon, mystery, reflection, the tides, irritability, moodiness, introversion; (Reversed) 'lunacy' chaos, madness, emotionality, or (subjectively) the muse, seat of the archetypes, the creative process.

ARRIVALS (Z)

XIX THE SUN, an Agent of CONSCIOUSNESS (Key 19)

Conscious awareness, universal energy, the active principle, warmth and light; the direct son and heir of the god of heaven (Surya, Apollo, Helios, Ra, Jesus, Allah); creative and guiding; rational and visible reality, daylight; the yang, power, the masculine; rising and setting, constancy, return, resurrection; turbines, teamwork, activity, energy, fuel, productivity; vital to life; health, vibrancy, growth, play, healing; the center, the ego; (Reversed) egotism, burnout, hyper-rationality, illness, or else (subjectively) fire yoga (agni), the supra-conscious.

XX JUDGEMENT, An Agent of Awakening (Key 20)

The Call (To Awakening); owning one's truth, self-proclamation, the defining moment, stand and deliver; rising up, salvation, conscious responsibility, coming to completion; regeneration, illumination, actualization, deep discrimination; unmasking, revelation, rebirth, resurrection, sounding your horn, drum rolls, outcome and resolution; (**Reversed**) judgmental, self-criticism, comparative mind, condemnation, or else (subjectively) inner certainty, critical thinking, self-acceptance, self-accreditation.

XXI THE WORLD, an agent of INTEGRATION (Key 21)

Dance of life, spirit manifest in worldly existence, one world, the kingdom, elemental harmony, the act of creation, ecstasy, completion, integration, perfection; squaring the circle, the Self, the soul of the world (anima mundi). Shiva Nataraja, (King of the Cosmic Dance) symbolizing the union of space and time within evolution. Associated with the zodiac, the entire tarot pack, the Great Mandala. (**Reversed**) fragmentation, decompensation, hallucinatory voices, or else (subjectively) the inner world, sub-personalities, the collective unconscious, other-worldiness, Earth as seen from inner space.

XXII THE WELL, an Agent of RENEWAL (Key 22)

Replenishment, healing waters of salvation; sublime aspirations; the 'silver cord' attaching man to the center; rebirth, nourishment, refueling. "When the well's dry, we know the worth of water" (Ben Franklin). Medicinal rites, baptism, purification, resurrection; related to 'the lake' as with fishing--symbolic of drawing out and upwards the numinous contents of the deeps; divination, mystic contemplation; (**Reversed**) sterility, the barren, resistance, addiction, disease, ghostly realms, wasteland, death by drowning, purgatory, or else (subjectively) catharsis, "wishing well," meditative cleansing of the mind, resting in healing bliss awareness.

XXIII THE RIVER, an Agent of FLOW (Key 23)

The mindstream, "the watercourse way" (Watts), the Tao; journey, passage through change, river of time, the eternal, Michael Jordan, impermanence; floating, fluidity, natural flow, going with the flow, downstream, free flow, "being in the zone" when time vanishes; non-attachment, groundlessness; evolution, "Never the same river twice" (Heraclitus), time-travel; all channels, currents, streams (metaphysical); navigation, the riverboat and raft; life, blood, the cradle of civilization, sacred river (Nile, Ganges, Mississippi, Styx etc.); fertility, floods, Oedipus, Buddha, Huck Finn; **(Reversed)** blockage, flooding, stagnation; or else (subjectively) flow, effortlessness, not making problems out of problems.

XIX THE RING, an Agent of WHOLENESS (Key 24)

"Wholeness, conjunction, cosmic union, the round, 'coincidentia oppositorum'; the "I/Thou," inclusion, fidelity, eternality; the 'ouroburos' (snake biting its own tail) i.e. the Self in totality, the mandala. Also tied to "the remaining link" of the chain; the relationship of the future; light radiated from the ring symbolizes eternal wisdom and transcendental illumination. In Tolkien trilogy, "The One Ring" (aka The Ruling Ring, The Ring of Power) is made of simple gold, but virtually impervious to damage, destroyed only by throwing it into the pit of the volcano; the wearer is partly "shifted" into the spiritual realm. **(Reversed)** power lust, incompletion, infidelity, or else (subjectively) Circle of Seers, withdrawing projections, nonduality.

XXV THE DRAGON, an Agent of INTIATION (Key 25)

The primordial enemy with whom combat is the supreme test. Things animal, adversarial, instinctive, terrorism, perhaps evil; something terrible to overcome; confronting the collective shadow; the way through all things--He who conquers the dragon is a hero; initiatory tests; slaying the monster; assoc. with plagues, sickness, giants, ogres. Passage through the gates, beyond terrestrial identification and limitation; is strong and vigilant with keen eyesight, used to guard temples and treasures, as emblems of imperial power. "Come not between the dragon and his wrath"(Shakespeare). **(Reversed)** inner demons, wrathful deities, bullies, disease, or else (subjectively) direct encounter with Man's deepest shadow fears, tantric initiations, secret societies of the future.

XXVI THE GREAT WEB, an Agent of INTERBEING (Key 26)

Interwoven nature of all existence, the law of resonance, "an inescapable network of mutuality"(Martin Luther King), deep ecology, the world-wide-web, the veil, the Gateless Gate, superstrings, interdependency, "interbeing" (Thich Nhat Hanh); Buddhist doctrine of "mutual co-arising" (dependent origination)—"all things co-arise"; "engi" (Japanese) arising in relation; linkage, correspondence, "nothing is isolated inside its own existence and everything is linked by a system of correspondences and assimilations" (Eliade). Related to Hindu 'maya', the weaver of appearances and the cosmic web of illusion (of separate existences); fabric of space-time, the drum, spiders, also Indra's Net, "the vast net extending throughout space where at each crossing point a radiant jewel reflects all others ad infinitum." **(Reversed)** disconnect, enmeshment, a snare, isolation, or else (subjectively) compassion for all beings, cosmic sympathy, citizenship of worlds.

0 THE FOOL, an Agent of POSSIBILITY (Key 0)

"Spirit in search of experience," total potentiality, possibility, open field, open space; undifferentiated spirit; everything that can be, Journey of The Keys, freedom to make mistakes (without karmic consequence); beginner's mind; crazy wisdom; the divine child, the puer aeternus. Without guile, innocence, wonder, the bumpkin, Parsifal; distinguished from the others because it's unnumbered (the zero); outside movement, becoming, or change; eccentric, a clown, the master/fool, unconscious/supraconscious, alpha and omega; **(Reversed)** foolishness, menace, imbecile, imposter, humiliation, stupidity, or else (subjectively) emptiness (shunyata), No-mind (Zen), final liberation, crazy wisdom, the unconditioned mind.

+9 THE TRAVELER, an Agent of SPIRITUAL INDIVIDUATION (off grid)

Signifies the unlimited potential for spiritual traveler to enter The Nine Paths at any point or mind moment as all situations, obstacles and mental states are accepted as fundamentally workable and amenable to this approach. The Traveler's mind is over-run with images, ideas, memories, attractions repulsions, habits, passions, goals, pain, pleasures, fears, emotions, fixations, fantasies, and other constructions. I effect, if you have experienced change, pain, or conditionality in your life, by definition, you are a traveler. This card may be used as a "significator" (agent of present identity or circumstance) or be included in divinations.

THE FOUR ELEMENTS, an Agent of Quaternity (off grid)

Many advanced cultures of the ancient world used a set of primary archetypal elements as metaphors to explain recurrent patterns in nature, and also, differences in perception and typology. The "doctrine of the elements", i.e. fire, water, air, and earth, is added to TNP to account for ordinary surface reality and the experiential sensations of the natural world. The single card generally points to the entire Minor Arcana of traditional tarot, and suggests local, ordinary, worldly, or "domestic" concerns when the card appears. Includes all four-fold structures, i.e. The Four: directions, seasons, natural forces, levels of the Intermediate Territory, Jungian Personality Types, tarot suits and courts, Kabalistic worlds, (Buddhist) Noble Truths, (Hindu) Yugas, and so forth. The card is reminiscent of T. S. Eliot's immortal poem The Four Quartets (1944) its sanguine reminder to all spiritual travelers:

> When we get to the end of our seeking
> We will find out where we've always been
> And know it for the first time.

Appendix D

Suggested Spreads for TNP

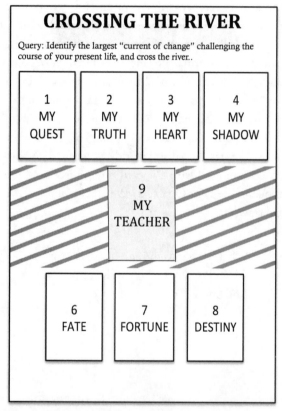

CROSSING THE RIVER

Query: Identify the largest "current of change" challenging the course of your present life, and cross the river..

| 1 MY QUEST | 2 MY TRUTH | 3 MY HEART | 4 MY SHADOW |

9 MY TEACHER

| 6 FATE | 7 FORTUNE | 8 DESTINY |

FATE represents the power or agency that predetermines and orders the course of events.

FORTUNE points to the bumps in the road, the specific occurrences, interfaces and developments in the human story.

DESTINY claims the hidden power believed to control what will happen in the future.

(Optional): Divine Position 9 via numeric reduction of the eight previous cards.

Three and Five Card Spreads

Basic instruction: Formulate question, shuffle exhaustively, fan face-down (below), and select to each position. Turn one card at a time, apprehend directly, then interpret with an eye to "the click." Move to the next card.

THREE CARD SPREADS

General instruction: Formulate question, shuffle exhaustively, fan face-down (below), and select cards to each position. Turn one card at a time, apprehend directly, then interpret with an eye to "the click." Move to next card.

Use any triadic configuration to widen perspective.

1   **2**   **3**

Examples:

DOMAIN	Position 1	Position 2	Position 3
OCCURENCE	Appearance	Reality	Necessity
DESIRE	Sex	Fame	Fortune
EQUILIBRIUM	Friend	Enemy	Stranger
JOURNEY	Departure	Transfer	Arrival
MY THREE BODIES	Physical body	Mental body	Emotional body

The Celtic Cross Spread

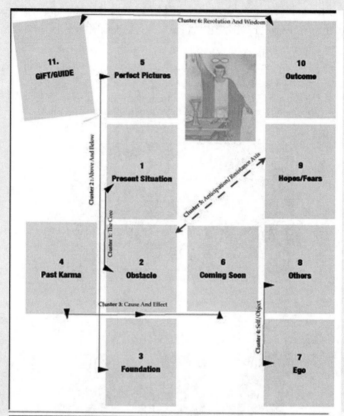

CLUSTER	POSITIONS	MEASURES
ONE: THE CORE	(1) Present Situation & (2) Obstacle	Establishes "the problem" and sets the therapeutic contract
TWO: ABOVE AND BELOW	(5) Perfect Pictures & (3) Foundation	Interplay of goals & visions with ground of being
THREE: CAUSE AND EFFECT	(4) Past Karma, (2) Obstacle, & (6) Coming Soon	The temporal/ process dimension, i.e. unfolding in time and causation
FOUR:SELF/OBJECT	(7) Ego & (8) Others	Combines self-perception and how significant others view us here.
FIVE: ANTICIPATION/ RESISTANCE AXIS	(9) Hopes and Fears & (2) Obstacle	How expectation conditions experience, and when fearful blocks our heart center (2)
SIX: RESOLUTION & WISDOM	(10) Outcome & (11) Gift and Guide	A barometer of destiny, free will, and karma

Contemplative Practices

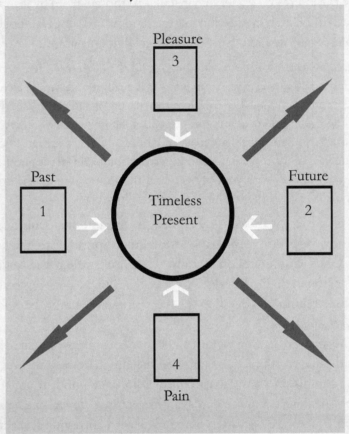

The Nondual Spread

Rest your mind in the timeless present while mixing the cards effortlessly.

Pleasure

3

Past

1

Timeless Present

Future

2

4

Pain

Once in tune with a natural flow, fan deck and randomly select the four positions. Contemplate your mandala intuitively without pressure to obtain something.

THE ZEN HERDING PICTURES

The Ten Ox-Herding Pictures are well known to Zen Buddhism. The commentary for each of these profound metaphorical stages is rich with scholarship and interpretative insight, well beyond our purposes here, and I invite the interested reader in particular to those offered by Josh Bartok and the late Tibetan meditation master, Chogyam Trunga Rinpoche. For example, regarding Picture 3: "Glimpsing," Trungpa writes:

> You are startled at perceiving the ox and then, because there is no longer any mystery, you wonder if it is really there; you perceive its insubstantial quality. You lose the notion of subjective criteria. When you begin to accept this perception of non-duality, you relax, because you no longer have to defend the existence of your ego. Then you can afford to be open and generous. You begin to see another way of dealing with your projects and that is joy in itself, the first spiritual level of the attainment of the bodhisattva.[2]

I first present the classic Zen images in traditional sequence, then the same images into a 10 card "Ox-Herding" Spread using the familiar Celtic Cross Configuration. Finally, I have substituted the traditional images with ten divined TNPs. As the bull in this allegory represents the enlightened mind, the question for the reading will simply be *"How best to catch the bull now?"*

The ten ox-herding pictures and commentaries presented below depict the stages of practice leading to the enlightenment at which Zen (Chan) Buddhism aims. **Instruction:** calm your mind of unnecessary distraction, shuffle and fan cards, and select face down, one at a time, for each position. Go slowly, contemplate each correspondence in your experience between designated position and selected card, wait for click, then move to next position.

---

2. "Searching for the Ox: The Path to Enlightenment in 10 Pictures," Josh Barok and Chogyam Trungpa Rinpoche, *The Lion's Roar,* March 4, 2015.

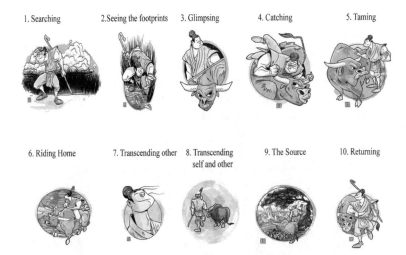

1. Searching 2.Seeing the footprints 3. Glimpsing 4. Catching 5. Taming

6. Riding Home 7. Transcending other 8. Transcending self and other 9. The Source 10. Returning

Translating Ox-herding Pictures into The Ox-Herding Tarot Spread

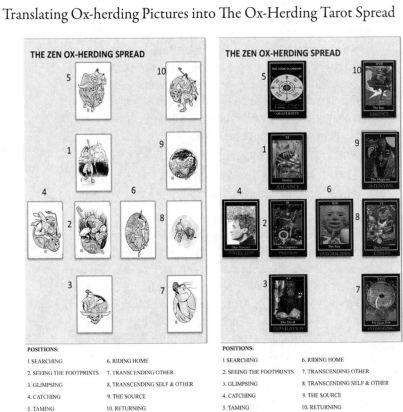

THE ZEN OX-HERDING SPREAD

POSITIONS:

1 SEARCHING   6. RIDING HOME
2. SEEING THE FOOTPRINTS   7. TRANSCENDING OTHER
3. GLIMPSING   8. TRANSCENDING SELF & OTHER
4. CATCHING   9. THE SOURCE
5. TAMING   10. RETURNING

THE ZEN OX-HERDING SPREAD

POSITIONS:

1 SEARCHING   6. RIDING HOME
2. SEEING THE FOOTPRINTS   7. TRANSCENDING OTHER
3. GLIMPSING   8. TRANSCENDING SELF & OTHER
4. CATCHING   9. THE SOURCE
5. TAMING   10. RETURNING

GAMES of TNP

Games are best played in **small groups of four to six** or larger meetings where table or floor space can accomodate multiple small groups working simultaneously. One TNP deck is used per group. A *designated dealer* is first chosen or divined (by the highest trump card drawn in each circle). An example is:

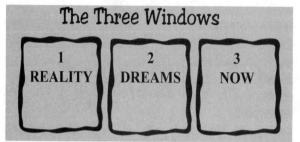

Instructions: [Allow as much time as needed. Recommended 60-90 minutes per group of six]. **Prepare:** With deck in hand, dealer joins group in meditative 5-10 minutes of natural quiet, mixing and cutting the deck effortlessly, passing it around for other players to do likewise while emptying the mind of all distractions. Once in tune with a natural flow, the dealer fans deck and invites all players to randomly **select three cards placed face down** in front of them. The cards are interpeted through the words:

Through this window of reality I see_____
Through this window of dreams I see_____
Through this window of now I see_____

The game proceeds simply and organically. Starting left of dealer, **Player 1** observes: *"Through this window of reality I see"* then turns first card over and freely associates (without pressure to force meanings). Response can be succinct or impressionistic; there are no right and wrong answers. The object is never winning, but learning. **Follow-up:** after Player 1 opens a particular window, all players in turn "follow-up" by offering non-evaluative feedback, such as: *"Through this window, I see for you ..."* (**Note:** Passing without explanation other than "I pass" is always permitted). Continue around until Player 1 has opened all three windows, then move to Player 2, and repeat full procedure until each player has opened all three windows. **Avoid interpretative analysis.**

Appendix E

Correspondences

HERMETIC CORRESPONDENCES

	KEY	ZODIACAL	KABBALISTIC
1	MAGICIAN	MERCURY	BETH (power)
2	PRIESTESS	MOON	GIMEL (wisdom)
3	EMPRESS	VENUS	DALETH (life)
4	EMPEROR	ARIES	HEH (speech)
5	HIEROPHANT	TAURUS	VAV (thought)
6	LOVERS	GEMINI	ZAIN (movement)
7	CHARIOT	CANCER	CHETH (sight)
8	STRENGTH	LEO	TETH (hearing)
9	HERMIT	VIRGO	YOD (work)
	KEY	**ZODIACAL**	**KABBALISTIC**
10	WH FORTUNE	JUPITER	KAPH (grace)
11	JUSTICE	LIBRA	LAMED (coitus)
12	HANGED MAN	WATER	MEM (virtue)
13	DEATH	SCORPIO	NUN (smell)
14	TEMPERANCE	SAGITTARIUS	SAMEKH (sleep)
15	DEVIL	CAPRICORN	AYIN (anger)
16	TOWER	MARS	PEH (riches)
17	STAR	AQUARIUS	TZADDI (taste)
18	MOON	PISCES	QOPH (mirth)
	KEY	**ZODIACAL**	**KABBALISTIC**
19	SUN	SUN	RESH (fertility)
20	JUDGEMENT	FIRE	SHIN (vices)
21	WORLD	SATURN	TAU (peace)
22	WELL	URANUS	KAPH FINAL
23	RIVER	NEPTUNE	MEM FINAL
24	RING	PLUTO	NUN FINAL
25	DRAGON	ASC, NODE	PEF FINAL
26	GREAT WEB	DESC, NODE	TSADDI FINAL
0	FOOL	AIR	ALEPH (balance)

X

Y

Z

Eastern teachings often utilize numbers to identify and retain the full body of practices. Tarot begins in vision-logic and in time naturally deepens to subtler bandwidths of awareness. These charts may further help further amplify Keys from Buddhist and consciousness perspectives.

KEY BUDDHIST CORRESPONDENCES BY NUMBER		WILBER'S LEVELS OF CONSCIOUSNESS
THE NOBLE EIGHTFOLD PATH This is the path the Buddha taught to those seeking liberation: 1. Right Understanding 2. Right thought. 3. Right speech. 4. Right action. 5. Right livelihood. 6. Right effort. 7. Right mindfulness. 8. Right concentration. Tarot Key: 8 Strength/Life Force	**THE FOUR NOBLE TRUTHS** This was the Buddha's first and fundamental teaching: 1. The existence of suffering 2. the origin of suffering 3. The cessation of suffering 4. The path of the cessation of suffering. Tarot Key: 4 The Emperor/Dominion	**THE INTERMEDIATE TERRITORY** Consciousness Realms of the Tarot of the Nine Paths **VISION-LOGIC** The "higher mind" (Aurobindo) Dialectical, integrative, synthetic. Establishes networks of relationships. Highest structure of the personal realm. Synchronisitic, non-linear, systemic
THE THREE KINDS OF SUFFERING The Buddha taught we can understand different kinds of suffering through these three categories: 1. The suffering of pain. 2. The suffering of change. 3. The suffering of conditionality Tarot Key: 3 The Empress/Passion	**THE FIVE HINDRANCES** These are the classical hindrances to meditation practice: 1. Desire, clinging, craving. 2. Aversion, anger, hatred. 3. Sleepiness, sloth. 4. Restlessness. 5. Doubt. Tarot Key: 5 The Hierophant/Spirit	**THE PSYCHIC LEVEL** When the power of inner sight is more direct than the power of thought. The 6th chakra or "third eye." Marks the beginning of transpersonal insights and subtler levels of self-reflection. **THE SUBTLE LEVEL** Seat of the archetypes. Platonic Forms. Subtle sounds and audible illuminations. Transcendent insight and absorption. Home to personal deity-forms.
THE FOUR METTA PHRASES Send loving kindness to yourself and others by using these phrases or words-sthat have personal meaning for you: 1. May I be free from danger. 2. May I be happy. 3. May I be healthy. 4. May I love with ease. Tarot Key: 4 The Emperor/Dominion	**THE EIGHT VICISSITUDES** According to the Buddha, we will experience theses throughout our lives no matter our intentions or actions: 1. Pleasure and pain. 2. Gain and loss. 3. Praise and blame. 4. Fame and disrepute. Tarot Key: 8 Strength/Life Force	**THE CAUSAL LEVEL** The Unmanifest Source. The Abyss (Gnosticism). The Void (Mahayana). The Formless (Vedanta). Effortless insight culminating in nirvana (Vipassana) **THE UNCONDITIONED MIND or NONDUALITY (Off Grid)**

Appendix F

Growth Cycles

APPENDIX F
TNP GROWTH CYCLES
BASED ON NUMERIC REDUCTION

1900	10	1915	16	1930	13	1945	19	1960	16
1901	11	1916	17	1931	14	1946	20	1961	17
1902	12	1917	18	1932	15	1947	21	1962	18
1903	13	1918	19	1933	16	1948	22	1963	19
1904	14	1919	20	1934	17	1949	23	1964	20
1905	15	1920	12	1935	18	1950	15	1965	21
1906	16	1921	13	1936	19	1951	16	1966	22
1907	17	1922	14	1937	20	1952	17	1967	23
1908	18	1923	15	1938	21	1953	18	1968	24
1909	19	1924	16	1939	22	1954	19	1969	25
1910	11	1925	17	1940	14	1955	20	1970	17
1911	12	1926	18	1941	15	1956	21	1971	18
1912	13	1927	19	1942	16	1957	22	1972	19
1913	14	1928	20	1943	17	1958	23	1973	20
1914	15	1929	21	1944	18	1959	24	1974	21
1975	22	1990	19	2005	7	2020	4	2035	10
1976	23	1991	20	2006	8	2021	5	2036	11
1977	24	1992	21	2007	9	2022	6	2037	12
1978	25	1993	22	2008	10	2023	7	2038	13
1979	26	1994	23	2009	11	2024	8	2039	14
1980	18	1995	24	2010	3	2025	9	2040	6
1981	19	1996	25	2011	4	2026	10	2041	7
1982	20	1997	26	2012	5	2027	11	2042	8
1983	21	1998	27	2013	6	2028	12	2043	9
1984	22	1999	10	2014	7	2029	13	2044	10
1985	23	2000	2	2015	8	2030	5	2045	11
1986	24	2001	3	2016	9	2031	6	2046	12
1987	25	2002	4	2017	10	2032	7	2047	13
1988	26	2003	5	2018	11	2033	8	2048	14
1989	27	2004	6	2019	12	2034	9	2049	15

A Tarot practice is to calculate Growth Cycles and Year cards from dates, by locating the corresponding Key on the map. It can stimulate a fascinating reappraisal of historical patterns, offer a parallel universe to linear time, and orient oneself esoterically to Time, and the passing of years.

The year 2018, in this light, numerically reduces $(2 + 0 + 1 + 8 = 11)$, and is thus viewed as a Justice year. One may contemplate any chosen year through this lens, and make choices and decisions with an awareness of the "arcanic backdrop" in TNP.

A careful inspection of Growth Cycles reveals the curious ways in which number patterns flow through Time, and occasionally take an unexpected leap, observed in calendric years.

With the expansion and re-tuning given in TNP, some years now correspond to the emerging agencies that did not consciously exist before (22-26). Their arrival casts some interesting reconsideration of what was and what will come with respect to number correspondences.

Cycles of Time are affected only slightly in the TNP Model, but as we saw with Waite's reordering of Strength and Justice in 1909, the ramifications in metaphysical space can reach cosmic proportions.

Growth Cycles and "destiny years" can be calculated for general interest, planning and strategy, birthdates, special numbers, past or future-viewing, and historical events. Destiny years reflect symbolic alignment with, or ripening of, a specific archetypal pattern of unfoldment in the fabric of time. Uniquely, the tables are calculated from the 27 Principles, and re-tuned accordingly, a refinement of constellations based on the 22 card arcana (see Arrien or Greer, 1987).

Virtually any date can be translated into a destiny year, even the present date, and then be used to springboard into a full reading. In TNP, when a particular Key is determined to correspond to a year or number series, one may consult The Matrix to ascertain its Path and Stage for a more in depth orientation. Below is an example of how this is done using Christmas 2099.

December 25, 2099 = 12 + 25 + 2099 = 37 + 2099 = 2136 (Destiny Year). 2136 = 2 + 1 + 3 + 6 = 12 Hanged Man, an Agent of Surrender. The final Christmas of the century, therefore, will be a day of surrender. Hallelujah!

(12) Hanged Man is in Transfer (Y) stage of Path 3, Joy, i.e. Empress →Hanged Man →World.

Contributing Sources

Ammann, R (1991). *Healing and Transformation in Sandplay;* [in foreword by Donald Sandner], Open Court, La Salle, Illinois.

Anonymous (1985). *Meditations on the Tarot;* Element Classic Editions, Massachusetts.

Arrien, Angeles, (1987). *The Tarot Handbook: Practical Applications of Ancient Visual Symbols;* Arcus Publishing Company, Sonoma, California. (1993) *The Four Fold Way: Walking the Paths of the Warrior, Teacher, Healer and Visionary;* Harper, San Francisco. *The Nine Muses: A Mythological Path to Creativity* (2000), Tarcher, New York.

Aziz, Robert, (1990). *C.G. Jung's Psychology of Religion and Synchronicity;* State University of New York Press, New York.

Benjamin, Marina (2004). *Rocket Dreams: How the Space Age Shaped Our Vision of a World Beyond;* Simon and Shuster, New York.

Butler, Bill, (1975). *Dictionary of the Tarot;* Schoken Books, New York.

Campbell, Joseph, (1949). *The Hero with a Thousand Faces;* New World Library (Third Edition, 2008), New York.

——— (2011) *The Power of Myth,* with Bill Moyers; Anchor, New York.

Campbell, Joseph, and Roberts, Richard (1982). *Tarot Revelations;* Vernal Equinox Press, San Anselmo, California.

Crowley, Aleister, (1969) [Originally published in 1944]. *The Book of Thoth: A Short Essay On The Tarot of the Egyptians;* Samuel Weiser, York Beach, Maine.

DuQuette, Lon Milo, (1997). *Angels, Demons & Gods of the New Millennium: Musings on Modern Magick;* Samuel Weiser, Inc., York Beach, Maine.

——— (2003) Understanding Aleister Crowley's Thoth Tarot

——— The Chicken Qabalah of Rabbi Lamed Ben Clifford: Dilettante's Guide to What You Do and Do Not Need to Know to Become a Qabalist; Welser Books, 2010.

Edinger, Edward F. (1984). *The Creation Of Consciousness: Jung's Myth for Modern Man;* Inner City Books, Toronto.

Evans, Rand B, (1999) *Outlook For Psychology;* The Monitor, APA Millennial Edition, December 1999.

Fenner, Peter (2016). Natural Awakening: An Advanced Guide for Sharing Nondual Awareness, Sumeru Press.

——— (2007). *Radiant Mind: Awakening Unconditioned Awareness,* Amazon Digital.

Getting, F. (1980). *Fate & Prediction: An Historical Compendium of Palmistry, Astrology, and Tarot;* Exeter, New York.

Giles, Cynthia, (1992). *The Tarot: History, Mystery, and Lore;* Simon and Shuster (Fireside) New York.

Glickman, Michael, (2009). *Crop Circles: The Bones of God;* Frog Ltd., England.

Greer, Mary K. (1988). *Tarot Mirrors: reflections of personal meaning,* Newcastle Publishing Co, North Hollywood.

——— ((1987) *Tarot Constellations: Patterns of Personal Destiny;* Newcastle Publishing Co, North Hollywood.

——— (1984) *Tarot For Yourself: A Workbook For Personal Transformation;* Newcastle Publishing Co, North Hollywood.

Houton, Jean (1992). *The Hero and the Goddess: The Odyssey As Mystery and Initiation;* Ballantine Books, New York.

Johnson, Robert A (1986). *Innerwork: Using Dreams & Active Imagination For Personal Growth;* Harper & Row, New York.

Journal of Addiction Science & Clinical Practice (2015). Volume 10 (1):8.

Jung, C. G. (1961). *Memories, Dreams, Reflections;* Vintage Books, Random House, New York.

Jung, C. G. [edited by Joseph Campbell] (1975). *The Portable Jung;* Viking Penguin, New York.

Jung, C. G. (1953-1979). *The Collected Works* (Bollingen Series XX, 20 Volumes); Trans. R.F.C. Hull, Trans; H. Read, M. Fordham, G. Adler, & W. McGuire, Eds.; Princeton University Press, Princeton, New Jersey.

——— Volume VI: *Psychological Types* ((1921).

——— Volume VII (Part 1): *Two Essays On Analytical Psychology* (1926, 1928).

——— Volume VIII: *The Structure and Dynamics of The Psyche* ((1947/54, 1952).

——— Volume IX: (Part 1): *The Archetypes and The Collective Unconscious* (1934/1950).

——— Volume XI: *Psychology and Religion: West and East* (1938, 1943, 1944, 1950).

----- Volume XV: *The Spirit In Man, Art, and Literature* (1930).

Jung, C. G. (1973). *Letters: 1906-1950.* Princeton University Press, Princeton, New Jersey.

Jung, Carl G., *Man and his Symbols;* Doubleday & Company Inc., Garden City, New York, 1964.

Kalff, Dora, M.(1980). *Sandplay: A Psychotherapeutic Approach to the Psyche;* Sigo Press, Boston.

Kaplan, Stuart R., (1978-2005). *The Encyclopedia of Tarot,* (Volumes I-IV), US Games, Inc., Stamford, Conn.

Kellog, Joan, (1978). *Mandala: Path of Beauty;* ATMA, Inc., Belleair, Florida, 1978.

Mansfield, Victor (1995). *Synchronicity, Science, and Soul-Making,* Open Court, La Salle, Illinois.

Krippner, Stanley, (2004). *Varieties of Anomalous Experience;* American Psychological Association.

Lovecky, Deirdre (1990). "Warts and Rainbows: Issues in the Psychotherapy of the Gifted," *Advanced Development,* Jan., 1990)

McDonald, Kathleen (1984). How To Meditate, a Practical Guide; Wisdom Publications, London.

Metzner, Ralph (1971). *Maps Of Consciousness;* Collier Books, New York.

Mitchell, Stephen (1991). *The Enlightened Mind;* Harper Perennial, New York.

Newman, Kenneth, D. (1983). *The Tarot: A Myth Of Male Initiation;* A Quadrant Monograph [published by the C.G. Jung Foundation for Analytical Psychology, New York.

Needham, Joseph (1943). "Integrative levels: a revaluation of the idea of progress,"in *Time: the refreshing river;* Allen and Unwin, London.

Nagy, Marilyn (1991). *Philosophical Issues in the Psychology of C.G. Jung;* SUNY Press, New York.

Nichols, Sallie (1980). *Jung and Tarot: An Archetypal Journey;* Samuel Weiser Inc, York Beach, Maine.

O'Neill, Robert V. (1986). *Tarot Symbolism;* Fairway Press, Lima Ohio.

Ouspensky, P. D. (1976). *The Symbolism of Tarot: Philosophy of Occultism in Pictures and Numbers,* Dover, New York.

Oxford Dictionary of World Religions. (Bowker, John (1997), Oxford University Press, Oxford, UK.

Peat, F. David (1987). *Synchronicity: The Bridge Between Matter and Mind;* Bantam, New York.

Place, Robert (2011). *Alchemy and the Tarot: An Examination of the Historic Connection,* Hermes Publications, New York.

Pollack, Rachel (1980). *Seventy-Eight Degrees of Wisdom* (Part 1): *The Major Arcana;* Aquarian Press Limited, Wellingborough, Northhamptonshire, U. K.-----Part 2: *Seventy -Eight Degrees of Wisdom: The Minor Arcana* (1983).

Progoff, Ira (1973). *Jung, Synchronicity, and Human Destiny;* Delta Publishing Co., New York.

Reber, Arthur, S. (1985). *Dictionary of Psychology;* Penguin Books, London.

Riley, Jana (1995). *Tarot Dictionary and Compendium;* Samuel Weiser, York Beach, Maine.

Ritsema, Rudolf and Karcher, Stephen [translators] (1984). *I Ching: The Classic Chinese Oracle of Chang;,* Element Books Limited, Great Britain.

Roberts, Richard, and Campbell, Joseph (1982). *Tarot Revelations;* Vernal Equinox Press, San Anselmo, California.

Robinson, Marnia (2009). *Cupid's Poisoned Arrow, Healing and Harmony in Sexual Relationships,* North Atlantic Book.

Rohrig, Carl (1993). *The Rohrig Tarot Book;* Bluestar Communications, Woodside, California.

Room, Adrian (1988). *Dictionary of Contrasting Pairs;* Routledge, London.

Rosengarten, Arthur, E. (1985). *Accessing The Unconscious, A Comparative Study of Dreams, The T.A.T. and Tarot* [doctoral dissertation]; University Microfilms International, Ann Arbor, Michigan.

——— (1994). *Tarot As A Psychotherapeutic Tool;* self-published manual.

——— (2000). *Tarot And Psychology: Spectrums Of Possibility;* Paragon House Publishers, St. Paul, Minn.

——— (2009) *Rosengarten's Tarot of the Nine Paths, Advanced Tarot for the Spiritual Traveler,* Paragon, House Publishers, St. Paul, Minnesota.

Salinger, J.D, (1966). *Nine Stories,* Bantam Paperback.

Samuels, Andrew, Shorter, Bani, and Plant, Fred (1987). *A Critical Dictionary of Jungian Analysis;* Routledge & Kegan Paul Ltd, New York.

Teilhard de Chardin, Pierre (1922). Modern Spiritual Masters Series edition (May 1, 1999).

Tolle, Eckhart (2014), *Doorway Into Now.*

Vaughan, Frances, E. (1979). *Awakening Intuition;* Anchor Doubleday, New York.

Van Eenwyk, John (1997). *Archetypes & Strange Attractors: The Chaotic World of Symbols;* Inner City Books, Toronto, Canada.

Von Franz, Marie-Louise (1980). *On Divination and Synchronicity;* Inner City Books, Toronto, Canada.

Waite, Arthur Edward (1971). *The Pictorial Key To The Tarot;* Harper & Row [originally under Rudolf Steiner Publications], New York.

Watts, Allan [with collaboration of Al Chung-liang Huang] (1979). *Tao: The Watercourse Way;* Pantheon Books, New York.

——— (1957) *The Way of Zen;* Pantheon Books, New York.

Weinrib, Estelle, L. (1983). *Images of the Self; The Sandplay Process;* Sigo Press, Boston.

Zur, O. and Nordmarken, N. (2015). *DSM: Diagnosing for Status and Money Summary Critique of the DSM-5.*

Index